A RESERVATION UNDIMINISHED

A RESERVATION UNDIMINISHED

The Saginaw Chippewa Case and Native Sovereignty

Todd B. Adams, Gary Clayton Anderson, and R. David Edmunds

University of Oklahoma Press : Norman

Publication of this book is made possible in part through the generous assistance of the McCasland Foundation, Duncan, Oklahoma.

Library of Congress Cataloging-in-Publication Data

Names: Adams, Todd B. (Todd Baker), 1971– author. | Anderson, Gary Clayton, 1948– author. | Edmunds, R. David (Russell David), 1939– author.
Title: A reservation undiminished : the Saginaw Chippewa case and native sovereignty / Todd B. Adams, Gary Clayton Anderson, and R. David Edmunds.
Description: Norman : University of Oklahoma Press, 2024. | Includes bibliographical references and index. | Summary: "Two historian expert witnesses and a former assistant attorney general of Michigan recount the story of the legal case they participated in: how the Saginaw Chippewa Tribe succeeded in having its treaty-created Isabella Reservation recognized by the federal government as against the state of Michigan and non-Native American business interests"— Provided by publisher.
Identifiers: LCCN 2024016861 | ISBN 978-0-8061-9470-7 (hardcover)
Subjects: LCSH: Saginaw Chippewa Indian Tribe of Michigan—Claims vs. Michigan. | Isabella Reservation (Mich.)—Cases. | Indians of North America— Land tenure—Michigan—Cases. | Indian land transfers—Michigan. | Indians of North America—Government relations. | United States. Indian Reorganization Act. | Self-determination, National—United States. | Federal-Indian trust relationship. | BISAC: HISTORY / Indigenous Peoples in the Americas | HISTORY / United States / 21st Century
Classification: LCC KIH1688 .A33 2024 | DDC 346.7301/3089973330774— dc23/eng/20240528
LC record available at https://lccn.loc.gov/2024016861

The paper in this book meets the guidelines for permanence and durability of the Committee on Production Guidelines for Book Longevity of the Council on Library Resources, Inc. ∞

CONTENTS

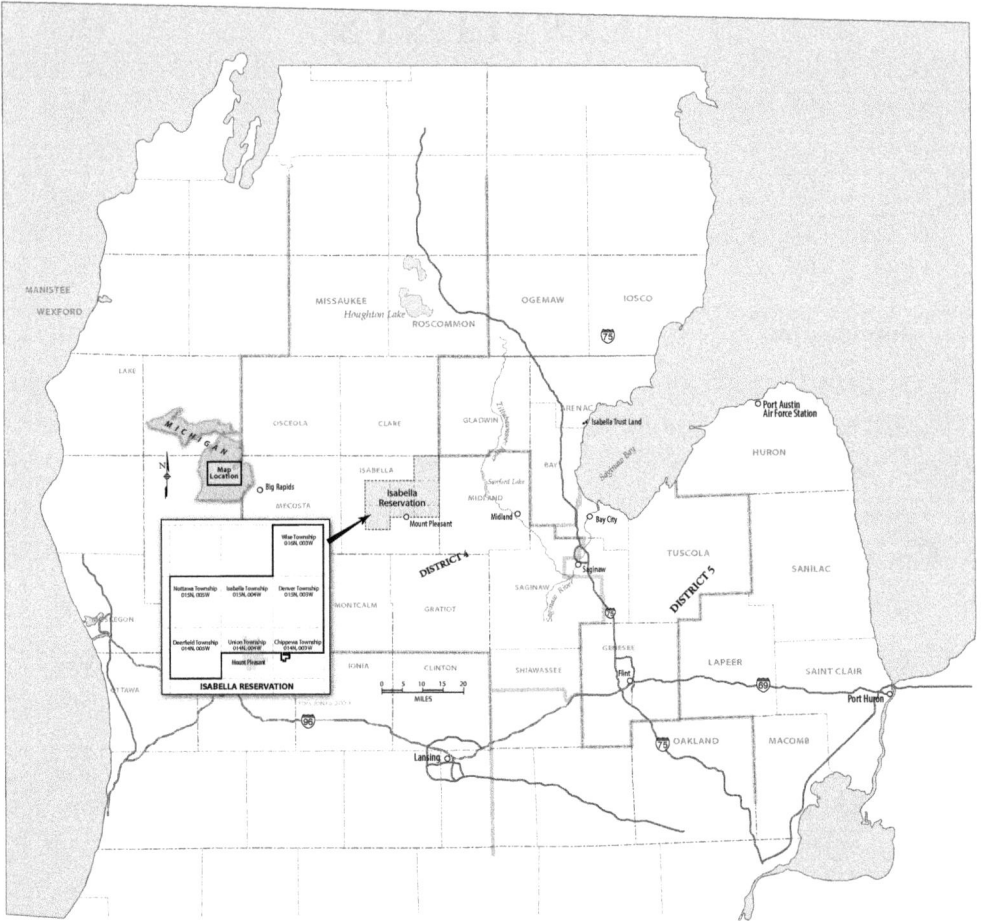

The Isabella Indian Reservation, central Michigan

INTRODUCTION

The federal government negotiated treaties with the Saginaw Chippewa Tribe of Michigan in 1855 and again in 1864. These agreements led to the creation of what the Saginaw Chippewas believed was a permanent Indian reservation, called the Isabella Reservation. As the years went by, the state of Michigan nibbled away at the privileges and legal rights that came with reservation status—Indian reservations were actual appendages of federal land and not subject to state jurisdiction—and soon came to assert jurisdictional control over most of the six townships that originally made up the reserve. In 2005 the tribe filed suit, contesting this jurisdictional authority, and the federal government, observing its obligations regarding "trust doctrine," joined the tribe in this suit. The state of Michigan, later joined by the city of Mt. Pleasant and Isabella County, disagreed, and the case went through a whirlwind of debate that involved multiple statements regarding issues both historical and present-day. Ultimately, one month before trial, the parties informed the court that they had agreed to arbitrate the case. Although general distrust and disagreement existed on all sides, a long period of negotiation began, which continued from 2008 to 2010.

The book that follows contains the story of this great debate and its conclusion. Grasping the story requires a clear understanding of the legal issues surrounding the court case, extending back to cases adjudicated in the 1980s into roughly 2005, as well as the United States

1

Supreme Court's assessment of what constituted Indian sovereignty. What becomes clear from the start is that Indian legal issues were, in effect, thorny and not always easy to understand. The lawyers on both sides understood that precedent favored them in certain areas but not necessarily in others. To gain clarity they turned to historians—five of them, two of whom worked for the federal government; one who worked for the state, county, and city; and one who worked for the Saginaw Chippewa Tribe. They examined Saginaw relationships with the federal government starting at the time of the Constitution and extending into the present. To publish all five reports would result in a book of considerable length, unruly and perhaps unreadable.

What, then, is this book? This introduction begins with some insight into the legal issues as decided by the courts in the years prior to the case. This brief section is followed by a historical outline of the general disagreements regarding the record of the Saginaw relationship with the federal government and the state of Michigan. This is not unusual: historians are hired to put the best possible face on the argument based on the historical record. The authors of this study have elected to publish the conclusions brought by the tribal historian, Gary Clayton Anderson, as well as those of one of the historians working for the federal government, R. David Edmunds, primarily because they present the overall historical picture, especially after 1860 and into the latter stages of the twentieth century. Thus, the book is a legal history augmented by a strong historical background outlining the lives and culture of the Saginaw Chippewa people. Also included are the thoughts and conclusions of Todd Adams, the assistant attorney general for Indian Affairs in Michigan, who graciously added considerable insight into the issues covered in this study.

The final section (chapters 7 and 8 and the conclusion) of the book turns once again to the legal aspects of the negotiated settlement. What did they mean for the tribe? What did they mean for the state, the city of Mt. Pleasant, and Isabella County? Answering these questions involves short interviews with people who participated in the negotiation (which began in 2008) and who implemented the agreement that followed (starting in 2010). We have tried to include as many individuals as possible, but some, including the tribal council, declined to be interviewed.

The shadow of the courtroom then fell over these historical reports and negotiations, and the Saginaw Chippewa Tribe found it quite difficult to cut through them. Reflecting the unfair nature of almost all the treaties negotiated between the federal government and Indian, or Native, nations, the US Supreme Court established canons of treaty construction that clearly favor Indian nations. Courts must interpret treaties as grants from an Indian nation to the federal government and not vice versa. The courts generally interpret the documents as the Natives understood them, not as nonnative American lawyers interpret them, either in the past or today. They often resolve all ambiguities in favor of the Indians; this legal conclusion is based on the fact that the federal government drafted the treaties and wrote them in English. These canons have the practical and intended effect of ensuring that an Indian nation keeps any land rights it had not expressly granted to the federal government through treaties.

States had often assumed control of a variety of local governmental processes in the late nineteenth century, including taxation, hunting and fishing rights, education, legal guardianship of children, and law enforcement. This occurred in part because in 1810 and 1823, the Supreme Court asserted that given the takeover of much of North America by the United States, the federal government owned all lands claimed by Indians. Sovereignty over these lands slowly reverted to the states as land was sold and counties were created, and cities, counties, and states constructed law enforcement agencies. The attitude of Andrew Jackson, expressed when he represented Tennessee in the Senate in 1817, is reflective of this view: he wrote that Indians had "only a possessory right" to their lands. He further stated that Congress, and later states, could enact whatever legislation they deemed necessary in dealing with Natives, often against their will.[1]

In 1831 (and again in 1832), Chief Justice John Marshall of the Supreme Court dealt with the issue of Native sovereignty within the context of the Cherokee Indian reservation in Georgia and Tennessee. The state of Georgia had enacted legislation that placed Cherokee lands under the control of newly created Georgia counties and then arrested missionaries who refused to leave these lands. Marshall—fearing reprisals from newly elected President Jackson and concerned for the future significance of the Supreme Court itself—refused to dismantle Jackson's new Indian Removal Act, signed into law in 1830, and cautiously reasserted the responsibility of the federal government to take care of

Indians and their lands, since they were "wards" of the federal government rather than independent nations. This, of course, was confusing because Congress had treated Indians as nations by the very fact that it negotiated treaties with them.[2]

Since the nineteenth century, hundreds of legal cases have gone through the courts as they have adjusted and adjudicated claims. Many more recent cases were launched by Indian tribes after Congress created the Indian Claims Commission in 1946. This act provided huge amounts of work for lawyers, historians, and anthropologists. Indeed, since 1953 the Supreme Court alone has reviewed, on average, two cases per year dealing with Indian claims. And it has often either created new law or rejected that which had been new law.[3] Since the mid-1980s, however, some cases stand out as being crucial to establishing precedent when it comes to *Saginaw Chippewa Indian Tribe of Michigan v. Jennifer Granholm, et al.,* Case No. 05–10296-BC, the subject of this study.

While many initial precedents might apply to the case, one of importance came in *County of Oneida v. Oneida Indian Nation of N.Y.,* 470 U. S. 226 (1985). Here the Supreme Court held that while the Oneida Indians had sold land to the state of New York in 1805 (which was illegal under the Indian Nonintercourse Act), they bought parcels of it back in the 1970s, which land the court then recognized as being under "aboriginal title," thus reasserting Indian sovereign dominion to this land. Yet the Oneidas sought only monetary damages in court; thus, general issues of sovereignty, such as taxation, were not addressed. Dissenting opinions in the case focused on an age-old legal precedent called "laches" (roughly, an unreasonable delay in making a claim). As the dissenting argument stated: "Ancient claims are best left in repose." In other words, claims such as this, if ruled in favor of an Indian tribe, would lead to considerable disruption of land titles, mostly titles held by non-Indians. Too much time had elapsed between the so-called crime and the attempt by the tribe to get recompense, or so the argument went. And, more importantly, dissenters argued that Indian land titles, if recognized by the federal government, would invariably lead to agonizing issues regarding taxation by cities, counties, and even states. Yet at the time of Oneida II, as it is often called, the dissenters in the court lost the argument.

The issue of laches came in front of the court once again in 2005. The case, which slowly made its way up from the appeals process, was *City of Sherril v. Oneida Indian Nation of N.Y.,* 544 U.S. 197. While the Supreme Court did not reverse itself entirely in *Sherril,* the decision left considerable confusion regarding just where laches could, and should, be applied. In contrast to the earlier Oneida II case, which recognized aboriginal title, in *Sherril,* the issue hinged entirely on taxation, which the Oneida Indians refused to pay to state and local officials on lands that the tribe now owned within the boundaries of its ancient reservation. The court ruled that the Oneidas' long delay in seeking judicial relief from taxation precluded it from reviving its ancient sovereignty—obviously, a somewhat contradictory decision when compared with earlier Oneida cases. Some legal scholars have even suggested that this constituted a "new laches."[4]

These various cases played an obvious role in discussions that occurred regarding the preparation that went into *Saginaw v. Granholm.* The state promptly hired two historians to research the history of the Saginaw people and their two major treaties of 1855 and 1864. Professor Theodore J. Karamanski, of Loyola University in Chicago, produced "The Historical and Ethnohistorical Context of Hunting and Fishing Treaty Rights in Western and Northern Michigan." He concluded that Saginaw leaders clearly understood at the time the treaties were signed that various rights, including those relating to hunting and fishing, were "temporary and not perpetual." Further, he wrote that Saginaw rights to land (in essence, reservation rights) "extended only until the land is required for settlements." In other words, while the 1855 and 1864 treaties granted the Saginaw a six-township reservation, the very existence of the reservation disappeared as the Indians acquired land and citizenship.[5] While Karamanski's report does carry on into the twentieth century, only the last few pages cover the period of 1875 to the present, and no research supported conclusions after 1875; especially absent were records found in the National Archives on this later period.

Karamanski's conclusions were based on articles in the 1855 and 1864 treaties that led to "allotment," a legislative process that was designed to end reservation status. This policy divided reservations into 80- and 160-acre farms and gave individual Indians titles to these plots, thus leading, supposedly, to dissolution of the reservation. Allotment clauses in treaties were initially haphazard, poorly implemented, and confusing. The policy, however, was formulated into law in 1887 under the Dawes Act. While the later law would be applied to virtually every reservation in the United States (two exceptions were the Navajo and Red Lake reserves) Commissioner of Indian Affairs George Manypenny (1853–57) had included allotment in the dozens of treaties that he negotiated in the 1850s, including the initial one with the Saginaw Indians. Yet the Civil War disrupted the process, and allotment did not begin in earnest on the Isabella Indian Reservation in central Michigan until 1870, after the process was reinforced under the 1864 treaty. That treaty allowed the Indian agent to determine whether an Indian was "competent," and thus should receive a fee simple title to lands; if he or she were determined "not so competent," the title would have restrictions. Under a restricted title, the Indian could not sell his or her land. Professor Karamanski virtually concludes his report at this point, which likely occurred because the Indian agents between 1870 and 1875 issued competent titles to land to almost every applicant, allowing land speculators to purchase much of the reservation for below market value. Karamanski does conclude that while pockets of Saginaw Indians continued to live together on northern portions of the reservation, any semblance of reservation authority, or sovereignty, had ceased to exist.[6]

A second report commissioned by the state was produced by Professor Anthony G. Gulig, from the University of Wisconsin–Whitewater. Titled "An Historical Analysis of the Saginaw, Black River and Swan Creek Chippewa Treaties of 1855 and 1864," it actually supersedes Karamanski in claiming that the Saginaw, Black River, and Swan Creek Indians dissolved their tribal organization and that "language [in the treaties] was never intended to describe a defined piece of land set aside to be held in common [a reservation]." A "dissolved entity" would have little use for a reservation, as Gulig argues.[7] Such a conclusion came from looking at the allotment process from 1870 to 1875 only, when large numbers of Saginaw families received fee simple patents for 160 acres within the bounds of the reservation. Individual Indians received 80 acres.

It is unfortunate that in the early years, most allotments were given out in fee simple. In both Mount Pleasant and Detroit an "Indian Ring" (consisting of Euro-American Indian agents, local land and timber speculators, and state and federal officials and politicians) manipulated the process of handing out patents. Most Saginaw Indians who received full title to their lands just as quickly lost those lands to corrupt land speculators. This corruption was not corrected until after 1875, a period that neither Karamanski nor Gulig seriously researched. The government continued the allotment process into the 1880s and 1890s, issuing restricted titles, which meant that the lands could not be sold since the title still rested in the secretary of the interior. These were the sorts of questions, then, that the expert witnesses for the tribe, the federal government, and the state, county, and city of Mt. Pleasant attempted to address. How much land remained in the hands of Saginaw Indians? To what degree did they still maintain an Indian Reservation?

Two reports were written by historians hired by the tribe and the federal government. George Lynn Cross Research Professor Gary Clayton Anderson, from the University of Oklahoma, and the Watson Professor of History at the University of Texas, R. David Edmunds, filed these latter reports. These expert witnesses attempted to show just how the land issue evolved in northern Michigan and to what degree the Saginaw Indians maintained their reservation. They pushed the debate way beyond 1875, into the twentieth century. Professor Anderson's report constitutes chapters 1–4 of this study. Chapters 1–3 outline the early history of the Chippewa people through first contacts with European traders; summarizes the impact on the Chippewas of wars fought by European empires and by the nascent United States; traces the consequences of the various treaties wrought during the long nineteenth century (one of which created the Isabella Indian Reservation); and dissects the allotment scandals endured by the residents of that reservation during the 1870s and 1880s, when haphazard recordkeeping and outright fraud allowed land speculators and lumber buyers to rob the Saginaw Chippewas of their land and timber. Chapter 4 reveals the abject corruption that existed in Michigan, including the roles played by the "Detroit Ring" and various politicians, land speculators, and lumber buyers who pilfered Saginaw resources by manipulation of the allotment process.

While Anderson's report ends at the turn of the century, R. David Edmunds, in chapters 5–6, follows through with an examination of reservation status from the early twentieth through the twentieth-first century. Chapter 5 details the effects of the decommissioning, in 1888, of the Indian agency that oversaw the Isabella Reservation and outlines the growth of the Mt. Pleasant Indian School, whose supervisors were consequently saddled by the government with the tasks once handled by the agency. Chapter 6 covers the Indian Reorganization Act and the birth and growth of tribal self-governance throughout the century. Edmunds ends with a discussion of the economic vitality created by the Saginaw Chippewa Indian tribe in the late twentieth and early twenty-first centuries. Along the way, he shows that very little evidence—indeed, virtually none—can be found to support what the state's expert witnesses have argued—that the Saginaw people were anxious to abandon their reservation and assume citizenship.[8]

By the early twentieth century, the state of Michigan, Isabella County, and the city of Mt. Pleasant had assumed control of many normal sovereign Indian rights. These entities employed that power on all the lands within the boundary of the Isabella Reservation. Even so, as Edmunds discovers, tribal organization continued to function, often through the auspice of the Indian boarding school in Mt. Pleasant; by the 1930s, the Saginaw Tribal Council began to emerge and gain back some authority under the Indian Reorganization Act of 1934. It assumed the right to build and operate a gambling casino near Mt. Pleasant in the late twentieth century and found the resources to challenge the state and local governments abrogation of its treaty rights under the 1855 and 1864 treaties.[9]

The state of Michigan soon discovered that it faced a more daunting landscape than it expected, given its early overoptimistic belief that the *Sherril* decision, and the laches argument, would protect against the argument of tribal sovereignty. At the first meeting of the court, though, the state, county, and city officials asserted their primary argument: that "the affirmative defenses of res judicata, collateral estoppel, equitable estopped, acquiescence, impossibility, impracticability and laches, or any combination of these affirmative defenses" led to the obvious conclusion that tribal sovereignty, and the Isabella Indian Reservation, had ceased to exist sometime after 1875.[10]

There was some support for the state's argument. Article 6 of the 1855 treaty theoretically dissolved tribal organization, but with one caveat:

"except for the purpose of carrying into effect" the treaty itself. This article created even more confusion when the federal government negotiated the second treaty in 1864. The question seemed obvious: How could the government negotiate another treaty with a tribe that no longer existed? What is more, to what degree did Saginaw Indians understand the legal jargon? These historical issues—oftentimes issues that the state and its experts could not logically challenge—will be addressed in the chapters below.

And the confusion grew to even greater lengths. The incongruity of the United States negotiating a treaty with a dissolved Indian nation— and the Senate ratifying it—would have caused most negotiators to address the tribe's status. Some evidence suggests that they tried to do so in the last article of the 1864 treaty. Article 8 offered the following: "The eighth article of the treaty of August second, eighteen hundred and fifty-five, shall in no wise be affected by the terms of this treaty." Yet this clarified nothing: there was no "Article 8" in the 1855 treaty; it concluded with Article 7. The negotiators of the 1864 treaty may have designed this clumsy effort as a loophole to deny the existence of the tribe while at the same time using what mechanisms still did exist to allot lands to individual Indians, the primary goal of the 1864 treaty.

While the American negotiators in 1864 likely hoped they had resolved the issue of tribal authority, nothing could be further from the truth. This continuing confusion led the defendants in the 2005 case to look for other evidence regarding the existence of tribal authority. The most likely place for such evidence was in the journals negotiators (supposedly) kept for both treaties. The Bureau of Indian Affairs (BIA) had begun asking agents to keep such journals in the early part of the nineteenth century, and it was standard procedure to hire a clerk for that specific purpose. While such a journal did surface for an 1855 treaty negotiated with the Ottawa Indians of western Michigan, no journal came to light for either of the two negotiations with the Saginaw Chippewas. The loss of this evidence meant there was no direct evidence documenting how the federal commissioners explained the treaties to the Chippewa Indians.

As the historians on both sides of the case introduced their reports, it became obvious to Federal Judge Thomas L. Ludington of the Eastern

District of Michigan that the case was far more complex than the earlier Oneida cases of the 1980s or the Sherril case of 2005. Laches still lacked a clear definition, and it became increasingly apparent that there had not been a lapse of time—decades—from the point at which the Saginaws had lost the ability to implement much of their sovereignty (say, roughly, 1880) to the third decade of the twentieth century, at which point the tribe reorganized itself under the Indian Reorganization Act. At this point, Judge Ludington decided to attempt negotiation—some give-and-take on both sides.

The negotiation that ensued took two full years. So many problems were addressed in this decision that the printed agreement came to 175 pages. The main issues involved law enforcement, environmental concerns, hunting and fishing rights, Indian child welfare, and taxation. At the heart of the final judgment was the conclusion that "since its creation, the Isabella Reservation has not even been diminished or disestablished in any way."[11]

Finally, a number of years ago, Todd Adams, who was at the time the acting attorney for Indian Affairs in the state of Michigan, suggested to both Anderson and Edmunds that perhaps the settlement of the very complex issues surrounding the case would make a good story, one that should be published. It was not only important for the people of Isabella County to understand why the case was brought and how it was concluded, but also for the people of Michigan, and even the nation, to see how past abuses of Indians can be resolved in a fair and reasonable way. Adams read the reports here reproduced, offered suggestions, and then helped write the introduction and conclusion.

As Adams so clearly asserts, the work of many people—historians, lawyers, government officials—all came together to produce a workable solution to the thorny issues surrounding the Saginaw Chippewa Tribe and its relationship with the state of Michigan, Isabelle County, and city of Mt. Pleasant. By reading the chapters that follow, people of the state, and indeed the nation, can come to see that Native tribes have been abused in the past and that they deserve their day in court. The state of Michigan ultimately agreed to that, and the state and its people, both Native and non-Native, are better off for it today.

1

EARLY CONTACT

In 1608, when the French arrived and built a trading center called Quebec on the St. Lawrence River, the central Great Lakes region provided a homeland for many different Native peoples. Over the next forty years, French traders slowly penetrated the interior, reaching the lands north of Lake Ontario by the 1620s, lands inhabited by the Huron Indians. Traders soon thereafter reached eastern Michigan, traveling along the coast of Lake Huron well into the west by 1650. It was there, in the lands of northern Michigan and southern Ontario, that they first encountered people who called themselves "Anishinaabe," or, in their language, "good humans" or simply "the people." Numbering into the several thousands, they came to be called Ojibwe by the French, borrowing an Anglo corruption that later evolved into "Chippewa," a general term that has stuck until recently as the most frequently used name. Farther west in the region north and south of Lake Superior, Anishinaabes were often identified by the French as Saulteurs, another corruption that remains today as an appellation for these same people in Canada.[1] They all spoke a similar language, Algonquian, and had a similar economy and culture.

The largest political unit that existed among the Chippewa people was the residence band. It could number as many as two to three hundred people or perhaps as few as fifty. Band organization remained fluid, and people came and went, often with the seasons. Given the importance of hunting to the various bands, the Chippewa people seem to have adopted a patrilineal clan system (although evidence is scant) to offer band residents a place in their society—people being given clearly defined lineage identities—and to prevent incest. It was taboo to marry another member of the same clan; women often joined their new husbands in other bands.[2] Others from her clan might then join the exodus, thus contributing to the fluid makeup of each band. Leadership within a band usually devolved upon the most active, and sensible, male member of the largest family and could be handed down from generation to generation. And sustaining such a family depended on bringing new wives into the band. Thus, the negotiation of a bride price for wives became a significant event, often the most important decision that Chippewa elders—both men and women—made each season.[3]

The Chippewa people within this clan system retained strong respect for kinship identity. Names became crucial in maintaining kinship relationships, and one's grandparents took a special place. Nevertheless, within the clan, every member of the same generation was identified as "grandmother" or "grandfather." This created an atmosphere in which elders were highly respected and honored. Likewise, in the Chippewa kinship system a person's aunts and uncles also held a special place, but they were not any more important than others of that generation who came from the same clan or village, who also were revered as "aunts" and "uncles." All were responsible for raising children, and children, when they got older, thus felt a strong obligation to help anyone in the clan who was in need.[4]

While older couples who knew each other often negotiated the contracts of marriage for their children, this was not always the case. At times, uncles and aunts participated in what became a family affair. Uncles, in particular, spent considerable time with nephews, learning their private wants and desires. These were often considered when the clan sought wives for them. The same might be true for an aunt, who listened carefully to the wishes of a young niece. Once a match seemed likely, a representative of the family—usually from the male side—would approach the young woman's family with a gift. It could be a gun, a canoe, or even such a modest item as a shirt. If the gift was accepted, it meant that the marriage was agreed upon—or, more exactly, that the young people agreed to it. The consummation of the marriage usually happened in the home of the young woman, but the couple then retreated to live with the husband's family. Given the careful nature of the marriage customs, it seldom resulted in trouble. The Chippewas remained, then, a relatively peaceful people, living in their small villages, sustaining themselves through hunting and fishing.[5]

A second reason for congeniality related to the Chippewa Indians' view of sexual relations. Young women had considerable freedom both before and after marriage. Virginity in men and women had no special place; young men and women could and did have sex before marriage. Oftentimes, young women chafed at being left behind in a village when the young men went on an extended hunt. They occasionally eloped with a young suitor, without marriage, and became what is often called a "hunting woman." Once a hunting woman returned to the village, an arranged marriage was still viable, given the relaxed views that the Chippewas had toward sex. The only barrier to premarital sex was pregnancy, which Native women not only knew how to avoid but also to end.[6]

This is the world that Europeans encountered in the 1640s. The settlement at Quebec, unlike English competitors to the south in Virginia and Massachusetts, came to depend on the expanding fur trade for its economic security. French traders reached the Huron villages (the name Wyandot is also used to identify these Indians) that lay north of Lake Erie in the 1620s and had established outposts within their villages a few years later. Jesuit missionaries soon joined them, although they made little progress in converting the large communities of Hurons, who spoke Iroquoian rather than Algonquian. These Natives cultivated large fields of corn and beans near their permanent villages, which were surrounded by tall palisades. Given their horticultural economy, which fostered more consistent food supplies, the Huron populations numbered much larger than their Chippewa neighbors to the west: populations totaled at least fifty thousand in 1620.[7] With French *voyageurs* by their sides (the term referred to French traders who adopted Native lifeways), the Hurons soon became involved in the fur trade, leading brigades of traders into the interior of Michigan, where they opened commercial relations with the Chippewas. While French traders did little to develop communities or towns, they did establish a unique commercial relationship with the

Native inhabitants, called by one historian the "middle ground."[8] The argument suggests that two very different cultures, which possessed very different notions of economic and social processes, learned to respect each other and to work together for their common benefit.

Chippewa Indians lived communally; material items, such as those used in bride price exchanges, had symbolic meaning but had little quantifiable importance. Goods, such as food and clothing, were important because they fed and clothed the entire clan, rather than the individual.

Accordingly, the Chippewas immediately saw the benefits of manufactured goods offered by the French traders, such as guns, kettles, and even trinkets. And the Chippewas also recognized immediately the French traders' desire for beaver, otter, and lynx pelts. Since neither group had set measures of value for these items, trade became a reciprocal exchange. French traders laid goods on a blanket, and Chippewa leaders graciously accepted them and then instructed their young men to bring forward pelts. This exchange soon resulted in strong ties between the two groups, traders and Indians, that had political and military importance.

French traders would arrive in the fall, when the Indians went on their hunts, and leave with canoes full of furs come spring. To cement this relationship—to ensure that a particular trader got furs in exchange—the Frenchman offered presents to band leaders and would take a wife, often the daughter of an important man in the village. While this relationship would change over the years, and a series of "articulations" would ultimately reach a point where the price of goods became an issue, traders generally were treated as family and given kinship names.[9] While sources suggest that some French traders viewed these relationships as temporary, others came to recognize that the ties were, in part, like those common for hunting women. Traders often spent the winter months in a Chippewa village with a willing female partner, only to leave come spring for Quebec. The trader might or might not return the next fall to reestablish the relationship with his partner. While such flexible relationships were certainly new to Europeans, they amounted to a reasonable accommodation on the part of the Indians. They needed traders—and that need only grew as game became scarce—and women needed partners, since their potential Native partners could be killed in war or on the hunt. Moreover, female partners offered considerable aid to French traders; they processed food, made and mended clothing, and even, at times, acted as intermediaries with other hunting groups.[10] The arrangement amounted to what anthropologists call a "social relation of production," a practice peculiar to the fur trade and beneficial to both groups.[11] The offspring of the unions, called Métis, assumed important roles in Chippewa society thereafter.

While French traders might linger in a Chippewa village over the winter, this was a time of considerable activity for the clans. It was also the most difficult time of the year: snow hindered hunting and ice limited fishing. Hunting camps moved frequently to locales where game was more likely to be found. When hunts failed, the only alternative was to fish for sturgeon and trout from the numerous lakes and rivers or to rely on foraged foods, often prepared in early fall, such as acorn meal or roots. But during the seventeenth century, the hunts seldom failed, and the growing use of guns, which had a longer range than bows and arrows, meant a variety of game animals were often taken—deer, moose, bear, lynx, fox, and beaver, to name the most common. Indeed, anthropologist Marshall Sahlins has argued that the time a Chippewa hunter needed to sustain a village in food amounted some twenty-eight hours each week on the hunt.[12] And while the Hurons continued to plant crops each year, the Chippewas, at least in the early period, gave little attention to corn or beans. Their economy seemed strong and capable of sustaining them forever.

Given the strength of their economy, the Saginaw Indians remained free of what is generally called "material want." Their limited material possessions gave them a sense of freedom that does not exist in modern society. Since the food quest was intermittent, there was more time for leisure, more time for male and female camaraderie, and more opportunity to spend time with children. And the inclination existed to consume all stocks of food without much concern for the future—the sharing of food by all created a situation where hording was impossible. This could lead to a starvation diet when snows became so high that hunters could not get to game herds. But during such periods, all suffered together, as consumption was a communal affair. Changes to this somewhat idyllic life did start to appear, however, as more Europeans arrived in Canada.[13] And the appearance of these strange new people would lead to disruption, overhunting, and increasing social difficulties.

Near cataclysmic events soon changed the landscape of the middle ground. During the 1640s, pathogens the Indians had never encountered before entered the Great Lakes region. The most devastating was smallpox. Introduced by the French, it hit the Hurons in 1644 and lingered on into the later part of the decade. Thousands died; others fled. Making matters worse, the five tribes (or Five Nations) of the Iroquois Confederacy, neighbors to the south—the Senecas, Onondagas, Cayugas, Oneidas, and Mohawks—opened a war with the Hurons. The reasons for the conflict were complex. The Five Nations were developing extensive exchange relationships with newly arriving Dutch traders near Albany and likely were encouraged to attack the French allies and take control of the regions that produced beaver.[14] Dwindling supplies of beaver pelts in Iroquois lands also contributed. The Iroquois recognized the need to expand their hunting range into Michigan and beyond. By 1648 the conflict resulted in the destruction of the complex of Huron towns north of Lake Erie, and the survivors (perhaps only a few thousand) fled west into Chippewa lands.[15]

Disease may have wreaked as much devastation on the Algonquian people as the war itself. While some Chippewa bands had been moving south into central Michigan before the war, they retreated north in the decades after it began, only pausing when the French reached Sault de Marie in force. Other Michigan Indians, including Ottawas and Potawatomies, fled west into Wisconsin, where they remained in contact with the French but faced occasional assaults from the Iroquois and their allies. Jesuits built a mission near Sault Ste. Marie in 1668, and the region was claimed by France in a formal ceremony three years later. Another French post, Michilimackinac, appeared near the Straits of Mackinac a few years later, with a garrison of troops under Antoine Laumet (known in North America as Antoine de Lamothe, sieur de Cadillac), and French traders often visited Green Bay and even built occasional posts along the Mississippi River to the west.[16]

Commissioned a major a few years later, Cadillac convinced the French government to expand southward, back into Michigan, where they built a new fort in 1701 at what would become Detroit. He was able to do this because the Iroquois agreed to a peace treaty that year. Using his influence with many of the Chippewa Indians of northern Michigan and Wisconsin, he convinced several bands to follow him south, including groups that by the 1720s were identified as the Saginaw Chippewas. In the years that followed, the Ottawas, Potawatomis, and Miamis followed suit, returning to central Michigan.[17] Yet the relocation strategy failed when it came to the Fox (Meskawaki) Nation, whom the French encouraged to move closer to Detroit. The newly returned Indians were soon bickering among themselves, mostly over resources. Potawatomi-Ottawa groups brought the Chippewas and Hurons into a confederacy aimed at removing the Foxes. This led to a Fox attack on Detroit in 1711 and the tribe's eventual flight back into Wisconsin. Over the next thirty years, the French and their allies feuded with the Fox Nation, who raided French trading brigades while the Confederacy launched several attacks against Fox villages.

While the Saginaw Chippewas mostly stayed out of these expeditions into the west, they remained loyal to the French through these troubled times. Peace finally came to the region in 1737. By this time the Saginaw Chippewas had settlements along the western shore of Lake Huron as well as in the vicinity of the Aux Sable River. As had the other Indian tribes of Michigan, most Potawatomis and Ottawas had moved west, closer to the eastern shore of Lake Michigan. Various reports mention villages of Saginaw people in the 1760s and 1770s. Struggles for land and resources continued: farther east, the French and Indian War broke out in 1755, but the conflict had little impact on the Chippewa Indians, other than to occasionally cut them off from trade. The British victory, however, did lead to an attempt to deny the Chippewas and their neighbors gifts meant to ensure favorable relations. Thus, in the aftermath of the war, a rebellion broke out, led by Pontiac, the Ottawa war chief who convinced many different bands to join his assault on British outposts. Many different Algonquian speakers participated in Pontiac's failed rebellion (1763–64), including some Chippewa warriors from the Saginaw people.[18]

In the aftermath of Pontiac's rebellion, the law and order that the French had tried to establish—and had often succeeded in implementing—began to break down. This order was based on the giving of presents and reciprocity, and the British lacked the patience necessary to deal with tribal leaders; given their monopoly over western trade, British military officers seemed less interested in protecting that trade. On several occasions between 1764 and 1768, Saginaw Chippewa parties attacked British traders along the Ohio River, and British traders and their partners retaliated.[19] Worse, European settlers—who had steadily moved north up the Susquehanna River from Philadelphia and west from Albany, New York—increasingly encroached on Indian lands, killing Indians in the effort. By the time of the American Revolution, the frontiersman Daniel Boone also provoked Native ire by settling west of the Appalachian Mountains in what would become Kentucky. This led to outrage that swept Indian country, as bands in Ohio and Michigan formed a confederacy in the 1780s to deny the American victors in the Revolutionary War any more land.[20]

To what degree the Saginaw Chippewas cooperated with the Ohio Indian confederacy is a murky matter. Certainly, some of their men and perhaps their chiefs were involved and fought against the American invasion of Ohio in the mid 1780s. Perhaps they witnessed, or at least heard of, the assault by George Rogers Clark's rangers on northern Ohio Indian villages. Some no doubt joined the Shawnee and Miami leaders Blue Jacket and Little Turtle, who attacked and sent reeling Gen. Josiah Harmar's American army in 1790. A few also undoubtedly participated in the near annihilation of Gov. Arthur St. Clair's army that followed the next year. Given these victories, others likely joined the confederacy as it faced off with yet another American army led into Ohio by Gen. Anthony Wayne in 1794. This time, the superior training of Wayne's troops led to an Indian rout and the destruction of large amounts of Indian corn and food that had been stored in villages on the upper Maumee and Miami Rivers for the coming winter. The disaster led to the peace negotiation and land cession at the Treaty of Greenville the next year.[21]

The treaty itself had little to do with Saginaw Chippewa lands. It basically led to the acquisition of half of Ohio by the United States. The treaty line separating Indian lands from those acquired by the United States started at the Cayahoga River (the spelling used in the document), which runs through present-day Cleveland. Running south to a portage, the treaty line then turned west, to the Miami River, thence downriver to the Ohio River. While the land cession did not include Saginaw lands, no fewer than twelve Chippewa Indian leaders attached their signatures to the treaty. Among those with strong Saginaw ties were Mashipinashiwish, Kathawasung, Masass, and Nemekass. Several of the others were representatives of the Chippewas of Lake Superior and Sault Ste. Marie, which gives us some indication of the broad nature of the Ohio Indian confederacy at the time.[22]

In many ways, the Treaty of Greenville set the tone for future negotiations. Its initial articles established "peace and friendship" between the United States and the Indian nations. General Wayne appropriated the southern half of the future state of Ohio as well as certain other properties, including the British post then located on Mackinac Island in Lake Michigan. Furthermore, should any of the Indian signers want to relinquish more lands in the future, the treaty stipulated that they could sell only to the United States. For these concessions, the Indians were to receive some annuities, including a thousand dollars' worth of goods to the Chippewa Indians each year thereafter. Some measure of interest also centered on the growing problem of what has been called "settler sovereignty," or the notion held by many settlers that they had a right to settle on lands anywhere in the west. The treaty gave the Indians the right to evict such intruders. Finally, the Indians agreed to allow only licensed traders to enter their lands, traders who were sanctioned by the United States government. These terms were difficult to enforce, since most of these Indians remained loyal to the British and their traders, who still resided in Canada.

Perhaps the most compelling part of the treaty that the various tribes embraced was the language regarding fishing and hunting rights. Given their lifeways, fishing and hunting were crucial to their existence. Wayne recognized this and wrote into the treaty the right of the Indians to continue to fish and hunt on the ceded lands. This became a standard concession on the part of the United States and promoted future conflict: Who would determine when that right would be relinquished?[23]

Following the Treaty of Greenville, relatively peaceful relations returned to the region. US government officials often met Saginaw Chippewa leaders at the various forts that had been built across central

Ohio. While most of these bands remained along the rivers that emptied into Saginaw Bay, two others, the Swan Creek and Black River bands, moved slowly south, closer to Lake St. Clair. Here they had more frequent contact with Americans, and a regular dialogue began. As usual, it often involved the cession of Indian lands. The Swan Creek and Black River bands also developed more regular relationships with American settlers who crossed the northern boundary searching for good farmland. This eventually led to the negotiation of treaties that exchanged land for annuities, the first of which was signed in 1807.

Just after Thomas Jefferson was sworn in as president in 1801, the War Department initiated a series of negotiations with many different Indian tribes in the old Northwest. These nations included the Seneca, Wyandot (or Huron), Piankashaw, Delaware, Munsee, Shawnee, Potawatomi, and Sac and Fox Indians. Most of the treaties called for the cession of land to the American government, lands generally situated west of Albany and in the regions that bordered the northern bank of the Ohio River, extending into what would become southern Indiana and Illinois. The Sac and Fox treaty of 1804 even included land cessions as far up the Mississippi River as Rock Island.[24] As settlers pushed north and west out of the upper Ohio River valley, they naturally put pressure on the government to purchase Chippewa lands in southern Michigan.

The negotiation of 1807 was held at Detroit with the Saginaw Chippewas, as well as with various Ottawa and Potawatomi leaders. It led to the sale of much of northwestern Ohio as well as lands in southern Michigan. The northern boundary was an east-west line that extended from the outlet of Lake Erie, which forms the mouth of the Sinclair River, to a point due east of the Maumee River. In an interesting twist, the treaty provided two blacksmiths to aid the Indians in adapting to farming, and it ended the rights and privileges of the Indians to hunt and fish on these lands. One of the blacksmiths was to "reside with the Chippeways, at Saguina." While the exact location of Saguina is not indicated in the treaty, the phrase likely refers to the present-day city of Saginaw, which is located just south of the bay of that name. It seems to have become a permanent Chippewa-Métis community.[25]

While the War of 1812 disrupted efforts to convert the Chippewa people to an agricultural economy—there is little evidence that the blacksmiths were ever sent north—in the years that followed the war, the Saginaws signed several more treaties with the United States: one in 1815 to reestablish peace; and a second, far more key agreement in 1819. This latter treaty was negotiated by Lewis Cass, who came to play an increasingly important role in Chippewa affairs.

Cass, who had served as an officer under William Henry Harrison during the War of 1812, became territorial governor of Michigan in 1813, after Harrison's troops had retaken Detroit. He would later take a leading role in developing Andrew Jackson's policy of forced Indian removal while serving as Jackson's secretary of war. An early biographer of Cass would argue that the governor successfully negotiated for more Indian land than any other American official in history, a dubious distinction. Certainly, regarding treaty land cessions, he acquired considerably more land than his mentor, Harrison, who was referred to as "Mr. Jefferson's Hammer" when it came to inflicting Indian policy on Indians.[26]

The treaty of 1819 was negotiated at Saginaw, Michigan, at that time a fledgling trading post operated by Louis Campau. Cass had hired Campau to put up four log buildings—along with the trader's house, the first to be built in the town—and Cass spent roughly ten days at the post negotiating with somewhere between fifteen hundred and four thousand Indians. (They were so haphazardly camped along the river leading into the bay that an accurate estimate became impossible.) Cass had also taken the precaution of reading the 1807 treaty and had discovered that promised annuities had never been paid. He promptly wrote Secretary of War John C. Calhoun that he would simply take a "draft" from a bank in Detroit to acquire silver dollars and make the payment. A company of soldiers commanded by Cass's brother, Capt. John Cass, made the trip as well, to maintain order.[27]

The treaty followed an increasing pattern when it came to the Michigan tribes. They were treated as one group, which included Ottawas, Potawatomis, and Saginaw Chippewas, although the majority of Indians in attendance were Saginaws. Cass, the American commissioner, was an enterprising, congenial man, who soon came to play a major role in Saginaw history. Unlike some of his predecessors, such as William Henry Harrison, who had bullied Indians into signing agreements, Cass took a more measured approach, trying to convince Indians of the advantages of government annuities and presents. This, he said, would lead to agricultural independence. He also provided plenty of lubricant during negotiations, using as justification the fact that the British, just east of Detroit, often handed out kegs of rum to the Chippewas who visited them. According to an Indian trader who witnessed the negotiation, Cass brought into Detroit a stockpile of 662 gallons of whiskey, which was used at times to suppress opposition to the treaty. He also assured Indians that they would be allowed to fish and hunt on ceded lands for a long time, crucial to any agreement given the economy of the Indians.[28]

After the opening address, Cass faced a barrage of indignation from Chippewa leaders. The chief spokesman of the tribe, Kish-kaw-ko, was a staunch opponent to any land sale. But he was soon incapacitated: "He had put himself out of condition at the close of the first day by drinking, and remained in a state quite unpresentable as a speaker for the residue of the time." His opposition, and apparently some violent actions while drunk, led to his arrest by the army, and he eventually "died in prison at Detroit." Kish-kaw-ko's replacement, O-ge-maw-ke-ke-to, answered Cass with a rejection that seemed to be supported by most of the other leaders present. He was "quite young, not over twenty-five," and in bearing "graceful and handsome." "We are here to smoke the pipe of peace, but not to sell out lands," he began. "Our English father treats us better," he then noted. "He has never asked for them [land]."[29]

Cass struck back with increasing arrogance. "The Great Father at Washington had just closed a war in which he had whipped their Father, the English King and the Indians too," the commissioner responded. "Their [the Indians] lands were forfeited in fact by the rules of war." Even so, Cass confessed that he did not intend to confiscate the land, but rather provide for the future of Chippewa women and children. They, along with their men, would receive "ample tribal reserves . . . where they could spread their blankets and be aided and instructed in agriculture." This did little to persuade the Indians to cooperate; indeed, the council broke up with both sides seething with anger. At this point, the traders and Métis took over—men such as Whitmore Knaggs, Henry Conner, John Harson, and especially Jacob Smith, who traded on the Flint River. They soon presented Cass with a list of names—Indian,

Métis, and non-Indian—of men who, if given large reserves, might agree to the treaty. With this opening, Cass crafted an agreement that the Indians finally signed several days later. As the Indians affixed their clan seals to the agreement, Cass handed out the silver dollars, the traders present literally going to fisticuffs over them. Afterward, no fewer than fifteen barrels of whiskey were opened, and a melee followed in which both Cass and the traders feared for their lives. When Cass ordered the liquor handout to stop, Campau, who supposed that he had been cheated out of the money, confronted Cass and said simply, "Yes General, but you commenced it."[30]

The degree to which the Saginaws opposed the treaty of 1819 is difficult to determine. The money did help seal the deal. In reporting his success in September 1819, Cass wrote to the secretary of war that the Indians "were anxious to receive what they could speedily dissipate in childish and useless purchases, at the expense of stipulations which would be permanently useful."[31] The Indians had demanded annuity money in the form of specie, which could be used to purchase goods that were readily becoming available on the Michigan frontier. By this time, it was also obvious that hunting and the fur trade could no longer sustain them—or their traders—as game herds had become increasingly scarce.

The treaty led to the purchase of a vast domain in central and north-eastern Michigan, lands adjacent to the cession of 1807. The new line extended from present-day Kalamazoo north to Jackson and included the lands surrounding Saginaw Bay west to the central part of the peninsula, up to present-day Alpena. It also was the first treaty of its kind to include no fewer than thirty tracts of "reserve" land—their sizes ranged between 640 to 10,000 acres—for Indian leaders, their Métis relatives, and traders. These tracts were to be surveyed and titled in fee simple, allowing their owners to sell them for profit. While tribal leaders often demanded lands that corresponded with the locations of their villages, several such grants were made to non-Indians who used native names, clear bribes to obtain the assistance of these acquisitive people in convincing elders to sign. Cass apologized to Secretary Calhoun for the large number of grants of this sort, explaining that they were necessary to obtain the treaty. Calhoun apparently thought the strategy a good one and sent the treaty on to the Senate for quick ratification.[32]

Given the fact that so much land had become available for settlement farther south in Ohio, Indiana, and Illinois, little settlement pressure was exerted on the surrendered lands in Michigan during the 1820s. The only conflict of interest dealt with fishing rights, as traders, seeing the demise of their profession, turned to other resources, such as exploiting the vast spawning grounds for whitefish and trout that existed in the straits that connected Lakes Huron, Michigan, and Superior. Indian superintendent Henry Schoolcraft recognized the growing controversy early in 1830, asking the secretary of war, who happened to be Lewis Cass, whether he had the right to issue licenses for exploitation to trade firms. The issue was not settled until 1834, when it was determined that some of the lands adjacent to Mackinac had been ceded in the Treaty of Greenville and that fishing grounds within this boundary could be exploited by non-Indians. Given weak enforcement, there took shape thereafter an industry that salted and shipped fish from various areas in the northern lakes to new markets at the bustling new cities of Cleveland and Buffalo.[33]

By the mid-1830s, the pressure of white settlement did finally become a problem for some of the Swan Creek and Black River Chippewas, who still lived in the vicinity of Lake St. Clair. Some had received tracts of land in the 1819 treaty and still retained them. Others who had tracts wished to sell and move farther north, away from encroaching whites. The main problem seemed to be the tendency of whites to steal oak and pine timber from reserves when the Indians were away hunting.[34] While some Indians who owned these tracts may have been willing to consider a sale, most could not legally sell land to whites even if they had a clear title. It was forbidden under the Intercourse Acts, including the main revision of the law, which occurred in 1834.[35]

Yet another reason for the willingness of the government to renegotiate the land reserves created by the 1819 treaty came from the wave of sentiment endorsing "forced Indian removal" that swept the west around the time that Andrew Jackson was elected president in 1828. Jackson had concluded as early as 1817 (when he was a US senator representing Tennessee) that Indians lacked clear title to their lands and that Congress had the right to remove them west of the Mississippi River.

Most of the attention was placed on the southern Indians—Cherokees, Choctaws, Creeks, Chickasaws, and Seminoles—primarily because their lands were needed for the expansion of the slave plantation system that produced cotton.[36] While some tribes north of the Ohio were moved west in the 1830s, there had been little pressure to remove the Saginaw Chippewas, given that their lands were mostly forest and not overly attractive to settlers who farmed. The new negotiations of 1836 and 1837 were mostly due to the lobbying of a handful of Swan Creek and Black River leaders who owned reserves.[37]

The result was a negotiation in Washington between leaders of the Swan Creek and Black River Chippewas, or those who lived closest to Detroit. They signed a treaty in the spring of 1836 in which the government agreed to sell their reserve lands to settlers, the proceeds of which would be paid after survey costs had been deducted. Nearly a year later, the Saginaw Chippewas from the bay signed a similar treaty ceding their reserves for lands in the west. While both agreements passed the Senate in 1837, that year the financial panic hit the country and land sales collapsed.[38] Finally, when it became obvious that land sales would never provide sufficient funds to support the Indians in a move west, the government renegotiated the terms of the land cessions, using the concept of "graduation," which was popular at the time. Under this plan, the land would be offered first at $5.00 an acre and gradually reduced to $.75 an acre over time.[39] This was supposed to assure the Indians that it would be sold.

This left the Saginaw Chippewas in a state of flux. They legally owned no land in Michigan but were allowed to live on lands until they moved west of the Mississippi River. The government abandoned this idea, however, after a small party of Saginaw chiefs traveled to Kansas and discovered that rather than rolling hills and oak groves, the land was flat and treeless. The decade that followed led to increasing uncertainty. The Mexican War shifted interest from Indian affairs in Michigan—and even the removal of Indians to the west—to Texas and eventually to gold in California. And since the deciduous forests of the eastern United States covered most of the lands north of Jackson and Kalamazoo, settlers had little interest in moving onto them. It made no difference that the Ottawa Indians agreed to a treaty relinquishing the western portion of Michigan that bordered the 1819 Saginaw land sale.[40]

Into this void came the administration of Franklin Pierce in 1853. Pierce appointed a new, seemingly sympathetic, commissioner of Indian affairs, George Manypenny, who set out to solve many of the "Indian problems" he inherited from previous administrations. He negotiated dozens of treaties in Iowa and Kansas, settling landless Indians on small reservations where they would hopefully start farming. Manypenny was not committed to the policy of removal that had dominated many of his predecessors. He felt it best to settle Indians where they were, on lands where they wished to live. He did believe, however, that Indians only needed sufficient land for farming and that large hunting estates were detrimental to the development of "civilization."[41]

As he assumed leadership of the Office of Indian Affairs, Manypenny soon realized that the Saginaw Indians of Michigan had not moved west of the Mississippi River—and had no intentions of doing so. And they were landless, in effect; they were squatters on government land, living in small conclaves of villages in the various river valleys that emptied into Saginaw Bay. A few had returned to Canada. Manypenny certainly realized that the government had basically reneged on its agreement to sell reserve lands, some of which were being overrun by squatters. He soon sought a new deal for the Saginaws, one that placed them on a reservation of their own.

2

THE SAGINAWS AND THE
NEW RESERVATION SYSTEM
OF THE 1850s AND 1860s

In the early 1800s, southeastern states became increasingly dissatisfied with the continued existence of Indian tribes within their boundaries. The addition of new lands acquired through the Louisiana Purchase presented a possible solution to this "Indian problem": remove tribes west of the Mississippi River. By creating a barrier between Indians and whites, conflict could be avoided and Indians would be given time to assimilate into white society. This notion of a barrier and the removal policy were eventually adopted by the federal government.[1]

At first, removal proceeded slowly. Through treaty negotiations, the government simply encouraged Indian tribes to voluntarily move westward. But since most Indians refused to leave, white Americans who lived in the new states west of the Appalachian Mountains demanded that they be forced to leave. Newly elected president Andrew Jackson, a westerner, agreed in 1829 to remove Indians and supported a bill in Congress that brought forced removal the next year. By 1840 the bulk of the Cherokee, Creek, Chickasaw, Choctaw, and Seminole tribes had been removed to the Indian Territory.[2] Tribes in the Northeast and Midwest were also forcibly relocated.[3] In total, roughly one hundred thousand Indians were removed from both the northern and southern states to lands west of the Mississippi.

Federal removal policy was ultimately hindered by the speed of westward expansion of non-Indian settlement. Once Euro–American settlers reached California and Oregon by the 1840s, the effort to remove and relocate tribes outside of the states was doomed. Nevertheless, pressure was exerted on the federal government to make available large segments of land that had been promised Indians in the West. But the rapid Euro-American settlement west of the Mississippi River left no place to resettle eastern tribes. A new policy was needed—one that separated Indians from whites and settled them on lands where they could supposedly be "civilized." Often these lands were close to American settlers, or even lands that they had owned for centuries.[4]

In his annual report to Congress in 1848, Commissioner of Indian Affairs William Medill proposed a solution: given the fact that whites wanted more land, it would be necessary to confine Indians to what he called "colonies," or reservations. Initially Medill thought in terms of creating two such colonies: "one north, on the headwaters of the Mississippi, and the other south, on the western borders of Missouri and Arkansas."[5] Congress initially balked at creating large reservations that would have many different Indian tribes living on them. The problem was then handed over to the new commissioner, Luke Lea, in 1850.[6]

Lea had no experience with Indian issues; he was a Mississippi lawyer and politician who sought a federal cabinet position after failing in his bid to become governor of Mississippi. But after serving as commissioner of Indian affairs for just a few months, Lea had already developed his own solution to the "Indian problem." Instead of creating two large reservations as suggested by Medill, Lea proposed that several smaller reservations be created, thereby reducing the need for the removal of additional tribes. In his 1850 report to Congress, Lea stated: "There should be assigned to each Tribe, for a permanent home, a country adapted to agriculture, of limited extent and well-defined boundaries; within which all, with occasional exceptions, should be compelled constantly to remain until such time as their general improvement and good may supersede the necessity of such restrictions."[7]

Immediately thereafter, Lea attempted to implement this policy. He tried to create Indian reservations in California, Minnesota, and Texas without success. In 1851 and 1852 federal agents negotiated treaties with California tribes that would have created nineteen such small reservations within the state. But the Senate refused to ratify these treaties, in part because the California congressional delegation still wanted all Indian tribes removed from the state.[8] In 1851 Lea also negotiated a treaty with the Dakota (or Sioux) Indians of Minnesota that would have established a reservation for that tribe along the Minnesota River. The Senate, however, removed this provision at ratification.[9] Finally, Lea attempted to convince the Texas state legislature to set aside lands for Indian reservations, but the state did not do so until well after Lea had left office. Thus, Lea's vision for a reservation system was not implemented during his term.[10]

In 1853 George W. Manypenny, an Ohio businessman and newspaper editor, was appointed commissioner of Indian affairs by President Franklin Pierce. Like his predecessor, Manypenny believed that Indian tribes should be assigned to small reservations that would become their permanent homelands.[11] His most succinct views emerge in his annual report to Congress in 1855. The Indian, he began,

> must have a home; a fixed, settled, and permanent home. . . . [Soon] there will be no place to remove the Indian population. The policy of fixed habitations I regard as settled by the government, and it will soon be confirmed by an inevitable necessity; and it should be understood at once that those Indians who have had reservations set apart and assigned to them, as well as those who may hereafter by treaty have, are not to be interfered with in the peaceful possession and undisturbed enjoyment of their land.[12]

By now, senior government officials had come to support the creation of a reservation system, and Manypenny was permitted to begin treaty negotiations with tribes across the country.

Between 1854 and 1857 Manypenny's administration concluded an unprecedented total of fifty-two treaties, nearly all of which provided for the creation of Indian reservations. While the language used to create these reservations varied, they always promised a "homeland." The 1854 treaty with the Menominees established "a home, to be held as Indian lands are held" along the Wolfe River in Wisconsin.[13] The Kickapoos signed a treaty the same year, receiving a "reservation for a permanent home" consisting of 150,000 acres of land in Missouri (literally the same size as the later Saginaw Isabella Reservation).[14] Despite differences in terminology, Manypenny viewed all of these treaties as creating permanent reservations. Through these treaties, Manypenny also added a new wrinkle to the reservation policy first articulated by Lea. Most of Manypenny's treaties either allowed or required that the reservation lands be allotted to individual Indians. For example, the reservation set aside for the Kaskaskias and Peorias in 1854 contained the following definition for allotment: "Excepting and reserving there from a quantity of land equal to one hundred and sixty acres for each soul in said united Tribe."[15] This allotment policy catered to the general belief that owning private property was an essential part of American life and would expedite the civilizing process then underway with Indians. By being assigned individual farms, Indians would soon see the value in improving them. This would create a livelihood to support their families.[16]

Manypenny's success in implementing the reservation system during his term as commissioner of Indian affairs had a profound effect on federal Indian policy. His successors generally accepted this policy and continued to pursue it, as evidenced by Secretary of the Interior Jacob Thompson's 1860 report to Congress:

> I am strengthened, then, in the conviction expressed in my last annual report, that the only plan that holds out any hope for the decaying aboriginal races, is to confine them to smaller tribal reservations, having well-defined exterior boundaries, so that the intercourse laws can be enforced thereon, and to divide these reservations into farms of moderate dimensions, to be held in severalty by the individual members of the Tribe, with all the rights incident to an estate in fee simple, except that of alienation.[17]

Thus, during the 1850s and 1860s the term "reservation" was specifically tied to relatively small tracts of land set aside for Indians who were to be assimilated into American society through farm programs, school systems, and missionary activity. The now well-established policy guaranteed that Indians would receive a permanent homeland and that the newly created reservations would have well-defined exterior boundaries so that the Intercourse Acts of 1834 could be enforced within those boundaries. Finally, the new policy prescribed that eventually the reservations would be divided into 160-acre farms and allotted to individual Indians.

The 1855 Treaty with the Saginaw Chippewas

The federal government's relationship with the Saginaw, Swan Creek, and Black River bands (hereafter collectively referred to as the Saginaw Chippewas) mirrored its general federal policy toward Indian tribes. The Saginaw Chippewas found support for the creation of a homeland for them from a variety of individuals, including Methodist missionary George Bradley, who had lived among them for a decade by the 1850s. He argued in 1852 that the federal government should "colonize them, and give them a territory of land say 6 miles square." The term "colonize," a euphemism for enclosing them on a reservation, had been used by Commissioner Medill in his 1848 annual report, which Bradley undoubtedly had read. Bradley continued: "Let each man or family own his land in fee simple with this base prohibition to prevent him from selling or alienating to any white man."[18] Bradley knew that the government owed the Saginaw Chippewas funds under previous treaties, and thus they had a good argument for demanding a new negotiation of their situation in Michigan.

The obligations owed the Saginaw Chippewas by the federal government were substantial. As well as a permanent annual annuity of $2,500, the government had agreed under an 1838 treaty to pay the Indians proceeds from the sale of 102,400 acres of land that they had ceded. Since the sale price per acre was high, government officials believed that few of these lands had sold, and any funds accrued from them would be far below what the Indians expected.[19] But a concise accounting also had not been done, and the Indians had received nothing from the sales.[20]

The Saginaw Chippewas were not the only Indians in this position. Other Chippewa and Ottawa bands in Michigan had signed removal treaties with the United States that promised substantial financial compensation that had not been forthcoming. They were owed $200,000 in exchange for their ceded lands.[21] By the 1850s this annuity money was past due, and these Indians had failed to remove from the state.

The Michigan Indian agent working under Manypenny became increasingly aware of these problems and the need to solve them. While serving in Michigan in 1853, Agent Henry Gilbert penned a long letter to Commissioner Manypenny in which he called upon the government to "set apart certain tracts of public lands" for the Saginaw Chippewas. Each member of the individual band should "own and occupy eighty acres of land." Title to each plot, Gilbert advised, "should be vested in the head of the family & the permit to alienate [the land] should be withheld." Gilbert further suggested to Manypenny that all the land within the reservation should be "withdrawn from sale & no white person should be permitted to locate or live among them."[22] Manypenny, who, as discussed above, was a strong advocate for creating a national reservation system, agreed and requested Commissioner of the General Land Office John Wilson to survey central Michigan for land in December 1854.[23] Wilson selected sixteen possible townships in Isabella County and requested that Manypenny designate six that were most desirable. Wilson believed that "only about two-ninths of the whole surface [of the sixteen townships] has been disposed of," and these sold lands were primarily located in the southernmost townships, which had been on the market for the longest time.[24]

Agent Gilbert continued to press as Manypenny worked to implement the land selection. In a letter to Manypenny dated April 12, 1855, the agent noted that most of the better lands were "being so rapidly absorbed" by Anglo settlers in Michigan that the government needed to act quickly if lands were to be reserved for the various tribes who now wanted to stay.[25] Manypenny agreed, noting a month later that the "whole subject of their alleged claims and unsettled business" was then under review, as well as "the propriety of at once locating them permanently upon reservations."[26] Just a few days later, in anticipation of future treaty negotiations, President Franklin Pierce issued an executive order withdrawing all of the vacant land in Isabella County from sale.[27]

With land available for reservations, Manypenny planned for negotiations with the Ottawas and the Saginaw Chippewas to commence at Detroit in late July 1855. George Johnston, a Métis Chippewa who had served as an interpreter in earlier treaties, was contacted by Agent Gilbert to prepare the Indians for the negotiations. Johnston prepared a speech that was given to the various delegations.[28] He noted that they had already completed "the selection" of "delegates," and that their names had been sent on to Detroit. Johnston cautioned them to be "wise" in "making a selection for a location of land that may be allowed to you by your Great Father."[29]

With the careful selection of delegations complete, the first negotiation started on July 28. A clerk was assigned to keep a journal of the seven-day negotiations. Commissioner Manypenny set the tone, stating that the purpose of the council was to "aid you in settling upon permanent homes."[30] The Ottawas and Chippewas were allowed to select several townships as their reservations, and they were promised that the government would spend $200,000 on reservation improvements, including money for schools, blacksmiths, and agricultural implements.[31]

This treaty would serve as a starting point for negotiations with the Saginaw Chippewas, who concluded their parleys with the federal government just days later. While a journal of the Saginaw negotiations has not surfaced, the same promise that was made to the Ottawa and Chippewa tribes—that the lands identified in their treaty were to be permanent reservations—was undoubtedly made to the Saginaw Chippewas.

On August 2, 1855, a treaty was executed between the United States and the Saginaw Chippewas.[32] That treaty contained seven articles. The first provided that:

> The United States will withdraw from sale, for the benefit of said Indians, as herein provided, all the unsold public lands within the State of Michigan embraced in the following description, to wit: First. Six adjoining townships of land in the county of Isabella, to be selected by said Indians within three months from this date, and notice thereof given to their agent. Second. Townships Nos. 17 and 18 north, ranges 3, 4, and 5 east.[33]

Thus, two reservations were created: one consisting of six townships in Isabella County (the Isabella Reservation), and the other, two townships near Saginaw Bay (the Saginaw Bay Reservation).

As with most of Manypenny's treaties, Article 1 contained provisions for the allotment of Indian lands. The treaty specifically stated that the heads of Saginaw Chippewa families could select 80-acre farms within their reservation as prescribed by under the terms of the Ottawa and Chippewa treaty negotiated just a few days earlier. Farms of 40 acres were allowed to individuals. This process was to take five years, but a list of eligible Indians had to be completed by July 1856.

A peculiar paragraph within Article 1 also gave individual Indians the right to purchase lands, without limit, within the borders of the reservation.[34] While it was assumed that this right would allow assimilated Indians to expand their farms within the reservation, in reality, it soon afforded speculators an opportunity to manipulate the process and buy tracts from Indians in order to exploit the timber on them.

Article 2 of the Saginaw Chippewa treaty of 1855 set aside funds for reservation development, much like in the earlier Ottawa and Chippewa treaty. These funds totaled $82,000, while an extra $137,400 would be handed out as annuities over twelve years. Article 3 discharged the United States from any obligation regarding funds owed the tribe or lands promised under earlier treaties. Articles 4 and 5 provided for church lands and interpreters. Article 7 offered the obligatory statement regarding Senate ratification. Finally, Article 6 of the Saginaw Chippewa treaty provided that "the tribal organization of the said Indians, except so far as may be necessary for the purpose of carrying into effect the provisions of this agreement, is hereby dissolved.[35] This language was rather unique, although Manypenny did include similar language in the Ottawa Chippewa treaty negotiated a few days earlier: "The tribal organization of the said Ottawa and Chippewa Indians . . . is hereby dissolved; and if at any time hereafter future negotiations with the United States . . . should become necessary, no general convention of Indians shall be called; but such as reside in the vicinity of any usual place of payment, or those only who are immediately interested in the questions involved."[36] Because a treaty journal exists for the 1855 Ottawa Chippewa treaty, it provides interesting insight into the likely intent of the companion provision in the Saginaw Chippewa treaty of that same year.

In the 1800s the Ottawas and Chippewas were never a united tribe in any sense of the word; rather, they were organized in individual bands.[37] For ease of negotiating, however, the federal government gathered these individual bands when negotiating the 1836 Ottawa Chippewa treaty and simply referred to them collectively as "the Ottawa and Chippewa nation of Indians."[38]

During negotiations for the 1855 Ottawa Chippewa treaty, it became clear that the Ottawas and Chippewas held very different views about the best course for the future. The Ottawas originally seemed interested in obtaining only money, while the Chippewas insisted on being granted land. On the third day of negotiations, Waw-be-geeg, a Chippewa chief from the Upper Peninsula, requested that they each negotiate separately: "At the Treaty of 36, our fathers were in partnership with the Ottawas, but now, the partnership is finished and we who come from the foot of Lake Superior wish to do our business for ourselves."[39] Because his request was not immediately responded to, Waw-be-geeg raised it again toward the end of the negotiations: "I told you when I first came that I wanted to be separated from the Ottawas and you have not answered me. We have sat here and heard you talk to the Ottawas—while you paid no attention to us."[40] This time, Commissioner Manypenny did address Waw-be-geeg. He explained that while the Ottawas and Chippewas were to negotiate the 1855 treaty together, Article 5 of the treaty would separate the two tribes for all future negotiations: "The very case you suggested is met in the treaty—you are separated as you desire. This treaty you and the Ottawas must sign together is because the old treaty of 36 was made in that way, but here we have followed your suggestion and provide . . . that no general council shall be called [in the future]."[41]

This was the only discussion of Article 5 of the 1855 Ottawa Chippewa treaty contained in the treaty journal. Thus, the Indians would have understood that this clause was included to dissolve the fictitious grouping of the Ottawa and Chippewa nations as one tribe. It was not intended to otherwise alter the political functioning of the individual bands.

Likewise, it is reasonable to assume that Article 6 of the 1855 Saginaw Chippewa treaty meant that Saginaw, Swan Creek, and Black River bands, each of which were composed of one or more bands that had not previously functioned together as a political unit, were being brought together solely for the purposes of treaty negotiations. That larger, fictitious political unit that Manypenny had agreed to dissolve for the Ottawas and Chippewas was also to be dissolved by Article 6 of the Saginaw treaty.

It is, of course, possible that Agent Gilbert may have wanted these clauses inserted into the Michigan treaties for other reasons. He had previously stated in a letter to Manypenny his intent "that within three or four years all connection with & dependence upon the Government on the part of the Indians may properly cease."[42] Late during the 1855 Ottawa and Chippewa treaty negotiations he said: "I think we must fix a time, when your connection with the U.S. shall cease."[43] To speed up this process, Gilbert may have hoped to dissolve the political organization of the bands. If he did, however, there is no indication that he explained this to the Ottawas and Chippewas, and no federal document survives that suggests otherwise.

More importantly, Gilbert's views were not shared by Commissioner Manypenny. Manypenny never gave any indication that he sought to end the federal-tribal relationship, and no timetable for doing so was included in the treaty. Furthermore, Manypenny believed that the continued existence of a tribal or band council was necessary to the civilizing process. For example, when discussing the issue of who was to be considered "mixed blood" for purposes of the allotment process, he wrote Gilbert the following: "The Indians themselves, *in council,* by their own traditions & knowledge will doubtless greatly aid in arriving at the facts regarding the ancestry of those who may claim under the provisions for mixed bloods."[44] Consequently, there is no evidence that Article 6 altered or had any impact on the treaty's original intent, which was to create a permanent Indian reservation consisting of six townships in Isabella County, Michigan.

In his annual report to Congress, Commissioner Manypenny provided a brief but revealing summary of the 1855 Saginaw Chippewa treaty:

> New conventional arrangements, deemed requisite with the Indians in the State of Michigan, have been entered into with the confederate Tribe of Ottowas [*sic*] and Chippewas, the Chippewas of Saginaw, and the small band of Chippewas of Swan creek. *By them the Indians are to have assigned permanent homes, to be hereafter confirmed to them, in small tracts, in severalty.* Such guards and restrictions are thrown around their lands and limited annuities as cannot fail, if faithfully regarded and respected, to place them in comfortable and independent circumstances.[45]

This statement demonstrates that Manypenny viewed the 1855 Saginaw Chippewa treaty as having fulfilled the same purposes as other treaties he negotiated in the same period. He had confined the Indians to two small reservations in Isabella County and near Saginaw Bay. He had also assured them that those reservations would be their permanent homes. The treaty also created well-defined exterior boundaries along township lines so that federal laws could be easily applied throughout. Finally, the agreement divided the reservation into allotments to facilitate agriculture.

IMPLEMENTATION OF THE 1855 TREATY

The commissioner of the GLO in Washington, Thomas A. Hendrix, created the procedure for land selection for the reservation on September 8, 1855. He wrote acting Commissioner of Indian Affairs Charles E. Mix that the best way to accomplish this was for the commissioner to determine where the reservation would be located. Then, as Hendrix believed, "the necessary instructions could be given by [the GLO] for the reservations."[46]

Agent Gilbert followed this advice and selected six townships within Isabella County—Wise, Denver, Isabella, Nottawa, Deerfield, and one-half each of Chippewa and Union—for the reservation.[47] These six townships contained a total of 138,336.81 acres of land. Officials in the land office immediately went to their tract books in Washington, DC, and wrote in clear language above the six townships: "All this township [Isabella Township, in this case], embraced in the selection of six townships, for Indian purposes, under Treaty of 2nd August 1855." Where only half the township was needed, such as with Union Township, the statement read simply, "The North half of this township set apart" for Indian purposes. Similar statements were added in 1855 to notes from the earlier GLO survey.[48]

Despite the expeditious location of the Isabella Reservation, over the next nine years the federal government failed to complete the individual allotments of the reservation lands. Under the July 31, 1855, Ottawa and Chippewa treaty, government agents were to complete the selection of lands for the Indians by July 1, 1856; the same deadline was applied to the Saginaw Chippewas. But several Senate amendments to the treaties slowed ratification of the Saginaw Chippewa treaty, which was not ratified until June 1856, making compliance with this deadline almost impossible.[49] A second problem was faulty surveying that had been done in Michigan between 1838 and 1842. Several townships within the Isabella

Reservation had to be resurveyed, a process that dragged on into 1857 and 1858.[50] This, when combined with the confusion over "certificates" and "conflicts," each of which are discussed below, caused the federal government to miss the treaty-imposed deadline for individual land selection.

EARLY CONFUSION OVER "CERTIFICATES"

The allotment process was stalled in large part because three different Indian agents served the Saginaw Chippewas. Agent Gilbert remained in office until spring 1857; he was followed by A. M. Fitch, who served until 1861, when D. C. Leach was selected by the new Lincoln administration. Gilbert and Fitch were charged with beginning the process of allotment, which was supposed to be implemented in two stages. First, the Indians would select lands (either 40 or 80 acres), and after quickly checking to determine that no "conflicts" existed (i.e., that no one else claimed to own those parcels), they were to be given "certificates" for the land. Second, the land office in Washington was then supposed to recheck the selections to determine that no conflicts existed and, if satisfied, authorize the issuance of a patent.

While this process seems simple, when Agent Leach came to the agency in 1861, he found the office in disarray. Gilbert and Fitch had failed to issue certificates, the first step toward land selection. This had caused considerable anxiety within the Indian community. Leach outlined the problem in a letter dated April 23, 1862, in which he noted the many conflicts that had appeared as a result of the delays:

> From an examination of the files of this office, it appears that errors were discovered in the original list forwarded from this office by late Agent Gilbert—that a copy of the list was sent to his successor in office[,] late Agent Fitch, by late [Commissioner] Denver on the 21th day of October 1857, with instructions to make the necessary corrections—that the corrections in part were made by him and completed by me, resulting, by reason of the errors and changes in the selections made by the Indians by permission of late Agent Fitch, in the making of an entire new list, which was transmitted to you the 26th of July last [1861] and upon which [Commissioner] Edmunds' report of Conflicts in part is based.[51]

Some fifty-five conflicts had been discovered. These represented only the conflicts that were revealed by the plat book in Washington, DC, when the Indian selections were put forward.

Nevertheless, Leach was able to find other lands within the Isabella Reservation and put together a list of 497 selections of 40 and 80 acres that had no conflicts.[52] A second list attached to it included seventy-three Ottawas and Chippewas who had been allowed to settle on the Isabella Reservation.[53] In addition, some 109 selections were made on the Saginaw Bay Reservation, mostly in Township 17, range 3 west.

These early lists have survived in the National Archives and have several distinguishing aspects. First, the Indians are organized by band on the lists, each headed by a recognizable chief. This indicates both that the band chiefs were used by the federal government as a way of identifying Indians entitled to participate in allotment, and that band leadership continued to operate as it had for centuries. Second, the lists show that both Gilbert and Fitch allowed the Indians to pick out the parcels of land they wanted. And finally, the lists reveal land selection patterns demonstrating that individual bands, which represented extended kin, or clans, wished to remain together.[54]

Certificates were sent to Agent Leach on May 9, 1864, and issued to the Indians that summer. In total, 570 certificates were handed out to the Saginaw Chippewas and other Ottawas and Chippewas on the Isabella Reservation. Certificates were not issued to the Indians on the Saginaw Bay Reservation, however. Ultimately, these Indians were given a second chance to select land within the Isabella Reservation.[55]

Just as the certificates were being handed out, Agent Leach was replaced by Richard Smith. Unfortunately, Smith did not know which lists to use in issuing the certificates, and he used older lists. Some years later, during the Grant administration, Commissioner of Indian Affairs Ely Parker attempted to grapple with the with the situation: "After the change in selections by certain Indians, under Agent Fitch . . . the certificates were issued, by some mistake for the old selections, instead of the new, in lieu of the old."[56] Given the growing confusion, Secretary of the Interior J. P. Usher ordered the GLO to "deny all applications for the purchase of any lands embraced in the Reservations of the Chippewas" and to suspend the issuing of certificates.[57] In sum, nine years after the signing of the 1855 treaty, no patents had been issued to the Saginaw Chippewa Indians. Even the certification process, which was only a promise of land, had been mishandled and was largely incomplete.

Conflicts within the Isabella Reservation

When Agent Gilbert began the selection process, he discovered that several military warrants had already been issued for lands within the Isabella Reservation. This was important, because the Saginaw Chippewas could only select their allotments from the "unsold public lands" within reservation boundaries, and it was unclear whether military warrants should be considered "sold" lands, thus creating a conflict. It would soon be discovered that issues with military warrants were not the only conflicts regarding reservation lands. Lands had been legitimately sold, canal lands had been set aside, the state of Michigan claimed swampland within the boundaries of the reservation under an 1850 law, and each township, by law, had to reserve one section for schools.

Initially, the Indian agents and other government officials thought the military warrants consisted of thirteen parcels, descriptions of which were sent on to the agent in Michigan. In light of the minimal nature of these claims, Commissioner Manypenny simply ignored them.[58] Later, however, it would be discovered that some 10,524 acres of land had been claimed from military warrants.[59]

Besides military warrants, the sale of public lands in the region that became the Isabella Reservation commenced as early as 1838. But land in the United States was somewhat expensive, costing $1.25 an acre, and no sales appeared within what would become the reservation until about 1850. The passage of the Graduation Land Bill in 1854 expedited land sales in Michigan, allowing land that had been on the market for at least ten years (which included land within what would become the Isabella Reservation) to be sold at $1.00 an acre; land on the market for fifteen years would sell for 75 cents an acre; and that available for twenty years a mere 50 cents an acre.[60] These price reductions led individuals to purchase some 6,849 acres of land with the boundaries of the Isabella Reservation before the land was taken off the market by the May 1855 executive order.[61]

Perhaps more land within the reservation boundary would have been claimed by warrants or even purchased had it not been for a growing survey scandal in Michigan. The scandal involved the original surveying that had been done between 1838 and 1842. The surveys in the central part of the state, those connected to the Ionia Land Office, were defective, making it almost impossible for citizens to purchase land the farther one went north, including the region that would become the central and northern portions of the six-township reservation. Some ninety-one townships were affected by the malfeasance. Congress appropriated funds to resurvey the state, work that was not completed until late 1857.[62]

This resurvey in particular affected the swampland claims of the state of Michigan, which, in the end, included approximately 14,121 acres within the Isabella Reservation.[63] The Swamplands Act of 1850 charged the secretary of the interior to make out "an accurate list and plats of the lands" described as "wet and unfit for cultivation."[64] This occurred in every state in the union. Based on the fraudulent surveys in Michigan, which had yet to be discovered or corrected, the government and the state agreed on such a list in 1852, only to discover the next year that the inaccurate surveys made it impossible to issue patents for swamplands.

While the secretary of the interior approved the state list on October 27, 1853, when the governor of Michigan asked that the patents be issued, the same secretary refused, seeing the need by this time for new surveys. Many years later, in *Michigan Land & Lumber Co. v. Rust* (1897), the US Supreme Court ruled that legal title was vested in the United States until the patents were issued and that the determination of what lands constituted swamplands rested with the secretary of the interior.[65] Even so, between 1850 and 1857 the swamplands grant was, according to the Supreme Court, "in the process of administration."[66] What all this meant was never determined. Nevertheless, the federal government turned over all the swamplands within the Isabella Reservation to the state, amounting to 14,121 acres.[67]

According to a general survey of the plat books in Michigan's General Land Office, over 34,000 acres of the Isabella Reservation fell under the category of "conflict," due to claims for swampland, canals, land purchases, military warrants, and schools. This still left a large portion of land for Indian allotments.[68] Agent Fitch reported 102,645 acres of "unsold" lands to the GLO, which was probably quite accurate.[69] There is no evidence to suggest that the Saginaw Chippewas were told that 40 percent of Chippewa Township (only one-half of which belonged to the reservation) had already been sold to white Americans. Over 20 percent of both Wise and Nottawa Townships would be taken by the state as swampland, and 20 percent of Deerfield was already occupied under warrants. While a sizable parcel of land remained for the promised reservation, the integrity of the borders had been breached—contrary to what George Manypenny had planned in 1855—and the loss of land base became even more pronounced as post–Civil War America entered a period of urban boom. The towns of Chicago, Cleveland, and even St. Louis needed timber, one commodity that the Indians supposedly possessed.

3

A NEW TREATY AND THE GREAT
MICHIGAN LAND SWINDLE

By the 1860s, problems with implementing the Treaty of the Chippewa of Saginaw of 1855—including debates over conflicts and pressures from the growing white community with its economic interest groups—eventually led to a discussion regarding a possible new treaty for the Saginaw Chippewas. Federal officials were aware of these problems early on, but the Civil War intruded at the expense of federal intervention. Some Saginaw leaders supported the push for a new treaty. As early as December 3, 1855, a delegation of Indians who were supposed to settle on the Saginaw Bay Reservation signed a petition asking that two more townships be added to their reservation, since "the greater portion of them [Townships 17 and 18] are selected by the state as swampland."[1] Agent Fitch later confirmed that these lands were swampy, describing them as being "entirely unsuited for agricultural purposes."[2] Two days later, Agent Gilbert reported a similar complaint on behalf of the Saginaw Chippewas of the Isabella Reservation. "There is so much swampland that they are much annoyed in choosing their locations," he wrote to Commissioner Manypenny.[3]

The Saginaw Chippewas had another concern that grew with time, which was ensuring that enough land remained to take care of future generations of their children. In a petition to President Lincoln dated February 15, 1864, they made this clear. The land selected for them, they said, did not make any provision for our young men and women to have any land when they should be of age. Now we are so situated here on our Reservation in Isabella County, that if the land is brought into market and white men come and settle among us, we fear it will disturb us very much and break up our settlement. Now we desire to take our last payment of ($18,800) Eighteen Thousand Eight hundred Dollars in land now in the Reservation—and so guard ourselves and our children from being scattered again, and that the needful steps be immediately taken to make the section of land.[4]

The concept of using annuity money to buy land for future generations was novel. But federal officials also knew that other factors were at work: whites were agitating for a treaty that ended Indian ownership of the lands near the bay. Powerful railroad and lumber interests were expanding northward and westward, and the two townships were in their path.

Central Michigan at this time had vast forests that lumber barons sought to exploit. Railroads built in the 1860s made such exploitation possible.[5] Bay City and Saginaw, which had some eighty mills by the late 1860s, wanted access to timberlands, especially those north of the Isabella Reservation.[6] A powerful political lobby emerged that represented these economic interests. Congressman Austin Blair from Michigan, who served on the US House Land Committee, was often able, as the president of the Flint & Pere Marquette Railroad put it, to "say a good word" for railroad builders. Railroad and timber interests would benefit if the government could convince the Saginaw Chippewas to relinquish the Saginaw Bay Reservation (Townships 17 and 18) and consolidate the various bands on the Isabella reserve, thus freeing up land along the route that went from the bay area into Clare, Michigan, a new town just north of the Isabella reserve.[7]

Given such pressures, Agent Leach informed Washington that the Indians were willing to move "to the principle [sic] reservation in Isabella County" and give up their land claims on the bay.[8] The government finally agreed, and with little apparent opposition, H. J. Alvord joined Leach in negotiating a new treaty with the Saginaw Chippewas, which was signed on October 18, 1864. Alvord seemed to suggest that it was the government that wanted the change, declaring in open council that the Great Father wished that the Saginaws "should all live together upon one reservation."[9] Regardless of the interests at work and the express desires of the individual parties, a treaty was concluded that fundamentally changed the relationship between the Saginaw Chippewas and the federal government.

THE 1864 TREATY

Articles 1 and 2 of the 1864 Saginaw Chippewa treaty eliminate any ambiguity that may have existed regarding the status of the lands reserved for the Indians and the boundaries of the reservation. After stating that the three bands (Saginaw, Swan Creek, and Black River) relinquished all claim to lands at Saginaw Bay (Townships 17 and 18), those articles provided that:

> The said Indians also agree to relinquish to the United States all claim to any right they may possess to locate lands in lieu of lands sold or disposed of by the United States upon their reservation at Isabella, and also the right to purchase the unselected lands in said reservation. In consideration of the foregoing relinquishments, the United States hereby agree to set apart for the exclusive use, ownership, and occupancy of the [Saginaw Chippewas], all of the unsold lands within the six townships in Isabella county Reserved to said Indians by the treaty of August 2, 1855.[10]

Unlike the 1855 treaty, this language explicitly refers to the land as a "reservation." Additionally, in a striking admission, by stating that the Indians now gave up the right to claim other lands outside of the reservation should lands "upon" the reservation turn out to have been "sold," the treaty established that sold lands existed within the boundaries of the Isabella Reservation but that they did not affect the status of the reservation.

Article 3 outlined the number of acres each Indian was to receive and also guaranteed the means by which selectors were to receive patents "in fee simple" for the lands. The agent, acting for the secretary of interior, was to determine which among them was "competent," and thus "qualified by business habits to manage their affairs," and those "not so competent," which included Indians who were "idle . . . wandering . . . or [of] dissolute habits, and all orphans." If a person was judged "not so competent," the patent would become inalienable; the land could only be sold after securing permission from the secretary of the interior.[11] While the treaty sought to secure the process of allotment, selection, and Indian ownership, Article 3 opened a Pandora's box for fraud. Indian agents were given the power to determine competency, and several of them later openly conspired with Michigan land speculators, railroad interests, and lumber buyers by designating nearly all Saginaw Chippewas as "competent," even though few would have fit this standard at the time.

Article 3 also specifically recognized the Saginaw Chippewa bands' continuing governmental system by providing the largest allotments to "chiefs" and "head-men." More fundamentally, the 1864 treaty as a whole resolved any doubt that Article 6 of the 1855 treaty could have dissolved the Saginaw Chippewas' "tribal organization." After all, a treaty could not be negotiated with an entity that no longer existed. No new dissolution provision was included within the 1864 treaty, leaving tribal organization completely intact.

The 1864 treaty made one other major change: it abrogated an article in the 1855 treaty that stated that after ten years, all unselected land within the reservation boundary was to be opened to purchase by anyone. The 1864 treaty clearly stated that allotments were to be given to "each other person [Indian] now living, or who may be born hereafter, when he or she shall have arrived at the age of twenty-one years." In other words, the entire reservation—or seemingly all reservation lands not purchased or claimed through warrants by others—was to be filled with Indian allotments; excess land was to be held in trust for future Saginaw Indian generations.[12]

The 1864 treaty was a very different document than the 1855 treaty. It resolved any ambiguities that may have existed in the earlier agreement. It was negotiated with the Saginaw Chippewa council, and the treaty made no reference to dissolve that organization. The federal government would now be locked into a continuous, long-lasting relationship with the Saginaw Chippewas, which is what the Indians wanted. Government agents would be involved in allotting land on the reservation and discussing issues with the council—or its later replacement, the Saginaw Business Committee—well into the twentieth century.

The Lincoln administration embraced the 1864 treaty. Commissioner of Indian Affairs William P. Dole had openly proclaimed that the policy of the United States was to "recognize Indians who still continue their tribal organization as wards."[13] Secretary of the Interior John P. Usher sent the document to the president, concluding that the agreement had been made "at the Isabella Indian Reservation," in the state of Michigan, clearly indicating that a reservation would exist under it.[14] President Lincoln affixed his name to the document, identifying the agreement as having been made at the "Isabella Indian Reservation."[15]

The entire Michigan congressional delegation came to accept the existence of the Isabella Reservation. While they desired to have an open land policy and lobbied strongly to have the Saginaw Bay Reservation opened for sale, they also acknowledged that "the reserve at Isabella has been made perpetual."[16] Using such words as "perpetual" seemed almost unbelievable in this age of exploitation, but the congressional delegation thought that the Saginaw Bay lands that were exchanged for complete control of the lands in the six townships to the west were worth it, especially since the lands in the interior seemed of little use—at least at that time.

THE AFTERMATH OF THE 1864 TREATY

Given the Civil War, it took the Senate nearly two years to ratify the 1864 treaty. During this time the lands on the reservation became increasingly valuable for their timber, as the country experienced an urban boom. Given the failure to ratify the agreement, though, nothing was done regarding the patenting of land deeds, even though agents attempted to implement the process. After several botched attempts, the commissioner of Indian affairs finally sent Special Agent H. J. Alvord to assess the conditions of all the Ottawa and Chippewa reservations in Michigan, many of which fell under the same allotment process as the Isabella Reservation. Reporting in late fall 1866, he found "eighteen reservations, varying in size from fractions of sections to several townships in extent." While the reservations were "widely scattered," all fell under the same agent, who had found it inconvenient to visit them all, given travel conditions. No plans similar to the Saginaw allotment had been attempted on any of them.[17]

Despite the scant attention it was paid by the various agents, Alvord was impressed with the Isabella Reservation, more so than the others.

"The moral and social condition of the Indians [at Isabella] is better than at any other reservation in the state," he concluded. The Saginaw Chippewas also had made the best agricultural progress. In closing, Alvord included a map "showing the several reservations in Michigan."[18] The existence of these reservations in Michigan had become so pronounced that Agent Richard M. Smith, who replaced D. C. Leach in 1867, elaborated on them in his first report to the commissioner of Indian affairs. Smith argued that the present "reservation system," the one designed by Lea and Manypenny, was the "best method yet devised to rescue them [the Indians] from their wild and savage state." The Indians had already made considerable improvements, and the allotment of lands would add to this progress. Such action, he believed, would lead to "inalienable home[s]" for the Chippewa people and make them "free from molestation of the whites."[19]

State officials in Michigan agreed with this assessment. By this time, most of them took the existence of the reservations for granted. In April 1868 Secretary of Interior O. H. Browning received a long letter from O. M. Barnes, a Michigan developer and president of the Jackson, Lansing & Saginaw Railroad. He confirmed the existence of the Isabella reserve, but he wanted to know why the government had not opened Townships 17 and 18 to settlement. Surveying was mostly the problem.[20] Further pressure came in the form of a letter, addressed to Secretary Browning, composed by the entire Michigan congressional delegation. Dated June 5, 1868, it was signed by Senators Zachariah Chandler and M. Howard, along with congressmen T. W. Ferry and J. H. Diggs. They urged the allotment of the Isabella Reservation and the sale (although this was illegal under the new 1864 treaty) of any excess land to settlers. Obviously, they had not read the entire agreement but were receiving pressure from constituents regarding access to the timber on the reserve.[21] Developers wanted the land all across Michigan to be patented so that they could purchase the timber. Nevertheless, in a rather telling statement, the congressmen openly acknowledged, once again, that "the reserve at Isabella has been made perpetual."[22]

Similar sentiments could be found among the white population of Isabella County, which had reached four thousand people by 1869. They wrote a petition that suggested the need to expedite the selection process, arguing that the Indians should be given their lands in "fee simple"—or patents—without restrictions on sale. They were far less generous in describing improvements made by the Indians. "These leading white citizens contended that the Indians "are now literally shut up within the limits of their reservation, which upon sides presents an unbroken barrier against an intermingling with the whites." The white settlements had "not only reached to but passed beyond and surrounded the reservation which stands as a solid and unbroken wilderness in our midst with not a single comfortably passable road through it.[23] The statement certainly confirms that the six-township reservation was highly visible and clearly defined.

THE POLITICS OF THE "DETROIT RING" AND
THE SELECTION PROCESS

Given the growing political pressure from Michigan citizens, politicians, the lumber industry, and railroads, Commissioner of Indian Affairs Ely S. Parker investigated the land selection process over the summer of 1869. Afterward, he issued a long report that documented an appalling failure of the previous agents to do their duty. Commissioner Parker ordered the new agent, James W. Long, who assumed duties in July 1869, to proceed to the reservation to confirm what selections had been made and to make new ones where necessary. Long was also to determine which Indians were "competent" and which were "not so competent."[24]

On assuming the job, Agent Long found a growing, aggressive group of land speculators and lumber buyers entrenched on the southern end of the reservation at Mt. Pleasant and living east of the reserve at Saginaw and even in Detroit. Trespassing occurred on Indian lands almost daily, as lumber operators, often with questionable sales contracts, cut Indian timber. Agent Smith in 1868 had tried to prosecute those who purchased the timber from lands held by certificates (those issued in 1864), since patents had not yet been issued by the government. Federal Judge S. S. Whitney rendered an opinion to Agent Long in August 1869 that such purchases were legal.[25] The judge concluded that it had been the intent of the federal government to allow the Indians to use the resources on lands issued under certificates—to start farming or lumbering, or even to build buildings.[26]

Even more threatening to Indian resources, Long discovered that a major land sale had occurred involving nearly 15,000 acres directly in the heart of the Isabella Indian Reservation. The purchasers were Saginaw Chippewa Métis Charles H. Rodd and A. J. Campau, who had bought the land in the fall of 1864. They paid $1.25 an acre. Rodd and Campau, who could legally purchase land under the old 1855 treaty— but not under the new 1864 treaty—did not have the funds necessary to make such a purchase, however, and the money came from lumberman Ezra Rust. The purchase thereafter was known as the "Rust Purchase."[27] Using Indians as a front to acquire lumber resources, or simply buying timber from individual Indians who had certificates, had become common practice by 1869.

The right of Indians to purchase land within the reservation had been rescinded under the 1864 treaty, and the question quickly became one tied to the timing of the purchase.[28] Several small purchases, uncovered by Agent Richard Smith, had been made prior to the 1864 treaty.[29] While Smith had learned of these purchases and considered them to be inconsequential, he never knew of the much larger Rust Purchase, which supposedly had been kept from the public by the two Métis who bought the land. Long informed the commissioner of Indian affairs of it in late 1869. There is no question that Long, who later became a developer himself, was better connected with land speculators than Smith, who was a rather out-of-touch Methodist missionary.[30]

A group soon emerged at Mt. Pleasant that intended to defeat the Rust Purchase. Mill operators Timothy P. Jerome and George Williams joined forces with forces with missionary George Bradley to oppose it. They held a council with the major Isabella Chippewa Indian leaders in late fall of 1869, where the chiefs and clan heads signed a contract in which they agreed to sell to Jerome and Williams all the timber within the Rust Purchase for a price to be set by Bradley or some other "disinterested" person. The sale was contingent upon Jerome and Williams being able to set aside the Rust Purchase in federal court. The operators convinced the federal prosecuting attorney in Detroit, A. B. Maynard, to file suit to negate the Rust Purchase just before Christmas 1869.[31]

Prosecuting Attorney Maynard, Jerome, and Williams were all Republicans who were connected to a group of politicians called locally the Detroit Ring. While Republican congressmen John F. Driggs and Austin Blair were initially part of the ring, they soon became embroiled in a massive political fight with its leader, Senator Zachariah Chandler, primarily over government patronage. When Driggs and Blair broke with the ring, a huge fight erupted over control of the Rust Purchase. The winners would have much to say about the process of allotment on the Isabella Reservation.[32]

It was under these conditions that Agent Long began sending lists of Indian names into Washington and preparing to issue patents. He realized that the Rust Purchase was going to be challenged, so he informed the commissioner that he would not select land within the Rust tract, supposedly waiting for the legal action to take its course. There was plenty of land within the six townships to accommodate the Indians, and he wished to avoid this growing fight over the purchase.[33]

Meanwhile, Long adopted a new method of listing the Indians on selection lists. While earlier agents had listed them by their bands, with the chief at the head, Long printed up new charts in which each page represented a particular section of land within a particular township. As he noted to Commissioner Parker, he "divided the lists into books of townships," which were in turn "subdivided into sections, making reference to the maps comparatively easy."[34]

It seemed like a simple change. Five to ten Indians were listed on a page under a heading beginning with "township," at the top, followed by "section." By each Indian name there was a legal description of tracts ranging from 40 to 80 acres. When sufficient Indians had been selected to fill the section, a new section, or page, was used. Long had revolutionized the business; no longer would speculators try to purchase thousands of acres, exposing themselves to litigation, like Rust had done. Rather they could concentrate on finding the Indians who owned these smaller parcels and buy them outright. It was only necessary to have the actual lists that Long had prepared, which, when organized section by section, also allowed the purchaser to get a better idea of the quality of timber being purchased. By controlling the lists, Long had an extremely valuable tool for land speculation since he could sell the information to purchasers.[35]

Over the spring of 1869, Agent Long fine-tuned this new selection process. He had the old certificate list—the 497 names—added to his new listing system that organized the Indians by townships and sections. After carefully looking over some additions by the missionary, Bradley, Long discovered that 152 claims conflicted with the Rust Purchase, and he removed them. He also removed, without explanation, 138 names of Indians who were "not entitled." In all some 600 Saginaw Chippewas remained on his new lists, many of whom had received certificates; other names that followed were Ottawas and Chippewas, some of whom were from other reservations. The final list numbered over a thousand individuals. Long submitted this revised list to Commissioner Parker in February 1870, asking that patents be issued immediately to the Indians on it. Given that Long had avoided making selections within the Rust Purchase, or on lands already patented before May 1855, he declared that there were "no conflicts." Long had even avoided conflict with a few squatting homesteaders, who he felt had a claim to land even though they knew they were invading an Indian reservation.[36]

Finally, alongside nearly every one of the 600 Saginaw names, Agent Long wrote "competent" to assess the ability of these individuals to take care of their own affairs. His justification included a gross exaggeration: "They are hard at work on well tilled farms which I have no doubt they will keep."[37] Actually, as missionary Bradley pointed out, "There are from 600 to 700 families entitled to make selections of land on the reserve a portion of which are living on it." He believed that many more would have entered the reservation, or "would have been here," had they been sure of getting their patents. Bradley's comments seem to suggest that many Saginaw Indians were not even on the reservation in October 1870, let alone competent to make selections. Indeed, Long was doing it for them, keeping the records himself.[38]

Over the summer and fall of 1870, various groups lobbied to have the patents issued. Congressman T. W. Ferry did his utmost to lobby for the issuing of patents. The commissioner of the GLO, J. S. Wilson, became an ally of the Detroit Ring. He prodded Commissioner Parker to send Long's lists on to his office, "with a view to issuing the patents at an early period as desired by Mr. [Congressman] Ferry."[39] George Bradley addressed "An Appeal for the Indians" to President Grant in

October 1870, calling for the issuing of the patents, followed by a petition—which Bradley organized.[40]

The only opposition to the process came from congressmen Driggs and
Blair, who had broken with Ferry and Chandler. Congressman Driggs
had obtained a copy of the "swindling contract," as he called it, that ring
members Jerome and Williams had made with the Indians, one "worth
$500,000 in which doubtless [A. B.] Maynard and probably Judge L [an
unidentified judge] are also interested." Driggs had sent the contract on
to Congressman Blair along with yet another Indian petition. He wanted
Blair to take the Chippewa Indian petition to "Parker, [secretary of interior Columbus] Delano and Grant," hoping to reveal "the gang." Driggs's
petition, signed by a number of Indians, contended that the Saginaw
Chippewas wanted the Rust Purchase sold "to the highest bidders" and
the money deposited into a trust supposedly for the Indians.[41]

As the fight over the Rust Purchase reached the newspapers, embar-
rassing the politicians involved, Agent Long did his best to convince
government officials that both the Rust Purchase and the Jerome and
Williams contract were not in the interests of the Indians. Since arriving in the area, Long became involved in speculation himself. He had
purchased land and plotted a new town called "Longwood" within the
Isabella Reservation. Long was aligning himself with local attorneys
and speculators living in Mt. Pleasant, rather than with Jerome and
Williams, or with Driggs and Blair.[42] Nevertheless, Long's days as agent
were numbered. President Grant had adopted a new "Peace Policy" as
a cornerstone of his Indian policy, and with it came the general belief
that only church ministers, or devote Quakers, should serve as Indian
agents. There might have been other factors that led to Long's quick
dismissal—speculation on and purchase of land or perhaps opposition
to the Detroit Ring certainly did not endear the agent with either the
government or the power brokers in Michigan.[43] Long quickly settled at
Longwood and became involved in politics and real estate speculation.

Previous agent Richard Smith replaced Long. Smith, a Methodist
minister who easily met the necessary qualifications to be an agent
under Grant's policy, seemed somewhat oblivious to the speculation that
was underway at Mt. Pleasant and Saginaw. To his dismay, he did soon
learn of the large numbers of contracts that Indians had signed in which

they sold their timber, often for pennies on the dollar; on occasion, they even sold land that they expected to receive patents for. He believed such deals might number six or seven hundred. Smith had talked with Long about this problem in May 1871, after taking the job, and both men agreed that such contracts were "wholly unauthorized." Under the Intercourse Acts of 1834, it was clearly illegal to purchase virtually anything from Indians, including land or personal property such as timber.[44]

Smith received no response to counter these purchases from Commissioner Parker, who was about to resign his office. The agent did approach US Attorney Maynard, who informed the secretary of the interior.[45] Secretary Delano, in a short response, simply informed Smith that he should "prosecute any person found trespassing upon or fraudulently endeavoring to obtain possession of the lands referred to."

Delano never defined "fraudulent endeavors" or specified under what law the prosecution was to proceed. However, he did ask Attorney General A. T. Akerman to "prosecute all persons found trespassing upon these lands," a request that seems to have been ignored.[46] Agent Smith had no intention of leaving the issue alone. His growing criticism, however, came too late as Jonathan Knox was made a "special agent" in the spring of 1871, charged with bringing the patents out from Washington and issuing them to Indians. Knox was a close friend of the man that the Grant administration had selected to succeed Parker as the new commissioner of Indian affairs, Francis W. Walker, who would soon become the target of Indian reformers bent on correcting some of the wrongs then being perpetrated on Indians.[47]

To what extent the Saginaw Chippewas understood the whirl of events surrounding their land is difficult to determine. Unlike the Métis, the majority likely knew little regarding the issue of deeds or the nature of sales contracts. According to Bradley, many were often off in the woods working in lumber camps or hunting and fishing. Even Agent Long, who judged almost all of them to be "competent," admitted in his final annual report that of those on the reservation, most spoke English only "to some extent."[48] A later Indian agent, George W. Lee, noted in 1876 that virtually all of the Saginaws adhered "to their native language," suggesting that hardly any spoke or understood English.[49] With little knowledge of English, the Indians had little chance to avoid the massive land transfer that was about to occur.

The Patents

By May 1871, Agent Smith knew that patents were being prepared in Washington. Smith also knew that when land certificates had been issued some years before, timber speculators often were able to buy the timber for prices ranging from $.50 to $1.50 per thousand board feet, well below market value. Even as the patents were being prepared, the selling of timber and land was occurring on the Isabella Reservation at an alarming rate. Smith suspected that the sales involved much of the land scheduled to be patented.[50] Smith did seem to blame Long, however, writing the commissioner in June:

> It has been reported to me that allotments of land have been made, by mistake I presume, to Indians now residing in Canada and that parties on this side of the line have been purchasing the pine timber standing thereon with the view of lumbering it off. How this is I of course cannot say, as my predecessor in office, late Agent Long, did not turn over to me neither register, or lists of those Indians nor maps or plats of the selections made by them under his direction.[51]

Unfortunately, Smith's growing suspicions regarding land speculation and a hoped-for investigation and prosecution of illegal timber sales ended that October, when the steamer *Coburn* went down in Saginaw Bay. He perished in the accident.[52]

Long presumably kept the lists and plats for obvious reasons. They were incredibly valuable, since they indicated which Indian would receive, through patents, individual 80-acre tracts of land. Just how Long marketed this information is unknown, but a group of speculators, mostly from Mt. Pleasant, soon invaded the reservation with that information at hand and convinced Indians to sell their patents, through use of quitclaim deeds, for virtually nothing.[53]

Speculators in land and timber convinced Saginaw Indians to sign deeds that were then recorded in the local courthouse at Mt. Pleasant. According to an investigation conducted by the government in 1876, most were offered $10 to $15 for their land; the government interpreter was the intermediary who set up the contracts. Most of the Indians were told by the interpreter, or by speculators and town officials, that they would not receive their land patents from the federal government unless they signed the deeds. When threats did not work, whiskey was distributed in large quantities.[54]

The contracts themselves mostly were written by Mt. Pleasant lawyers. Speculators who worked with county officials included Irving E. Arnold and Long, of Mt. Pleasant, and Alexander Andre, of Saginaw.[55] Many of the contracts have survived. Nearly sixty original "Warranty Deeds" exist in the Andre Papers that show timber and land being transferred from Indians to Andre starting in March 1871. These deeds cover nearly 5,000 acres.[56] A typical deed conveys "all the Pine Trees and Timber standing, lying and being on the above described land." Since the speculators had some concern that the government might change the land selected during the final process of patenting, the lawyers solved this by adding: "And full permission is hereby given by said first party to said second party to insert the proper description of said land in this deed."[57]

Like Andre, Irving Arnold amassed a huge amount of land. In one sale, advertised in the September 22, 1881, issue of the *North-Western Tribune* and discovered by historian Ella V. Powers, Arnold offered 5,040 acres of land in Nottawa, Chippewa, Wise, Denver, and Isabella Townships—all formerly Indian lands within the reservation.[58] John Leaton and William B. Brown owned 33,000 acres within the Isabella Reservation by 1881. As historian Powers, whose father had witnessed the frauds, noted: "It was easy to get an Indian signature on a deed when he was drunk."[59] Indeed, Arnold, Andre, and Leaton amassed altogether nearly 45,000 acres of Indian land, roughly 64 percent of that allotted in the early 1870s, claiming the land through warranty deeds.

In June 1871, just before the patents to this land were issued, the director of the GLO did bring to the attention of Commissioner Parker, who was himself a Seneca Indian, the fact that only 24 Chippewas had been judged "not so competent" out of the 1,040 on Long's list.[60] Parker, however, was increasingly under fire for supposed graft within the bureau, and with his resignation in August 1871, and the loss of Smith to a steamer accident two months later, the last hope for placing restrictions on the deeds disappeared.

Special Agent Jon Knox, a clerk in the BIA, handed out the patents. He arrived in August, the very month that Walker became the new commissioner, reporting with apparent pleasure to Walker four months later that "it is estimated by the best judges" that no more than one-fifth of the patented lands remained in the hands of the Indians not long after being issued. "All classes of citizens of the state," Knox concluded, believed that "the sooner the reservations are disposed of . . . the better it will be for the Indians." Such a stark admission suggests that Walker expected such a resolution.[61]

George Betts replaced Agent Smith late in the fall of 1871. He was, in a word, corrupt. He ran the agency until the spring of 1876, when an investigation revealed that a lumber ring had worked hand-in-hand with Knox, and later Betts, in securing Isabella Reservation lands. As more patents were handed out late that fall of 1871—very likely directly into the hands of speculators, who simply presented deeds to the agents—Betts and Knox quietly collected 670 more Saginaw names for land selections. They finalized this list at Isabella City in January 1872.[62]

This time Jerome, Williams, and Arnold, key Detroit Ring members, secured many of the Saginaw Chippewa names that were placed on this second list: some of them came from gravestones or from Indians then living in Canada. Lumberman Arthur Hill, who then found himself opposing the ring, noted in a private letter to Congressman Blair that "we can show that Jon. J. Knox, Special Comr. [commissioner], has at different times received money from certain men for improper favors."[63] Hill and others were obviously upset that the Detroit Ring, as represented by Jerome, Williams, and Arnold, had bribed Betts to turn over his land location selections. (Special Agent Knox joined Betts in this endeavor.) This had left the local Mt. Pleasant speculators—such as Arnold, Andre, and Leaton—suddenly in the cold.

Complaints came into the commissioner's office from lumber operators who were not part of the ring but knew exactly how it worked. C. H. Gage, an important East Saginaw lumberman, demanded to know what had happened to "[Agent Robert] Smith's Papers," meaning his selection lists. Obviously, he had no idea that Long had refused to turn them over to Smith in early 1871. Gage, however, was fully aware of Betts's collusion with Jerome and Williams, and he wanted it investigated. He charged that these men were given the lists made by Betts and Knox and that they had purchased the lands in question even before the agent and special agent had departed for the East to collect the patents. "The whole thing is considered a swindle by many good men in the [Saginaw] valley," Gage concluded.[64]

Two of those "good men" were John C. Leaton and Arthur Hill of Mt. Pleasant. They watched carefully as Betts and Knox concluded their work on the new, or second, lists in January 1872. Leaton and Hill then asked to see them. Upon being refused—obviously, they had already been promised to the Detroit men—they followed the two government agents to the train station in Clare. After Betts and Knox had retired for the night, Hill and Leaton convinced the station manager to let them "borrow" the trunk carrying the government papers. Leaton and Hill stayed up all night copying the lists—some 670 Chippewa names with land descriptions—and returned the trunk in the morning. The lifting of the names was soon discovered, and the two men were brought to trial in Detroit in April. Betts used the theft to vindicate his conduct; the lifting of the names revealed the "character of these men," he wrote.[65]

More affidavits and petitions followed. One came from none other than Arthur Hill and John C. Leaton. They claimed that even after they had offered to "pay the usual fees" for the lists, Betts had refused to turn them over. This explains why they "borrowed" them at the train station.[66] A second petition called for a presidential investigation. Congressman Driggs sent the document on to Blair in Washington, DC. It was signed by eighty-two land speculators and lumber buyers and merchants from the Saginaw region, presenting "many and grievous charges of bribery and corruption . . . especially in the management of the affairs of the . . . Isabella Reservation."[67]

Driggs wanted Blair to take the petition directly to President Grant, for if Senator Chandler heard of it, he would certainly prevent Grant from getting it or seeing it. "To bring to light this whole matter," Driggs argued, will "interfere with the great money power that binds the Chandler Ring [i.e., the Detroit Ring] together." The ring, with Chandler at the head, as Driggs identified it, "embraces not only the Jeromes-Rusts-Williams, [but US Attorney] Maynard, [Commissioner] Walker, Ferry, Godfry, J. J. Bagley" (the latter soon to be the next governor of Michigan), and others.[68] The growing fight over Indian pine land had led to a gigantic struggle for the political control of Michigan.

As Betts and Knox continued collecting Indian names and shipping them off to Washington, they apparently failed to keep track of the numbers involved. When Michigan congressman W. D. Foster finally asked Commissioner Walker to report on the allotment process on the Isabella Reservation, noting that someone had told him that some 1,900 selections had been submitted and that the reservation had a total population of only 1,464 Indians, even Commissioner Walker asked Betts for an explanation. The figure of 1,900 selections seems to have come from the Saginaw faction, whom Foster apparently represented.[69]

Betts never really responded to Foster's assertion. He did write that such allegations were only the plotting of Democratic opponents. Betts noted: "Rumors afloat in regard to land matters on this reservation" were simply tied to the upcoming election (in November 1872). "I am very sure if these patents [the 670 pending] could be on hand for delivery *as soon as possible*," he wrote Commissioner Walker, "it would produce a fine impression among the Indians. . . . The patents *due them* had best be *forthcoming, speedily,* or we will feel it at the polls."[70]

Walker allowed Betts to issue 663 patents at the Isabella Reservation in late August 1872, two months before the election. Only 15 of the recipients were marked "not so competent."[71] Senator Chandler did his part to maintain the power of the ring by awarding jobs in order to keep certain men quiet. During the summer of 1872, James Long, who had been pushed aside, became postmaster in Isabella City. Isaac A. Francher, who also found that more connected speculators had seized control of the process, had been given a similar post in Mt. Pleasant. In the elections that fall, President Grant won a decisive victory over the reform Republican candidate, Horace Greeley (who unfortunately died before the vote was counted), and Congressman Blair went down to defeat.[72]

Betts's annual reports for these years completely ignore the fraud and note that a solid community of Indians had settled on the Isabella Reservation. He referred to the Saginaw homeland as a "perpetual reservation [of] six adjoining townships."[73] In 1874 he indicated that about one-half of the three Saginaw bands still resided on the reserve and enclosed a survey chart showing that these Indians lived on over 11,000 acres of land.[74] They also continued to maintain their tribal council, a group that had petitioned the commissioner of Indian affairs asking for an investigation of the patenting process as early as September 1871.[75]

While the extent of the fraud will never be completely known, it appears from Betts's 1872 report that the Saginaw Chippewa Indians lost about 83 percent of the land allotted between 1871 and 1873. This amounted to over 60,000 acres. Since the 1864 treaty reserved the remaining land, at least 30,000 acres, for future Indian generations, and some Indians had actually been able to keep their allotments, there was still a substantial land base on the Isabella Reservation that needed to be administered.[76] At the time, the government seemed oblivious regarding how many allotments had actually been issued, but a later investigation for Representative Julius Houseman, conducted in 1884, revealed that agents had issued 1,778 patents. (Obviously some went to Indians who were either dead or living in Canada.)[77]

When Betts tried to push through one more allotment of three hundred names in 1875, the chiefs and clan leaders complained to the new commissioner of Indian affairs, J. Q. Smith. They claimed that Betts had removed the legitimate leaders of the tribe and substituted men who would do his bidding.[78] Smith, not privy to ring activities, launched an investigation. Of course, by this time, literally half of the reservation had fallen into the hands of land speculators and lumber buyers. They were making fortunes on land deals, and many began to build massive Victorian homes in Mt. Pleasant, some of which still stand today.

For the Saginaw Indians, this period of allotment was a disaster. While they had been given valuable land, most of them likely never knew where their allotments actually were. Certainly, very few of them ever moved to that land or tried to farm it. Most of the tribe slowly moved northward to escape the invading white population. The majority also continued to live as they had in the past, hunting and fishing and living a communal life. A few had acculturated to some degree, working in the expanding lumber industry either as loggers or laborers in the mills, but that number was relatively small in comparison to the tribe as a whole. If any of them even knew of the investigation that was to follow, they said nothing about it. The new commissioner did intend to stop the exploitation and stabilize the Isabella Reservation.

4

THE NEW ERA

The years of the Grant administration (1869–76) were marked with considerable fraud when it came to Indian affairs. Commissioners often worked with politicians who had open access to the secretary of the interior. These commissioners controlled agents who in turn found ways to steal from their charges, the Indians. In some ways, the so-called Gilded Age—Mark Twain's name for it—made sharp business practices acceptable. Some of those who abused the system felt that if Indians could not take care of their own business, they should be exploited. Reformers, however, were gaining ground during the last year or so that Grant was in office.

One change was the development of a new position within the BIA: special agents. They were highly paid men who were supposedly above corruption and were assigned to investigate possible corruption on reservations. Respected religious officials, such as Bishop Henry Benjamin Whipple of Minnesota, picked these men, all of whom seem to have given good service.[1] One such man, someone of impeccable honesty—indeed, he was so honest that Grant's last secretary of the interior, former senator Zachariah Chandler from Michigan, promptly fired him—was Special Agent Edward C. Kemble. Aware of possible fraud at Isabella, the BIA assigned Kemble to investigate in 1875.

Kemble discovered that the petition of chiefs demanding an investigation was in fact signed by eight of the twelve headmen who had signed the 1864 treaty. Furthermore, Kemble found that Agent Betts had worked in league with land speculators and lumber buyers. County officials conspired with the agent and speculators to acquire Indian land and timber. Those Indians who had supposedly received titles in fee simple were brought in front of the agent, or interpreter John M. Collins, told to mark a document, and then dismissed. The document was usually a simple bill of sale for the land that was to be allotted to the Indian. Without knowing, many Indians signed deeds for the sale of their lands even before the patents arrived. Others simply signed contracts that gave away their timber at ridiculously low prices.[2]

This information, including the fact that the agent and interpreter were paid roughly fifteen dollars per contract, went into Kemble's report. The news of the devastating report quickly reached Washington. Even though Chandler had just taken over the position as secretary of the interior—a job he may have wanted in order to protect the fraudulent land business—he was unable to stop the attention focused on Agent Betts, who had abetted speculators and profited in the effort. Chandler would get even, to a degree, by firing Kemble—who was promptly hired back by the new administration of Rutherford B. Hayes in 1877—but he also was forced to remove Betts. The new agent, George W. Lee, quickly discovered that of the over three hundred new selections that Betts had wanted the government to recognize in 1875, most were "for minors, and in the name of deceased persons who were not living at the time of the selections. . . . I find a large number of selections, perhaps 2/3 of the list of 1875, are by persons who have already had 40 acres."[3] Of those Saginaws who received lands in the period 1871–73, Lee believed that not one in twenty should have been judged "competent."[4]

The Impact of the Pine Fraud on Reservation Status

Despite the loss of considerable lands in the 1870s, the Isabella Reservation remained intact. This was so because there was still a land base—between 30,000 and 40,000 acres—and strong cultural and economic ties within the Saginaw community. Sometimes agents saw this strength as a weakness: "One great cause of their slow progress towards civilization," Agent Lee concluded, "is the tenacity with which they adhere to their native language." Most adults simply refused to speak English, "even when they can do so quite intelligibly." The native language remained a staple at home, and Chippewa parents never forced their children to attend school regularly.[5] In other words, they remained a distinct people, adhering to a "reservation culture," living communally, despite being surrounded by a white population.

The ties of the Saginaw Chippewas to their own religion also remained very strong. In their own history, the Saginaw Chippewas mention the importance of the Midewiwin in helping them through what they perceived as a troubled time—the late nineteenth century. The *mides,* who offered ceremonial rites, possessed the power to converse in the spiritual realm. These shamans practiced even as Methodist missionaries offered their own spiritual guidance and economic assistance.[6]

The Saginaw Chippewas continued to support their own political institutions. The tribal council remained intact, and when Betts tried to disrupt this Native political group by removing members, the entire community revolted. Special Agent Kemble described this council when he met with Saginaw leaders on February 8, 1876. The meeting he held with tribal members included "seventy-five members of the Tribe in attendance, including fifteen principal chiefs and head men." This strongly suggests that each band, or clan, had a representative in the council. This body met in their own "council house," located near the town of Isabella to the south. Most of the tribal members then lived in Rosebush, a community well north of the tribal headquarters. But seemingly, the tribe continued to cling to the lands near Mt. Pleasant, even though they owned very few acres there.[7]

Government officials also continued to refer to the Isabella Indian Reservation during the 1880s. Acting Commissioner of Indian Affairs Orlando Brown made this clear in a letter describing reservation lands in 1880: "That portion of the Isabella Reservation which has not been granted to individual Indians in fee simple, does not come within the definition of public lands, the same having been withdrawn from the public domain, and set apart in common with other lands as a reservation held in trust."[8] Federal officials—agents, judges, and prosecuting attorneys—became more inclined to protect Indian lands after the frauds of the mid-1870s were revealed. They soon came to see the state and its citizens as major predators and trespassers. This was part of a national critique of President Grant's administration, increasingly demanded by reformers who were gaining ascendency in Washington, DC.[9]

The new age was perhaps best expressed by Commissioner of Indian Affairs H. Price in 1881, when he was queried by a Michigan citizen, one S. D. Coon, regarding the status of the Isabella Reservation. Were "steps being taken to discontinue the said reservation," Coon asked? Price replied: "The legal title to the lands in question was acquired by the Indians under the above treaties . . . and that No Steps are being taken to discontinue the reservation."[10] The reservation could only be defined at the time as the six townships, as that was the only active definition ever used. Thus, the GLO continued to identify the six-township reservation on official maps, including one published in 1878.[11]

The Indian agent in Michigan seemed also to pay attention to more details, even asking for advice regarding the Intercourse Acts of 1834 in order to better protect his charges. This sometimes led to trouble; for example, Agent Lee discovered that a "trusted chief of the Tribe on the reservation," one George Bennett, had sold a team of oxen that belonged to the bands as a whole. Lee indicated that while he did not have "a copy of the laws in regards to Indians" (the Intercourse Acts), he did believe that it was unlawful for a white person to buy property, such as oxen, from Indians on a reservation, and he so notified the buyer, one A. B. Upton.[12] This apparently brought some resolution, but Lee still thought it essential "that all U.S. Laws bearing upon Indian Affairs" be compiled and sent to agents such as himself. Lee's growing awareness of problems may have stemmed in part from his own vulnerability. The Saginaw Indians did not like him and pressed him constantly for an accounting of annuity money and reservation land. The tribal council was becoming more assertive on a variety of fronts, even condemning Bennett for his attempts to sell oxen. The council also charged Lee with being too close to land speculators. By the 1880s, the Saginaw tribal council began to demand some answers. They sent memorial after memorial to Washington, demanding to be heard. While such petitions may have had only a minimal impact, Agent Lee was replaced in September 1882 by Edward P. Allen, who quickly became more attentive to the council and its wishes.[13]

The main issues that the Saginaw tribal council dealt with in the early to mid-1880s included the future allotment of lands (an attempt at selection had been made in 1878 with no patents issued); the disposition on unallotted lands of fallen timber that had been knocked down during a storm; and the right to determine just who was to receive lands in the future, as there were still thousands of acres to give out to young people who had just reached their majority. This last concern had emerged in 1881, when it was rumored that certain Pottawatomie Indians were to be included in land allotments on the Isabella Reservation. To deal with these new complaints, the commissioner authorized Agent Lee, and, soon thereafter, Agent Allen, to prepare new lists for allotment. All new allotments were to be made with many restrictions; most were to include "not so competent" status.[14]

Hoping to avoid the problems with allotment that Agent Lee had faced, during the summer of 1883 Allen called on the Saginaw tribal council on three separate occasions to help him in the selection process. The men met first at the Indian church in central Isabella Township, near Rosebush, and then at their "camp meeting ground," which was not far away. Since the only Indians eligible for land were young men and women who had reached the age of twenty-one after the last patents had been issued in the early 1870s, it was relatively easy to pick them out. Allen found that the council agreed to submit the names of eighty-two such individuals; he had another list of thirty-six others who might be considered but were being withheld "because of dispute as to their being entitled either by reason of non age, having had land before, or some other objection."[15]

White observers from Isabella County who watched this process were not entirely happy with it. Even before Allen finished, attorney A. M. Tinker, Isabella County clerk of court, complained that Allen had included "certain Indians on the Isabella Reservation" who were not eligible because of their age.[16] Allen answered Tinker by pointing out that he had classified all of the young women who were assigned land as "not so competent," primarily because men—such as Tinker, no doubt—preyed on them. As Allen put it, despite having taken large portions of the reservation already, "there are whites, as I have the best reason to believe, who stand ready to 'gobble up' their lands for a song the moment the Indian gets his patent."[17]

The seriousness with which Allen took his job is indicated by the questions that he raised during the process. Should an Indian receive land who had a Canadian father and a Saginaw mother? Allen also wondered if Indians who were deemed "semi-idiotic" or infirm were eligible. And what about "orphans?" Commissioner Price argued several of these individual cases with Allen in a May 1884 letter, becoming more confused with each debate. He finally lit on a conclusion that seemed to apply to them all: "You will submit this case to the Indians in council and report the result with a full statement of the facts."[18] In what was clearly a major reversal, the government grew more dependent on the Saginaw tribal council for sorting out such issues, letting them determine who was a member, who was of age, and who deserved land.

With a system that seemed to satisfy everyone other than lawyers in Mt. Pleasant, Allen proceeded to issue patents. Eighty-two were sent to the agent in March 1885, followed by another group of sixty-eight, sent out in February 1886. The latter group included the questionable ones from 1883, all of which, according to Allen, had been "carefully examined . . . all in open council." A few of these were determined to be "competent," but the vast majority were "not so competent," and thus the lands covered by them could not be sold, nor could the timber on those lands be sold unless the secretary of the interior agreed to the sale.[19] These allotments, almost all of which were for 40 acres of land, amounted to 6,080 total acres.[20]

According to the agent's report, the allotment process worked smoothly given the cooperation of the tribal council. In its aftermath, the commissioner of the GLO concluded that it was essential to create a "tract" book for the "Isabella Reservation." There were serious questions regarding conflicts over land titles. Such a book would outline reservation land, but more importantly, it would reveal the large number of conflicts that existed between it and the one used by the county clerk at Mt. Pleasant. The book was to be sent to the new agent, Mark W. Stevens, who took office after the New Year in 1886.[21]

THE TRESPASS ISSUE

The need for a thorough investigation of the trespass issue on the reservation had been growing for some time. Indian petitioners had called for such an investigation on several occasions, and given the new respect garnered by the tribal council, the commissioner of Indian Affairs decided to take on the issue.[22] Thus, in spring 1881, the secretary of interior directed the GLO to conduct such an investigation and sent Special Agent John H. Welsh to the Isabella Reservation to ascertain the degree of trespass on Indian lands and to prosecute trespassers.[23]

Throughout the summer, Welsh, who had special permission to work on the reservation—an indication that there was some under-standing by federal officials that a boundary for the reserve did exist—collected evidence. On some occasions, the amount of trespass was minimal, and the trespasser agreed to pay for the timber taken. Welsh collected money, on one occasion as little as $26.90, and turned it over to Agent Lee. Welsh also had a second charge; to measure the amount of downed timber and sell it, collecting some $260, which was sent to the federal treasury.[24] Welsh, however, seems to have allowed the most guilty trespassers to pay small sums, or he turned the evidence over to the federal prosecutor in Detroit, who did little with it.[25] While Welsh seemed unwilling to prosecute prominent lumber operators, the new allotments, which were handed out starting in 1883, seemed to satisfy most Indian leaders. Indeed, in the 1880s the land base of the reserva-tion increased substantially, given the fact that "restricted" deeds con-stituted "Indian lands."

Nevertheless, at least one report that reached the commissioner of Indian affairs suggested that Agent Allen had protected the more promi-nent land barons in Mt. Pleasant.[26] Troubled by the entire business, the commissioner of the GLO sent a second special agent, F. W. Warden, to the Isabella Reservation in the fall of 1886. Warden left Washing-ton with the knowledge that while the commissioner would consider allowing trespassers to provide compensation for "their liability under the law," there was an added element; the US attorney in Detroit had received instructions to begin prosecutions immediately. Agent Mark Stevens, who took charge in 1886, was also ordered to assist in the prosecutions.[27]

Since the GLO had not yet produced the tract book that it had once promised, Stevens first turned to the county records, hoping to get a clear sense of just what constituted Indian lands: those held in trust by the government for individual Indians (restricted), those held by the tribe in common, and lands that were to be allotted to young people. The county records were a mess; county officials had no idea regarding which lands were issued under "not so competent" patents (and thus were theoretically not taxable) or competent patents (titles that could be taxed). To complicate the issue, much of the land in the county had supposedly been "purchased," and the titles recorded in the courthouse. As far as county officials were concerned, they felt just in taxing all lands in the county. As Stevens put it: "The records of Isabella County are not reliable with reference to this question for nearly every description of land when 'NSC' patents have been issued such lands, as shown by county records, are owned by other parties who claim title as purchasers of the Indians." In other words, speculators continued to purchase lands in the early 1880s, often filing deeds on lands that were from "not so competent" patents. Based on these fraudulent deeds, the Michigan Board of Equalization granted the right to tax those lands.[28]

Stevens was rather aghast at the problem, which he realized had to be rectified. He launched a series of lawsuits against those speculators who used illegal deeds, filed in the county courthouse, to cut timber from Indian reservation land.[29] In July 1886, six such suits were filed against the biggest timber cutters in the county: William N. Brown, Brown and Leaton, John C. Leaton, Leaton and Upton, Thomas Pichard, and Phillip Gruett. Other smaller suits followed. Even those speculators who had paid some small compensation for illegal timber cuts were not exempt. When asked for an opinion, the US attorney general concluded that such compensation had nothing to do with the prosecution, which went forward. The federal government, while often remiss in the past in enforcing the Intercourse Acts that protected Indians and their land in Michigan, was now doing so.[30]

The evidence presented for trial was clear; Agent Stevens offered specific accounts in fifteen separate cases. Typical was the case of Jane Ne-se-get, who received a 40-acre patent in 1885, only to discover that one George Hersey was occupying the land and cutting timber based on a fraudulent title. He refused to leave and claimed to have purchased the land from John Leaton. The latter, for his part, was discovered cutting $400 worth of ash and elm on a 40-acre patent given to Adelia M. Wyman McDonald, using what amounted to a fraudulent questionable deed. Dozens of other examples were offered up by Agent Stevens. Making matters worse, after lands had been mostly cut clean of timber, they were abandoned by the original speculators who had held the fraudulent titles and were then sold for taxes. Once a new owner received a "tax title," Agent Stevens noted, it was almost impossible to overturn that contract in the state courts. Stevens concluded: "Millions of feet of valuable timber within the last five years have been cut off from vacant Indian lands and new selections where 'not so competent' patents have been issued."[31]

Over the next two years, the prosecution of timber theft continued, but the government found it difficult to overcome the local lawyers and the many changes that had occurred as land had been sold for taxes, retitled, and sold again. Agent Stevens assisted Special Agent Warden, who had been sent to Michigan by the land office. They both submitted long reports regarding the evidence that pointed to fraud. In one report relative to the fraud regarding titles, dated May 26, 1888, the acting commissioner of Indian affairs assured the commissioner of the GLO that the process was continuing. "Relative to the timber depredations . . . within the Isabella Indian Reservation," he said, the attorney general seemed resolved to prosecute, provided "good cause of action existed."[32]

The prosecutions frightened some Mt. Pleasant lumber operators and their attorneys; they wrote to the commissioner of the GLO requesting information. Mostly they sent in land lists, asking questions regarding the ownership of said land.[33] The ongoing investigation soon hit a snag, however, as the US Congress neglected to authorize funds to continue Agent Stevens in his job. The entire Michigan Agency—one that serviced nearly a dozen different tribes—was closed. Stevens left the agency in July 1889. While this did not end the prosecutions—indeed, convictions followed in the 1890s—the process seemed stalled by spring 1890. At that point, the commissioner of the GLO queried the commissioner of Indian affairs as to the status of the investigation. The commissioner could only respond that he would welcome the selection of a special agent from the land office to investigate the matter once again.[34] The commissioner of Indian affairs seemed to think that it was more appropriate for the land office to continue the investigation, rather than the BIA.

The bureau did not, however, abandon its charge to protect the integrity of the Indian reservation that had been created by the 1864 treaty. This became apparent when an urgent telegraph arrived in Washington from Agent Stevens just before he left office. Dated September 20, 1888, it stated that a mass invasion of homesteaders had suddenly appeared on unallotted reservation land, the interlopers claiming that the reservation had been opened to "homestead entry."[35] The federal land agent at Grayling (the Ionia land office had been closed) had authorized the entries, which according to the plat books amounted to no fewer than sixty claimants, for a total of over 2,500 acres.[36]

Meanwhile, a series of letters from local citizens arrived in Washington. Citizens such as James Anderson wanted to know if "Indian reserve lands" within Isabella County were "subject to private entry as homesteads."[37] A petition, organized by the Mt. Pleasant Business Exchange, an organization that had learned of the questionable nature of these homesteads, then reached Washington. This group argued that the unallotted lands on the reservation should be purchased through another treaty. Once in government possession, the lands then could be legally opened to homesteaders.[38]

Acting Commissioner A. B. Upshaw telegraphed Stevens, who had not yet departed, with a clear, decisive response to such queries: "General Land Office has telegraphed local officials to stop all entries on Isabella Indian Reservation." Just three days later, the acting commissioner sent yet a second message: "No law exists authorizing entry of land on Isabella Indian Reservation." Stevens was ordered to use whatever means to evict the trespassers under Section 2147 Revised Statues.[39]

Upshaw then sent similar letters to the various settlers who had written, including Anderson. "Indian reserve lands" were not subject to "sale or entry," the acting commissioner wrote. Many local residents had been at the point of concluding—without any legal evidence—that the reservation no longer existed and that vacant land was open to all. Despite the strong language from Washington, the problem persisted into the next year before whites finally gave up. Responding to J. H. Porterfield, a lawyer from Mt. Pleasant, the acting commissioner clearly stated: "No land in the Isabella Reservation is subject to homestead entry, and that a white man cannot obtain title to land in that reservation under the homestead or other land laws."[40] That same year, the GLO once again published an official map that included the six-township Isabella Reservation.

Canceled Patents and the Land Title Debate

While Congress had stopped funding the agent's position, assuming that one was no longer needed in Michigan, the correspondence dealing with the Isabella Reservation—and the problems associated with it—seemed to be on the increase by 1890. Various Indians who had received "not so competent" patents in 1885 suddenly discovered that whites had conflicting local titles, filed in the county courthouse. Many of these new patentees were young people who had been away at Indian boarding schools. They could read and write in English, and a few fired off letters to the commissioner of Indian affairs.[41]

A second conflict erupted over the fact that many patents had been printed, sent to Michigan, and then, for whatever reason, canceled. When the patents were reissued in 1885, it was soon discovered that whites supposedly had purchased the canceled patents—even though they had never been issued to Indians—in the 1870s and filed local deeds for them in the county courthouse. Those whites who held these so-called deeds, fearing the loss of the land, went into court and won a decision that indicated that a federal patent to land could not be canceled—even one that apparently had not been issued to an Indian in the first place—causing even more confusion.[42] The patents had been canceled when it became obvious to the agents in the 1870s that the Indians who had been issued the patents either did not exist or were not on the reservation. This, of course, does not explain how the individuals who filed titles got hold of enough information to create a quitclaim deed and file it in the courthouse.

Serious questions also arose after a "not so competent" patentee died. Judge Maxwell of Mt. Pleasant wrote the commissioner asking: "How does said restriction affect the heirs of the original 'not so competent'" allotment? The commissioner answered that the death did not affect the restrictions to the title, and the heirs would simply have to request that the secretary of the interior remove the restriction to the title.[43]

Suddenly, this created a new issue—determining just when a "not so competent" Indian—living or dead—could be judged competent and be allowed to sell his or her land. In the years to come, after the passage of the Dawes Severalty Act of 1887 and the allotment of most reservations in the United States, these issues would be resolved to some degree. But Saginaw Chippewa lands had been allotted very early, and the process was not well established when it came to these issues. And it did not help that federal administrations regularly changed in the 1880s and 1890s, further disrupting bureau business.

While land issues continued to enmesh the commissioner in Washington, local citizens and politicians lobbied for a final allotment of Indian lands. A special agent was selected in 1891 who was to ascertain how much land was left unallotted and divide it among qualified Indians. He was also to investigate the timber fraud situation and to untangle the mess that had developed over the "canceled" patents, which were at this time estimated to number 101. Of this number, some had been issued to Indians in 1883 and 1885, but no officials in Washington seemed to know how many.[44] The man selected for the job was E. B. Reynolds, who was then working in Wisconsin for the BIA.

Reynolds faced an impossible task. He had been ordered by the commissioner of Indian affairs to consult the Saginaw Chippewas in council and determine their views. The Indians, he discovered, were mostly angry and upset. A few apparently had never received patents promised in 1883; others were determined to prevent Ottawas and Pottawatomies from getting lands in what would be the last allotment; and, finally, some complained that even when they had patents, whites took their lands anyway, using force to keep them from taking possession. Any attempt at getting satisfaction from the local sheriff was futile.[45] And no one seemed to know what rules governed "not so competent" Indians who might wish to sell their lands or who had inherited a small parcel that was useless to them. The acting commissioner of Indian affairs finally concluded in June 1891 that "if the chiefs will unite in a certificate," indicating that it was in the best interests of a particular Indian to sell, then the secretary of the interior might agree to the sale.[46]

As Reynolds struggled through the summer, he tried to rectify what had become a massive land fraud problem. He asked the commissioner whether there was some recourse for those Indians who had received patents in 1885 for lands that had been patented in the early 1870s and then canceled. Usually, such lands had been sold and resold several times in the 1870s, since lumber merchants supposedly had purchased the canceled patents in "good faith." Apparently sick of the entire, ridiculous affair, the US attorney general ultimately concluded that the Indians themselves would have to seek redress in the courts. Federal officials seemed virtually incapable of dealing with so many conflicting claims and titles.

Reynolds stayed close to the Indians, rather than remaining in the more comfortable Isabella City or Mt. Pleasant, and called his location the Rosebush Agency. Some Chippewa leaders sent him appeals in writing. Joseph P. Gruett, for example, wrote the following: "Now Friend Reynolds, do something for us poor Indians and do it right away." Reynolds could find only 126 parcels of land still available for selection within the reservation bounds—lands that did not seem to be affected by the cancelled patent issue—but they were not enough to satisfy every young Indian who by age was now qualified for land. Reynolds issued the last patents—126—in November 1891 and prepared to file his last report.[47]

In this last written statement, he lambasted the Indian office for its failure to look after these Indians. He noted that the state of Michigan was preparing to tax all "not so competent" lands and that the Indians who had patents did not know what to do—whether to pay the tax, fight it, or simply stand by as the state confiscated their lands. Reynolds suggested that the Justice Department be advised of this and stop it. "It seems to me that it will be the shurest mockery to postpone this matter until the lands are all sold for taxes . . . or the timber is all removed there from under color of right or stolen outright." Reynolds's appeal went further. "They [the Indians] are poor, have little standing in the court of Michigan and I think would stand little chance of securing justice therein." They "looked to the department as the only source of help in this matter and I hope they will not look in vain."[48]

While the Office of Indian Affairs, or "the department," as Reynolds called it, seemed overwhelmed with problems associated with the Isabella Indian Reservation, there is still no question that federal authorities continued to identity and recognize the reservation and its existence, despite attempts by county officials to suggest that no reservation existed anymore. Yet government land office maps continued to clearly identify the six townships as the Isabella Reservation. Allotment, despite the alienation of land that often came with it, had had no impact on federal recognition of the reservation.

COMPETENCY, THE LAND ISSUE, AND THE BUSINESS COMMITTEE

As younger, more assimilated Saginaw Chippewas received land and made their presence felt with the tribal council, the bands became more demanding in their dealings with the US government. By 1890, just before Reynolds arrived, they put together their own list for allotments, using a printed sheet of paper entitled "Isabella Indian Reservation." The council asked that patents be issued "as shall be recommended by our chiefs and council." When Reynolds handed out the patents in 1891, he basically followed their wishes, marking almost all patents "not so competent."[49]

Saginaw Indians also compiled their own list of frauds, even accusing several Métis in their own tribe of abusing the allotment process. They knew for a fact that Joseph Bradley and Lyman Bennett, both tribal members, had used their wives to acquire more land than they were entitled. More significantly, they uncovered dozens of cases in 1890, which they listed numerically (they covered twelve legal pages), in which patents issued in 1885—supposedly for unoccupied land—were being claimed by others, mostly land speculators. Over the next year, more petitions came into the commissioner's office, one complaining because a patentee given land in 1891 was of "too light [a] complexion" to be an Indian.[50]

Such problems with competency only ballooned over the next few months. One H. A. Sanford, the owner of a shingle company in Mt. Pleasant, wrote a long, detailed letter praising Reynolds's care regarding the issuing of "not so competent" patents but then protested the case of one Daniel Bennett, who had received such a patent yet was clearly capable of handling his own affairs. Another Indian, John Mogg, who had been given a 40-acre allotment, had purchased land in another region and simply wanted to sell his allotment.

Harried by such complaints, Commissioner of Indian Affairs T. J. Morgan finally decided in March 1892 that if two "disinterested and competent" persons could attest to the competency of an Indian, and that the Indian provided a signed bill of sale, then the transaction might be granted by the secretary of the interior.[51]

This idea, short-lived, was soon replaced by another. In October 1893 the Department of the Interior ordered that a new special agent be sent to Isabella with instructions to help select five representatives of the bands to form a business committee that would be "attached to the Isabella Indian Reservation." They were to pass on recommendations to the secretary on the "not so competent" status of most of the reservation members.[52] This did not mean that the tribal council had dissolved itself. Yet some questions existed by the spring of 1892 as to the legitimacy of those chiefs. Young Cornelius Bennett had written the commissioner suggesting that a certain set of men should be recognized as leaders, while other members of the bands had gathered around a different set of chiefs. This conflict was likely tied to the growing divisions that existed between young, educated Indians, such as Bennett, and older, more traditional individuals.[53]

The business council that was organized in October was an elected group that the commissioner thought would not be affected by band factionalism. This group of five men would deal with land issues only, issues that were overwhelming the government. The idea of forming a business council was being introduced by the BIA on reservations across America at this time. The office formed a similar business council on the Wind River Reservation for the Arapahoe Indians in Wyoming in the same year as the Saginaw Chippewas organized one.[54]

Given the younger generation that became vocal in the 1890s, it is unsurprising that some conflict occurred. As the tribe turned to voting on chiefs and members of the business council, a number of younger men who were not hereditary chiefs were elected. Indeed, the five members of the business council contained two men in their thirties.[55] While the business council appeared to represent the more progressive factions within the Saginaw bands, one critic, Daniel Elk, wrote in 1900 that the business committee had become too inclined to grant sales, thus resulting in the Indians' loss of land: "The Indians are very anxious to appoint the New Committee for the Reservation, hoping they do Better for the Indians."[56]

There may have been some truth to this criticism, although few other Indians corroborated Elk's charges. One certainty, however, is that the

Isabella Reservation business council became more aggressive in asserting its presence as the years went by. The group increasingly noted the problems with the so-called canceled patents, and they requested that the government do an audit of this land.[57] The letter asking for the audit was signed by Chief Philip Gruett, as secretary for the business committee. The letter noted that a disturbing number of patents issued in 1885 and 1891 were for lands that white men possessed and refused to give up. They claimed titles from canceled patents, a problem that the government had tried to ignore in the past. The question increasingly became how many had been canceled and what could be done, if anything, to regain this land?

The answer was rather astonishing. According to the audit, completed in October 1895, some 108 patents had been returned to Washington, DC. Since the government assumed that the land had not been patented originally—a fair assumption given the fact that the patents had not reached Indian hands—much of it was reissued in 1885 and 1891. The various lists—the commissioner of the GLO found several discrepancies when comparing them—demonstrated that over 17,000 acres of land out of the total of roughly 70,000 issued in 1871 had the patents returned to Washington.[58]

While the commissioner's office recognized it had a serious problem even before Gruett's letter arrived, it found very few good answers to address the issues. It was blatantly illegal for land speculators and lumber buyers to get the name of a patentee and then file a quitclaim deed to the land, supposedly after purchasing it. But the local courts supported such activity. Initially, it was assumed that the federal attorney in Detroit could simply file suit against the interlopers. But this soon proved unworkable, as the commissioner of Indian affairs was forced to admit time and again to frustrated patentees: "Under the decisions of the U.S. Courts it appears that the Secretary of the Interior had not power to cancel the patent, though fraudulently obtained." All the commissioner's office could do was hope that the courts would reverse themselves. In reality, the issue had become an embarrassment. There seemed to be no solution.[59]

The growing fight over land only solidified the Saginaw Chippewas in their desire to remain together as a tribe and to maintain their reservation. When Special Agent Reynolds came to deliver the patents in 1891, the tribal council took two weeks in deliberating over each one.[60] And when Special Agent James A. Cooper came to organize the Saginaw Chippewa business committee in 1893, while he discovered considerable "factional feelings" among the Indians, he brought them together in council and they voted many times, until five clear representatives were selected. The men selected were, Cooper believed, "among the most intelligent of the Isabella Reservation."[61]

Since most of the lands allotted during the 1880s and 1890s were given without marketable patents, those that were not under conflict remained in Indian hands for many years to come. Well over 10,000 acres apparently were included in these latter allotments. But some trust land still supposedly existed, even though Reynolds assumed he had issued it all. Likely the total amounted to somewhere between 2,000 and 5,000 acres. Unfortunately, the federal government admitted to having little idea of the actual amount.[62]

CHIPPEWA VIEWS OF THEIR RESERVATION

Trying to assess how the leaders and people of the Saginaw Chippewas viewed their reservation by 1900 is complex. Certainly, they had faced much adversity in maintaining control over lands and had lost well over 60 percent of their lands to fraud. At times, agents gave insights into tribal views, but more often than not those same agents were greatly influenced by white settlers and politicians. Numerous petitions signed by tribal leaders also are somewhat reflective of Indian views. But petitions were usually drawn up by white men or Métis, who also had agendas. Only after 1880, when some younger, educated Indians appeared at the reservation, did petitions increasingly reflect the will of the Chippewa people. Some sense of Chippewa views can be gleaned from these later documents.

Very early, writing generally of Chippewa views in Michigan, Agent Smith, who had spent eighteen years among them, found that while they were not competent to be given land in fee simple, they took very seriously the defense of their reservation lands and resources. They viewed the reservation as a communal homeland, much as Commissioner Manypenny had described when he helped create it in 1855.

"Settlers are regarded by the Indians as trespassers who have no business on the reservation," Smith wrote in his 1867 report. By this time the reservation had been surveyed, and the Indians had a fairly clear view of its boundaries. Even so, Smith admitted that most Indian leaders at that time had come to believe that allotment would be a good thing, or so surrounding white settlers had told them.[63] The missionaries also were instrumental in preaching for allotment—Smith being an exception—thinking it would lead to citizenship, agricultural productivity, and Christianity, which in fact, it did not.[64]

These views, held by many Chippewa leaders, had changed by the mid-1870s. After it became obvious that most Indians who initially received patents in 1871 and 1872 (fully five-sixths) lost their lands, Chippewa leaders came to hold an entirely different view.[65] They recognized that the allotment process led to land alienation. In Commissioner of Indian Affairs E. A. Hayt's annual report of 1878, the following was recorded regarding the views of Indian leaders on the Isabella Reservation: "So well have the Indians of Isabella County, Michigan, become convinced of their entire inability to protect their lands, that at a recent council with them, held by a special agent of this office, at which a number of allotments were made, they unanimously requested that the patents for the lands allotted be issued to them without the power of alienation."[66]

This reflects the continued desire of the Indians to protect their six-township reservation. Some members of the Office of Indian Affairs by this time also had concluded that notions of making these Indians citizens, and thus allotting them land in severalty, were highly premature. Further evidence of this failure comes in assessing the agricultural efforts, which at times were praised by corrupt agents. Certainly, agents put the best face on collected data when sending reports to Washington. Nevertheless, as late as 1878, there were only 13 yoke of oxen, 50 head of cattle, 100 hogs, and about 40 horses in the hands of Saginaw Indians on the reservation. Three more yokes of oxen were found among off-reservation Saginaw Indians. Many Indians, in other words, continued to work in lumber camps and to fish and hunt for a living, both on and outside the reserve.[67] While the reservation had become a homeland, this had not led to an agricultural revolution.

The thousand or so people who remained on the reservation were perhaps the best off economically. But they, too, suffered at times for lack of food. When this occurred, they consistently turned to their agent or petitioned their "Great Father" (the president) for help. The agents generally took money from agricultural programs and purchased food.[68] This sense of dependency on the federal government was consistently expressed in petitions that the tribal council sent east. In a "General Council" of Indians "living on the Reservation in Isabella County" in 1869, the petitioners addressed "the President of the United States."[69] Again, in May 1875, in the petition that ultimately brought the Betts regime down, Indian leaders "respectfully represent to our Great Father in Washington" a series of grievances.[70] Finally, in yet another petition dated August 1875, the Saginaw Chippewas closed with an appeal that, while likely not given much attention in Washington, certainly had much meaning to them: "We combine together as one man in shaking hands with our Great Father, Hoping he may have compassion upon his children in this prayer to the Great Spirit."[71]

A New Era?

Most of the Saginaw men who negotiated with the federal government in the 1860s and 1870s were in their forties or fifties. This began to change by the 1880s, when a new era had emerged on the reservation. One reason for the change was the fact that many young Saginaw men had joined the Union Army and fought in the Civil War. They quickly learned English while in camp. Other young people had been sent off to boarding school, where they were forced to learn English. After their schooling ended, they went back to the reservation. They wanted land and a future, and many wanted to marry.[72]

By the 1880s and 1890s, the tribal council became more direct in its dealings with reservation agents, and after 1889, with a host of special agents who came to Rosebush. The council's first success of this sort came in 1882, when it convinced Washington officials to fire George W. Lee, who, though not a bad agent, was generally disliked. The council presented evidence that Lee had not treated the tribe fairly in the distribution of annuities. The commissioner of Indian affairs agreed, replacing Lee with Allen in 1882.[73] Lee's downfall seemed to come after it became increasingly obvious that the timber mills in Mt. Pleasant, owned by many of the same people who had committed the frauds of 1871–72, were still trespassing on Indian lands and taking timber—and Lee was allowing it. The tribal council demanded an investigation, suggesting that even the sale of downed timber be postponed until more information could be gathered regarding its value.[74]

Agent Allen learned, to some degree, from this experience. He no longer questioned the authority of the council, a conclusion that seems apparent from his report of the first selection of lands undertaken in 1883. Allen drew up a list of eighty-two names and "took applications" from others. He then held three councils with tribal leaders, using "utmost caution" to explain the proceedings. At each council, he asked if anyone present had any objections to the people on the list. Allen "marked most of the men and all of the women as 'not so competent,'" which was exactly what the council wanted. The agent added, however, with some regret, "Many of them drink and many more are indifferent to their own welfare."[75] The commissioner of Indian affairs approved the list on November 13, 1885, "of lands selected upon the Isabella Indian Reservation."[76]

The tribal council also aided in the prosecution of trespassers, working with justice department lawyers on at least a few successful cases. Fully eight years after Stevens filed the first case, four guilty verdicts were obtained in federal court in Detroit. Fines of nearly $2,000 were levied against the four offenders, a hefty sum for the 1890s.[77] After two years of debate, it was determined that the recovered funds should go to the Indian allottees, although the sums sent to them were quite small, being reduced to cover court fees.[78]

The commissioner of Indian affairs believed that the Justice Department had a duty to support Indian allottees and defend their claims in court. In a letter to the US attorney general, Commissioner D. M. Browning made a succinct argument, saying distinctly that Indians were

> still in a state of pupilage and under the guardianship of the General Government. Under the same ground, I am clear that it has not been the intention of Congress, in any legislation so far, to put these Indians, who take

such separate allotments, entirely upon their own resources or to withdraw the Government's guardianship, supervision, and protection. . . . In other words, I am entirely clear that it is the duty of the Government to protect these Indian allottees in the enjoyment of their allotments. The only question is as to the manner of such protection.[79]

This policy included protecting whatever rights came with having a reservation, one distinctly guaranteed under a treaty.

In truth, however, the level of protection would change from administration to administration and the court battles would continue for years, well into the twentieth century.[80] This made it virtually impossible for the Office of Indian Affairs to extract itself from dealing with, and protecting, the Isabella Indians and their reservation.[81] By the mid-1890s, the bureau was constantly calling on the superintendent of the Mt. Pleasant Indian School—which was within the boundaries of the reservation and served Saginaw students—for help in solving problems on the reservation. So much correspondence came out of the commissioner's office regarding land and reservation issues that there is no doubt that, had Congress approved, the bureau would have added a new agent in Michigan.

The 1855 and 1864 treaties with the Saginaw Chippewas created a six-township reservation in Isabella County that was intended to be the Indians' permanent home. There is no question that the US attorney general, the secretary of the interior, the commissioner of Indian affairs, and virtually every agent who served in Michigan continued to call the six townships an Indian reservation throughout the 1890s. In 1893, at the insistence of the commissioner of Indian affairs, these same Indians even signed affidavits attesting that the last agent, Mark Stevens, had held a council meeting in which three chiefs were elected—Peter Bennett, Joseph Bradley, and John P. Williams—to lead, as they proudly noted, the "Isabella Indian Reservation."[82]

Over the years after the 1864 treaty, the Saginaw Chippewas lost much of their tribal sovereignty. The loss of land base led to the loss of other functions that many tribes in America enjoyed. Any tribal operational control over law and order had been completely lost, as local sheriffs and city police officers in Mt. Pleasant and elsewhere lorded over the Saginaw people, often with a heavy hand. While there was a well-run boarding school at Mt. Pleasant operated by the federal government, the Indians themselves had very little input when it came to the education of their children. And the federal government did little to protect the Indians from state and local taxes, even though the Indians themselves hardly ever benefitted from the advantages that these taxes provided for citizens. Mostly, the Saginaws did not vote or participate in local politics. All of these circumstances were tied to the implementation of the allotment process, which had been an outright failure.

Some public officials were beginning to recognize the errors made when this allotment process was in its infancy. In 1885 George Manypenny, while in retirement, stated that if he could have foreseen the results of the early allotment treaties that he negotiated in the mid-1850s and had gone ahead with them, he would have been guilty of committing a "high crime."[83] But neither he nor the Saginaw Chippewa leaders could have foreseen the mismanagement and outright fraud that led to the loss of much of their lands and their tribal rights.

Yet the loss of land base, while substantial, did not destroy the social, cultural, and religious glue that held together the Saginaw people. They continued to elect tribal councils and business councils—adapting tribal solutions to elements of government that the federal government encouraged—and to send protests on to Washington, DC. These were the actions of a Native tribe that continued to view its relationship with the federal government as one in which they had been placed on a reservation for their own protection and advancement. By the 1880s, while Congress seemed to have abandoned these Indians, the BIA and the executive branch of government did not, sending special agent after agent to investigate their circumstances. Certainly, as much letter writing went on during these later years as during the early formation of the reservation.

Even so, at the local level, county and state officials were hard at work trying their best to destroy any sense of sovereignty that the Saginaw Chippewas had by right of treaty. Taxation was central to such efforts, and many Indians were forced to pay local taxes, even though they were wards of the federal government and under such circumstances should have been exempt from those taxes. And while state and local officials infringed on tribal sovereignty, they also did little to elevate the tribe or care for needy people within it. The Isabella County poorhouse was mostly off-limits to Indians, as was medical help such as that offered indigent white people. It would take a new century—and a new awakening in the country as a whole, as well as within the federal agencies that administered assistance to Indians—to provide the help needed for the Saginaw people to regain the losses inflicted upon them by the process of allotment.

5

THE MT. PLEASANT
SCHOOL INTERREGNUM

In 1889, shortly after the closing of the Mackinac Agency, federal officials estimated that 630 Saginaw, Swan Creek, and Black River Chippewas composed the Isabella community; of these, about 500 lived on the Isabella Indian Reservation. Other Saginaw Chippewas formed small communities in the Chippewa River valley or near Saginaw Bay.[1]

The Indians on the Isabella Reservation no longer had an agent in Michigan, but they continued to rely on the federal government. Many of the Saginaw Chippewas still had not received the patents to their allotments, and although Indian agent Mark Stevens had sent in a schedule of their selections and patent requests to the Office of Indian Affairs prior to the closing of the Mackinac Agency, bureaucrats in Washington lost the applications. In response, the Chippewas compiled a lengthy schedule on their own and resubmitted it to Washington, but the Office of Indian Affairs refused to accept it until a new special agent could be appointed.[2] For budgetary reasons, officials proposed that the superintendent of the new Mt. Pleasant Isabella School administer the patent process, but no superintendent was appointed until April 1892, and the patents could not be awarded.[3]

As a short-term remedy, the commissioner of Indian affairs directed E. B. Reynolds, the Indian agent in charge of the Lac du Flambeau, La Pointe, and Red Cliff reservations in Wisconsin, to proceed to the Isabella Reservation, ascertain the eligibility of those Indians applying for patents and the amount and location of lands available for allotments, and send such information to Washington. The commissioner also instructed Reynolds to investigate "such matters as may be brought to your attention by the Indians, and inquire generally into their condition and needs, and make such recommendations to this office as you may deem necessary."[4] For all practical purposes, Reynolds was to function as the ad-interim Indian agent for the Isabella Reservation.

In March 1890, Reynolds met with the Indians on the Isabella Reservation and found they still adhered to their political relationship with the federal government. He reported that they blamed the federal government for the delayed issuance of the patents and pointed out that Indians on the reservation believed that the "Indian Office" was responsible for their welfare because "in their dealings with the government, they know of no other. And while they look to it [the BIA] for relief, they hold it responsible for any wrong which they conceive has been done them."[5] Reynolds also strongly recommended that a "special agent, or if this could not or cannot be done, then some person here [in Mt. Pleasant] be appointed" to oversee the issuance of patents and the lease or sale of timber on the allotments. According to Reynolds, "If some such arrangements are not made, . . . the Indian will keep but little benefit from his timber . . . [and] the unfortunate circumstances attending the non-delivered deeds will . . . attach to the new ones."[6]

The federal government also tacitly acknowledged its suzerainty over tribal government on the Isabella Reservation. In 1893, Commissioner of Indian Affairs Daniel Browning instructed Special Agent James A. Cooper, who was serving as the acting superintendent of the Mt. Pleasant Indian School, to meet with Indians from the Isabella Reservation and personally select five members of the Saginaw, Swan Creek, and Black River Chippewa bands to serve as a business committee to assist federal agents in the issuance of "not so competent" patents. After "visiting the reservation," Cooper found "more or less factional feelings existing among these Indians such as prevails among Indians generally."[7] On September 9, 1893, Cooper met in council with the "Saginaw, Swan Creek and Black River Bands of the Chippewa Indians on the Isabella Reservation," then (to his credit) provided federal supervision of an election in which five members were elected to the business committee.

Ironically, eight months later Browning again intervened in the reservation's government. In April 1894, he dispatched C. C. Duncan, another federal "inspector," back to the "Isabella Indian Reservation" to investigate charges of corruption against the business committee. In May, Duncan exonerated the "business committee of the Chippwa Indians on the Isabella reservation" from all charges.[8]

Federal officials initially intended that the superintendent of the Mt. Pleasant Indian School would function as an agent for the Isabella Reservation. The school, authorized by Congress in 1891, was constructed on two hundred acres of land adjoining the city of Mt. Pleasant. The institution officially opened with thirteen students on January 3, 1893, but students were housed and attended classes in downtown Mt. Pleasant until March, when the first school building was completed. During the 1890s both the enrollment and physical facilities at the school increased. By 1898 total enrollment reached 222 students, and the school had added additional classrooms, dormitories, a barn, and outbuildings. A decade later, eleven brick buildings had been erected, and in addition to attending classes, the students produced bumper crops on the school farm. In the 1920s student enrollment hovered between 275–300 students (from throughout the Great Lakes region and parts of the Great Plains), and the school offered academic classes as well as manual training programs in agriculture and in industrial and domestic arts. The superintendent oversaw thirty-five to forty employees, including teachers, matrons, cooks, carpenters, gardeners, and clerks, in addition to overseeing a diversified curricula and looking after school athletic teams and a band.[9] Obviously, the superintendent of the Mt. Pleasant Indian School had his hands full.

But federal officials in Washington also expected the school's superintendent to oversee the government's obligations to the Saginaw, Swan Creek, and Black River Chippewas and to the Isabella Reservation. Initially, the superintendents seemed willing to comply. In 1893, acting superintendent James A. Cooper had visited the reservation and had assisted the Saginaw Chippewas in electing a business committee to assist in the issuance of patents.[10] During the next two decades superintendents at the school met with this group and supervised the issuance of patents.[11] Superintendents at the Mt. Pleasant Indian School also looked after the welfare of reservation residents and periodically investigated charges of fraud in the administration of tribal and reservation affairs.[12] They also sent regular reports to the commissioner regarding conditions on the reservation. By 1915, however, the school had continued to grow, and even A. B. Cochran—a superintendent who had previously been "deeply interested" in the plight of Indians on the reservation and who had repaired old beds from the school dormitory and distributed them to needy Chippewas on the Isabella Reservation—was being overwhelmed by his dual responsibilities to both the school and the reservation.[13]

The superintendents of the Mt. Pleasant Indian School also were confronted by changes in the tribal government of the Indians on the Isabella Reservation. Although the tribal government of the Saginaw, Swan Creek, and Black River Chippewas supposedly had been terminated by Article 6 of the 1855 treaty, this provision of the treaty had proven meaningless, since tribal leaders had negotiated another treaty only nine years later (in 1864).[14] Moreover, Indian agents and other federal officials continued to meet with tribal leaders.[15] Indeed, a traditional tribal council had continued to function on the Isabella Reservation between 1889 and 1893, and several chiefs and council members had repeatedly written the president and commissioner of Indian affairs in regard to patents and other tribal affairs.[16] Federal efforts to formalize relations with the reservation leadership had resulted in the formation of the official business committee.[17]

The establishment of a federally sponsored business committee neither ended the political infighting among the Chippewas on the Isabella Reservation nor solved the dilemma federal officials faced in working with a reservation government. In contrast, since the business committee had the federal government's blessing, individual Indians or tribal political factions now addressed their complaints to the superintendent of the Indian school, the commissioner of Indian affairs, or other federal officials. Issues involving reservation politics that might previously have been solved within the confines of a tribal council meeting now were forwarded on to the school superintendent or his superiors for a final decision, and even those complaints sent directly to Washington often were forwarded back to Mt. Pleasant for the school superintendent's investigation.[18] The federally sponsored business committee continued to participate in the issuance of patents and other reservation business, but in 1906 the traditional council of the Chippewa Indians of the Isabella County reservation met and informed federal officials that they had formally appointed a "chief" or "chairman." Envisioning the council as a threat to federal influence on the reservation, the commissioner of Indian affairs informed a spokesperson for the group that the government did not recognize its legitimacy. The BIA would deal only with the federally "ratified" business committee.[19]

Written on a letterhead of an attorney in Mt. Pleasant, the letter, dated December 19, 1906, announced that the council of the Chippewa Indians of the Isabella Reservation had formally appointed a chief. This was a portent of things to come.[20] By the first decade of the twentieth century, tribal governments (whether "ratified" or not) on the Isabella Reservation sought professional legal assistance in their relationship with the federal government. Obviously, tribal government on the reservation continued, and by 1914 the tribal council had informally merged with the business committee. Represented by Joseph Bradley, a Saginaw Chippewa attorney, they threatened legal action against the federal government, claiming that the United States had denied them adequate payment from the sale of the tribal grist mill in 1872. Bradley also informed Commissioner of Indian Affairs Cato Sells that the Saginaw Chippewas planned to use such funds "for the purpose of bringing the true facts" of the government's alleged mismanagement of the allotment of the Isabella Reservation "before the Court of Claims." This court was just beginning to function as a place where Indians—as well as other citizens—could bring actions against the federal government. According to Bradley, "It is estimated that one-third of our reservation has not been allotted properly." He wanted some compensation.[21]

Eager to pursue such claims, during the fall of 1915 the council met regularly and expanded the scope of their inquiries.[22] They asked for a delineation of Chippewa hunting and fishing rights on the Isabella Reservation and requested that the government investigate the growing backlog of "heirship" cases on the reservation.[23] During the following decade they enlarged the scope of their grievances, also seeking reimbursement for timber cut illegally on reservation lands and claiming that federal officials owed them $1 million through its failure to protect tribal hunting and fishing rights. In 1927 they filed a petition to bring a suit before the US Court of Claims seeking payments for such damages.[24]

By 1930 the scope of activities initiated by the tribal council of the Chippewa Indians of the Isabella Reservation, originally founded in 1906, had so increased that the council was forced to reorganize. Ironically, in 1930 L. E. Baumgarten, the current superintendent of the Mt. Pleasant Indian School, was instructed to interact with the council as the legitimate spokesmen for Indians on the reservation, and he participated in their reorganization. The old business committee established by federal officials in 1893 was incorporated into the tribal council (condemned in 1906 as not "ratified" by federal officials), which now served as the tribal government for the Isabella Reservation. Moreover, by 1930 the council also had expanded the scope of its activities. It continued to represent Saginaw, Swan Creek, and Black River bands of Chippewas on the Isabella Reservation, but it also represented a larger contingency of Saginaw Chippewas who had scattered from the reservation to adjoining areas in Michigan or other states.[25]

The enlarged scope of activities generated by the tribal council of the Chippewa Indians of the Isabella Reservation did not bode well for superintendents of the Mt. Pleasant Indian School. As noted above, in addition to their role as school administrators, they served as de facto Indian agents to the Isabella Reservation, but after 1915 they were overwhelmed. The superintendents continued to play a key role in the issuance of patents, but the increased demands mounted by Indians from the Isabella Reservation markedly compounded their workload.[26] Superintendent R. A. Cochran, who previously had taken pride in his administration of reservation affairs, complained: "We have over 150 probate cases, hold hearings when required, also land sales, and handle applications for patents in fee; also appraise tracts when required and act in an advisory capacity in many ways to the allottees. We have the tract book for the reservation, plats and files, etc."[27]

Cochran particularly resented the growing number of heirship cases he was asked to investigate. In January 1916, he wrote to the commissioner of Indian affairs reporting that he had recently attended an heirship hearing, but that he had encountered difficulty in assembling those Indians involved in the case. Obviously upset over the expense and labor required to assemble the Indians, he complained:

This is a nonreservation school and we do not have funds of any kind for this work. During the years of 1871 and 1872 there were about 200 not-so-competent patents issued to the Indians of the Old Isabella Reservation. . . . I am not able to say just how many heirship cases there are among these Indians, but a great many of the original having died leaving estates unsettled. We have a large school and lots of work, two clerks, and really do not have the time to devote to this heirship work. Funds should be allowed for this purpose and an examiner sent to clean up these cases at an early date.[28]

In response, federal officials dispatched a special "Examiner of Inheritance" to the Isabella Reservation, but the agent did not complete the work, and Cochran again complained that "the work of the school . . . is very heavy" and he had neither the staff nor the funds to adequately pursue the heirship cases.[29] In April 1917, Cochran's superiors replied that they expected him to pursue the heirship cases, and when Cochran answered with a detailed letter explaining why "it will be impossible for this office to handle these heirship cases on account of [in]sufficient office force. . . . I cannot give them the consideration that they would require and at the same time run the school," the assistant commissioner of Indian affairs informed him that they hoped to send some assistance in the future, but "in the meantime . . . the Office will expect you to conduct the hearings and make proper report in regard thereto."[30] The promised assistance failed to arrive until 1923, six years later.[31] In the meantime the embittered Cochran was forced to labor on the heirship cases.

In 1924, Cochran left the Mt. Pleasant Indian School, but the superintendents who followed him also were forced to investigate patent and heirship cases.[32] In addition, they were burdened with investigations into growing controversies focusing on tribal claims against the government, on hunting and fishing rights, and surrounding the discovery of oil and gas on the reservation.[33] Moreover, in 1930 L. E. Baumgarten, who assumed the superintendency in 1926, was forced to assist the tribal council of the Chippewa Indians of the Isabella Reservation with their reorganization and formulation of bylaws.[34] But when the commissioner of Indian affairs asked Baumgarten to also conduct a census of the Saginaw Chippewa tribe, he repeatedly balked, arguing, as had Cochran, that "it could not be done with our present office force without additional help and additional funds." According to Baumgarten, the Saginaw Chippewas were "scattered far and wide," but "if the department permit me to give a census of the berths [*sic*] and deaths of the Indians living on the Isabella Reservation, this can be done without much difficulty."[35]

All the superintendents who had arrived at Mt. Pleasant assumed that the focus of their assignment would be the school. When additional administrative duties in relation to the Isabella Reservation also were assigned to them, they resisted such demands by claiming that the reservation no longer existed. There were some precedents for the claim. In 1902, a report by J. Franklin House, the superintendent of Indian schools, mentioned that "it can hardly be said that there are reservations in this state [Michigan]" because the Indians had taken allotments and received "no aid or support from the government."[36] Six years later, in 1908, a similar report by another visiting school inspector mentioned that the Mt. Pleasant Indian School "is situated . . . in about the center of what used to be the Isabella Indian Reservation."[37] In 1910, F. H. Abbott also described the school as located "in the heart of what was formerly the Isabella Reservation."[38] There are a few other scattered references in federal documents describing the Isabella Reservation as "old" or "former" prior to 1915, but they are uncommon and infrequent in comparison to references from this period (1900–1915) that portray the reservation as extant.[39] Moreover, like House, they seem to be based on the assumption that since the reservation had been allotted, it no longer existed.

In 1915, references to the reservation as "former," "old," or no longer in existence increased. That year, Superintendent Cochran, in reply to Elijah Elk's request for a heirship case investigation, replied that "all land on the Old Isabella Reservation had been allotted," while C. F. Hauke, a clerk in the Office of Indian Affairs who answered much of the correspondence from both Cochran and the Saginaw Chippewas, also informed Elk that he could expect a federal reply with "further references to land on the former Isabella reservation." Meanwhile, Cochran's disdain for the heirship cases had become so obvious that it was apparent even to the Indians. Joseph Bradley, the Saginaw Chippewa attorney who represented many of the Indians, reported: "I think an Examiner will do better than the Superintendent in Inheritance cases because the Superintendent's work in the school keeps him so busy." Bradley added that Cochran also did not like to make rulings in heirship cases because it "makes unpleasant feelings" among some of the Indians.[40]

Cochran's dislike of his increased workload continued. One year later, while complaining about the impending heirship cases burden, Cochran again referred to the "Old Isabella Reservation" and repeatedly declared that "this is not a reservation school."[41] In 1921, while lamenting that he had been asked to answer inquiries sent to other Indian agents in regard to the "old Isabella Reservation," Cochran replied to the commissioner of Indian affairs that "this office has always since the abolishment of the old reservation taken care of its affairs." Not surprisingly, he then provided a litany of the tasks he was required to perform for "the reservation."[42] Two years later, in 1923, when Cochran was asked to assemble Indians for other heirship case hearings, he informed the investigator that "the most difficult feature of this work here is that the heirs are scattered and sometimes hard to reach. We are not on a reservation."[43]

During the 1920s, a few other officials in the BIA echoed Cochran's sentiments. In 1920, E. B. Meritt, the assistant commissioner of Indian affairs, informed George Carpenter, a resident of Detroit who evidently had inquired about purchasing land on an "Ottawa and Chippewa Reservation," that such a reservation did not exist. In his reply, Meritt instructed Carpenter to contact Cochran in Mt. Pleasant for further information on the subject.[44] Whether or not Meritt was referring to the Isabella Indian Reservation is a matter of conjecture. Between 1921 and 1926, both Meritt and Chief Clerk Hauke described the reservation as "the former Isabella Reservation" in some of their correspondence with the Saginaw Chippewas.[45] Moreover, in 1924 O. Padgett, who served as the superintendent of the Mt. Pleasant Indian School from 1924 to 1926, also stated that he believed the reservation had "ceased to exist" after "all the land was taken up by allotment."[46]

Both L. E. Baumgarten and Frank Christy, the two final superintendents at the Mt. Pleasant Indian School, also occasionally commented that the reservation no longer was extant. In March 21, 1929, when a circular from Washington asked him to supply information on the Isabella Reservation in regard to over one hundred heirship or patent claims involving mineral rights, Baumgarten replied that "the old Isabella Reservation is practically a thing of the past and the few pieces of land still held in trust is such a small number that the Circular does not refer to this School."[47] The statement indicates, however, that Baumgarten associated reservations only with unallotted lands, or with lands held in trust ("not so competent" patents), and that he was unsure about the status of the reservation. In December 1929, Baumgarten replied tersely to a request by Ramona Village, a nascent tourist attraction in California, for a "picture of Indians, or picture or any kind of a Ceremonial Chamber" on the Isabella Reservation, by writing that "inasmuch as this is a school and as there is no reservation in Michigan, we have nothing to offer you.[48]

Baumgarten deflected comparable requests from public school students or teachers with a similar reply.[49] On several occasions, Frank Christy, who succeeded Baumgarten as school superintendent, also denied the reservation's existence. In reply to federal requests for detailed information about the reservation or its inhabitants, Christy also claimed that he could not supply data regarding healthcare or the efforts of home extension workers on the Isabella Indian Reservation since "this is not a recognized Indian reservation," and "there has been no Isabella Reservation in the ordinary meaning of that term for fifty years."[50]

But federal officials were not consistent in their assessment of the reservation's status. Prior to 1900, there were almost no statements by federal officials that the Isabella Reservation had ceased to exist, and during the following thirty years, while the reservation continued to be managed by the superintendent of the Mt. Pleasant Indian School, the predominant evidence that can be gleaned from federal documents is that the reservation continued to exist. In 1905, during his early tenure as superintendent of the school, R. A. Cochran referred to the reservation's continued existence when he reported on Indians living "on this reservation," or "the Indians of the Isabella reservation."[51] That same year, Charles M. McNichols, a special agent assigned to conduct a census of Ottawa and Chippewa Indians in Michigan, described part of the Saginaw Chippewas as living on "the Isabella Reservation, near Mount Pleasant," or "belonging to the Isabella Reservation."[52]

Even a letter written in 1907 from the acting commissioner of Indian affairs informing the newly formed tribal council that they would not be recognized by the federal government still referred to "the Ottawas and Chippewas of the Isabella County Reservation."[53] Additional correspondence from the acting commissioner in that year also informed a member of Congress that the "Superintendent of the Mount Pleasant Indian School [is] in charge of the Isabella reservation."[54] Meanwhile, the reports of the commissioners of Indian affairs, published annually during this era, continued to list the Isabella Reservation as a federal reservation.[55]

In 1912, correspondence between the acting commissioner of Indian Affairs and the US Geological Survey addressed the possibility of economic development or a reservoir on the "Mount Pleasant Reservation" in Michigan. Meanwhile, Superintendent Cochran and C. F. Hauke, both individuals who only three years later, in 1915, would declare that the Isabella Reservation no longer existed, corresponded extensively on the distribution of used beds from the Mt. Pleasant Indian School to reservation residents. In their letters they repeatedly referred to the reservation as being extant: Cochran asked to distribute the beds "to the Indians of this reservation," while Hauke granted Cochran the authority to issue the beds "to the Indians of your reservation."[56]

Cochran and Hauke continued to use present tense to refer to the reservation as existing through the late summer of 1915.[57] The official reports of the commissioners of Indian affairs continued to list the Isabella Indian Reservation as extant, but during the following decade Cochran, Hauke, and several other officials arbitrarily declared that the reservation had been abolished.[58] Other Indian agents in Michigan disagreed. At Barraga, Edward Clements, the special agent in charge of the Mackinac Agency, described the reservation as still in existence and pointed out: "It is my understanding that Indians of Isabella Reservation have been under the Mount Pleasant Indian School. . . . During the past several years certain matters having reference to the Isabella Reservation have occasionally been referred to this office but were finally referred to and disposed of through the Mount Pleasant Indian School."[59]

In November 1920, in an effort to clarify the reservation's status, the commissioner dispatched Inspector W. I. Endicott to Michigan to examine the reservation and its relationship to the Mt. Pleasant Indian School. In his report, Endicott disagreed with Cochran that the Isabella Indian Reservation had been abolished and suggested that the superintendent misunderstood the reservation's standing. According to Endicott, the reservation's status "appears to be little understood in the field." He recommended that due to the reservation's location, "the administration of the Isabella Reservation in Michigan be conferred upon the Superintendent of Mount Pleasant School."[60] In response, the assistant commissioner of Indian affairs wrote to both Clements and Cochran, informing them that the "Isabella Reservation Agency" (but not the reservation) had been abolished on June 30, 1889, and that the "administration of Isabella Reservation, Michigan," would be the responsibility of the superintendent of the Mt. Pleasant Indian School.[61]

Although Cochran—and Cochran's successors as superintendent of the school (O. Padgett, L. E. Bamgarten, and Frank Christy)—used the ploy that the reservation was nonexistent to avoid public inquiries and additional paperwork, other correspondence generated by Baumgarten and Christy also indicates that they envisioned the reservation as extant. In March 1929, Baumgarten reported to the commissioner of Indian affairs that questions had arisen "regarding Indian allotments on the Isabella Reservation."[62] Baumgarten also referred to the reservation as being in existence in correspondence concerning oil and gas rights and in discussing census records for "the Chippewa Indiana on the Isabella Reservation."[63]

Baumgarten's 1931 Annual Statistical Report to the commissioner of Indian affairs offers some insights into his analysis of the continued existence of the Isabella Indian Reservation. On those parts of the government forms that requested "agency or jurisdiction," Baumgarten listed "Mount Pleasant Indian School," but when the government forms specifically asked for a reservation, Baumgarten typed in "Isabella Reservation." In addition, the narrative section of the report provides clues into his previous use of the terms "old" or "former" to describe the Isabella Indian Reservation. In the narrative, Baumgarten describes the reservation in the present tense. For example, he points out that "the Saginaw, Swan Creek, and Black River bands of Chippewas," the contemporary Indians about whose activities he was reporting, are "the Indians of the Isabella Reservation." But he asserted that "the Mount Pleasant, Michigan, jurisdiction is, primarily, one of school activities. There, however, is some agency work to do in connection with the Old Isabella Reservation, of which there are still forty tracts, from five to forty acres each, held in trust for the original allotees, or heirs of the original allotees."[64] In other words, Baumgarten admitted that the reservation still existed but that he believed that the nature of the reservation had changed since much of the original reservation land base had been allotted and no longer was held in trust status by the federal government.

Baumgarten's superiors disagreed. Commissioner of Indian Affairs Charles H. Burke and his successor, Charles J. Rhoads, both referred to the Isabella Indian Reservation as being in existence, as did other officials in the GLO.[65] But the critical difference between Baumgarten and his superiors was the issue of allotment. The BIA official position was encapsulated in a letter by Rhoads to Edward Boyles, the deputy attorney general of the state of Michigan. On November 7, 1932, Rhoads wrote to Boyles regarding Saginaw, Swan Creek, and Black River Chippewa hunting rights. Rhoads agreed that the Chippewas were subject to state hunting and fishing regulations while hunting or fishing on "unreserved ceded land which has been sold or otherwise disposed of under the homestead law" (land ceded by the Chippewas by their treaties through 1864), but he pointed out that "a different situation arises, however, if, as is this case, restricted Indian land is involved" (land in the six townships that comprise the Isabella Indian Reservation). According to Rhoads, the dissolution of tribal organization or granting of citizenship does not necessarily have the effect of removing Indians from federal jurisdiction and control. Moreover, after citing several court cases, Rhoads informed Boyles:

> The conclusion that allotted land is not thereby excepted from a reservation and is still Indian country within the intention of Congress, seems to be the only reasonable and proper one. Otherwise Federal statutes relating to reservations and the Indian Country . . . would cease to apply, and thus Congress, charged with the duty to protect the Indians, would be held to have abandoned that duty entirely, when in fact it only extended to them the privilege of citizenship.[66]

Obviously, from the official perspective of the BIA, the Isabella Reservation had remained in existence since its establishment in 1864. In 1889, the Mackinac Agency had closed, but the reservation continued.

Non-Indian citizens in Isabella County and surrounding regions also envisioned the Isabella Indian Reservation as in existence. Private citizens inquiring about patents or other business on the reservation referred to the reservation as intact, as did local citizens who attempted to influence tribal politics on the reservation.[67] In 1890, the Mt. Pleasant Business Exchange wrote to federal officials requesting that "this reservation . . . be opened to homestead" and local taxation; otherwise it would remain "wild and unproductive in the midst of a most fertile country."[68] Other committees of businessmen wrote to their congressmen, urging the government to accelerate the patent process so that "the Indians entitled to the vacant lands on our reservation" could secure unrestricted titles to their allotments.[69] Reports from local newspapers described a broad spectrum of activities taking place on "the reservation," or by "the Indians from the reservation" at Mt. Pleasant.[70] Indeed, a circular prepared during the 1920s by the Michigan State Library in Lansing (an official agency of the state of Michigan), which was evidently sent in response to inquiries about the Mt. Pleasant Indian School, also lists the Isabella Reservation in existence in Isabella County.[71]

More significantly, the Saginaw, Swan Creek, and Black River Chippewas who lived on the Isabella Indian Reservation or in adjoining regions also envisioned the six townships as a reservation. During the four decades (1893–1934) when they found themselves under the jurisdiction of the Mt. Pleasant Indian School, their correspondence with officials in the BIA is replete with letters and petitions in which they refer to the continued existence of the Isabella Indian Reservation. The focus of these letters and petitions differed from decade to decade, but they reflect the Saginaw Chippewas' steadfast belief that the reservation was in existence. During the early 1890s the Indians sent numerous letters and petitions to federal officials urging them to hasten the issuance of patents on "this Indian reservation" and complaining that the "unclaimed land on the Isabella Reservation" should be allotted to young Saginaw Chippewa men and women who had reached the age of twenty-one years.[72]

Other correspondence from the first two decades of the Mt. Pleasant school interregnum focused on tribal politics. Several letters complained that Chief Joseph Bradley "denied the right" "of fellow Chippewas" on "this reservation" to select their own land allotments and that he was "ruining this reservation."[73] In 1896, Elijah Cup-taw-quootd charged that Bradley and the other members of the business committee appointed by federal officials "have got this Isabella County Indian reservation almost all in ruin," while Bradley, writing from the "Isabella Indian Reservation," admitted that "things are getting a little mixed" but placed the blame on other members of his committee.[74] Daniel Elk probably reflected the sentiment of many Saginaw Chippewas when he wrote in 1900 that the Indians "are very anxious to appoint the new committee for the Reservation." In 1906, the council of the Chippewa Indians of the Isabella Reservation rose to challenge the government supported business committee.[75]

During the decade between 1910 and 1920, the Chippewas' assumption that the Isabella Indian Reservation still existed can be found in their correspondence requesting that officials should pay funds that the Saginaw Chippewas believed were still owed to them by the federal government. Letters from this decade also reflect, among other things, Chippewa concerns over hunting and fishing rights and the inheritance of patents and allotments. For example, in 1914 Joseph Bradley, the former chief and member of the business committee who served as an attorney for the tribe, inquired about $1,025 allegedly owed to the tribe from the sale of the reservation grist mill in 1872. Bradley indicated that the Chippewas intended to use the funds to pay off old debts and to investigate irregularities in the allotment process on "our reservation." In the same letter, he also asked if the Indians were "under the restrictions of the State game laws when hunting, confined to only our reservation."[76] There are many examples of references to the Isabella Indian Reservation as being extant in Chippewa letters referring to heirship cases. Typical references can be found in letters written to the commissioner of Indian affairs: one, by Elijah Elk, refers to "the "indians in the reservation of isabella Co"; another, by George Bradley, comments on the arrival of an examiner of inheritance "to the Isabella Reservation."[77]

Correspondence by Saginaw Chippewas during the 1920s and early 1930s also reflected the Indians' belief that the reservation still existed and mirrored Joseph Bradley's 1914 request for money. In 1921, Pot-Tar-Sung wrote to the commissioner of Indian affairs demanding to know "who is our agent in this Isabella County Indian Reservation. And also how do we stand by getting our rights against (the) U. S. Government? Is there any show [?] that we will get our money soon?"[78] During the Great Depression, other Saginaw Chippewas also requested federal funds. In August 1930, Adam Smith and sixteen other Chippewas wrote to the commissioner stating they had no car and "nothing to eat" and "need our money bad." The money, they claimed, was "in [the] Isabella County reservation." Two years later, Anna Norman, a Native American woman also seeking assistance, reported to Commissioner Charles Rhoads that she had lived most of her life on "an Indian Reservation in Isabella County."[79]

Finally, in 1930, when the Chippewas on the Isabella Indian Reservation created a more formal structure for their tribal government, the minutes of their organizational meeting reflected their assumption that the reservation was still extant. Those delegates at the meeting who were not part of the reservation community were specifically designated as "Representatives from outside the Isabella Reservation."[80]

On June 30, 1889, the Mackinac Indian Agency closed, and the supervision of the Isabella Indian Reservation was assigned to the superintendent of the Mt. Pleasant Indian School in Mt. Pleasant, Michigan. The superintendent exercised jurisdiction over the reservation for the next four decades, assisted at time by special agents dispatched to the reservation by officials in Washington. The annual reports of the commissioners of Indian affairs for these years and official correspondence from the records of the BIA and the GLO illustrate that federal officials believed that the Isabella Indian Reservation continued in existence. Superintendents at the Mt. Pleasant Indian School (primarily R. A. Cochran and L. E. Baumgarten) periodically wrote that the reservation had ceased to exist, but these statements reflected their resentment of the increased workload forced upon them by heirship cases, patent selections, census reports, and other bureaucratic duties associated with the administration of the reservation. In contrast to their statements that the Isabella Indian Reservation had ceased to exist, Cochran, Baumgarten, and other employees of the BIA also issued contradictory statements affirming it existence.

Cochran's and Baumgarten's superiors attested that the Isabella Indian Reservation was in existence. In 1921, Assistant Commissioner of Indian

Affairs E. B. Meritt informed Cochran that although the Isabella Reservation agency had been abolished in June 1889, the reservation continued in existence and that Cochran was obligated to administer it.[81] In 1932, in contrast to Baumgarten's assumptions that the allotment of reservation lands terminated reservation status, Commissioner Charles Rhoads asserted that the federal government considered allotted lands on the Isabella Indian Reservation to be part of the reservation and that the reservation still was in existence.[82]

Statements by non-Indian citizens of Isabella County and surrounding regions and articles from local newspapers also indicate that the general public believed the Isabella Indian Reservation to be in existence during the four decades from 1889 through the early 1930s. Letters and petitions from Saginaw, Swan Creek, and Black River Chippewas also indicate that Indians living on the reservation and in surrounding areas envisioned the reservation to be in existence during this period.

Between 1889 and 1934 the Isabella Indian Reservation continued in existence.

6

THE INDIAN
REORGANIZATION ACT

In 1932, Franklin D. Roosevelt was swept into the presidency, and the reforms of his New Deal administration were implemented in many parts of the federal government. John Collier, the former director of the American Indian Defense Association, who generally opposed Indian boarding schools, was appointed commissioner of Indian affairs. In February 1934, the Mt. Pleasant Indian School was closed, and all facilities, including land, buildings, and most of the furnishings were transferred to the state of Michigan.[1] Frank Christy, the last superintendent of the Mt. Pleasant School, was assigned to a similar position as superintendent of the Tomah Indian School in Wisconsin. Christy still exercised supervision over the Isabella Indian Reservation, but Jere Charlow was appointed "clerk in charge" of a new BIA branch office in Lansing.[2] In June 1934, Congress passed the Indian Reorganization Act (Wheeler-Howard Act), which was designed to end the allotment process, encourage tribal communities, and reorganize tribal government.[3]

Eager to participate in the opportunities provided by this legislation, the Saginaw Chippewas on the Isabella Indian Reservation wrote to federal officials inquiring about their eligibility for incorporation under the act and even submitted a preliminary constitution and bylaws for the government's perusal.[4] Charlow informed the Indians that they must first vote on whether they wished to "come under the Wheeler-Howard bill," which they affirmed in an election on June 17, 1935.[5] Yet before they could officially organize under the Wheeler-Howard Act, Assistant Commissioner of Indian Affairs William Zimmerman informed the Saginaw Chippewas they first needed to qualify "in only one of two ways." Applicants must be "either a recognized tribe or group of tribes," or they must be "Indians who do not constitute a recognized tribe, but reside on one reservation."[6]

Zimmerman informed the Saginaw Chippewas that they did not qualify under the first provision. Although the federal government had negotiated a treaty with tribal chiefs in 1864, had assisted in the plebiscite of the business committee for the tribe in 1893, had repeatedly met with that committee, a tribal council, or their representatives since the 1890s, and had supervised the formation of a formalized tribal political structure in 1930, Zimmerman argued that Article 6 of the 1855 treaty had "dissolved their tribal organization." Yet Zimmerman completely discounted the previous claims and statements made by Indian agents R. A. Cochran, C. F. Hauke, L. E. Baumgarten, and even Frank Christy, the current superintendent of the Tomah Indian School in Wisconsin, that the Isabella Indian Reservation had been abolished or had ceased to exist. According to Zimmerman, the Saginaw Chippewas did qualify for inclusion under the Wheeler-Howard Act because they were "Indians residing on a reservation." Zimmerman pointed out: "The reservation of your group of Indians is the Isabella Reservation which is still recognized as an Indian Reservation by this office. Your group also comes under the term 'Indian' as defined in section 19 of the Reorganization Act in view of the fact that your group is composed of descendants of members of a recognized tribe, residing on June 1, 1934, within the boundaries of an Indian reservation."[7] Ironically, previous disclaimers aside, the continued existence of the Isabella Indian Reservation was the critical factor enabling the Saginaw Chippewas to organize as a recognized tribe under the Wheeler-Howard Act.

Indeed, the reservation's existence was so critical to the Saginaw Chippewa reorganization attempts that Zimmerman advised the Indians to change the preamble of their proposed constitution from "We, the members of the Saginaw, Swan Creek, and Black River Bands of Chippewa Indians of the State of Michigan" to "We, the Indians residing on the Isabella Reservation in the State of Michigan." The change, according to Zimmerman, "would make it clear that the persons organizing under this constitution are all Indians residing on the Isabella Reservation." Zimmerman also instructed them to include a clause stating that "no person may be a member of the tribe unless he is a resident of the reservation at the time of the adoption of this Constitution and By-laws." After the "organization was formed," Zimmerman assured the Indians, "the organized group can adopt the Indians in the various districts outside the reservation." Zimmerman also informed the Chippewas that they must extend membership to any Indian person living on the reservation who was "one half or more Indian blood," and that "it will not be legally possible for this organization to extend its jurisdiction to lands outside the reservation even though they should be restricted lands belonging to members of this organization unless such lands should be transferred to the tribe." Zimmerman made several other recommendations, and in August 1936 the proposed constitution and bylaws were returned to the "Indians Residing on the Isabella Reservation in the State of Michigan" so they could make the suggested changes.[8]

During the late summer and fall of 1936, the Saginaw Chippewas on the Isabella Indian Reservation met with Jere Charlow, the chief clerk at the Lansing BIA office, and integrated some of Zimmerman's and other agents' suggestions into their constitution and bylaws.[9] On March 27, 1937, the Saginaw Chippewas of the Isabella Reservation approved the new amended constitution and bylaws by a vote of 109 to 5.[10] During the following summer, the tribe proposed a corporate charter to enable it to pursue economic activities on the reservation. In October 1937, the "Corporate Charter of the Saginaw Chippewa Indian Tribe of the Isabella Reservation of Michigan" was approved by the secretary of the interior. According to Assistant Commissioner William Zimmerman, "This completes the organization of the Saginaw Chippewa Indian Tribe of the Isabella Reservation of Michigan in accordance with sections 16 and 17 of the Indian Reorganization Act of June 18, 1934 (48 Stat.984)."[11]

In 1938, less than one year after the corporate charter of the Saginaw Chippewas had been approved, an "Economic Survey of the Saginaw Chippewa Indian Tribe of Michigan" was conducted by a credit agent employed by the federal government. The report indicated that 414 members of the tribe resided on the reservation, but many did not own land. Only 120 acres were owned in fee simple, while 1,666 acres were still restricted under the "not so competent" status of the old patents, but much of this acreage had become so divided among the original allottees' heirs that the parcels were too small for agricultural development.[12] Forty Indian families on the reservation owned their own homes with assorted outbuildings, but many others lived with relatives or in rented residences. A handful of Chippewas owned a few horses, cattle, and swine. Many kept small flocks of poultry. A few Indians were small farmers, but most worked at off-reservation jobs, as oilfield workers, or as itinerant laborers. Some Chippewa women produced baskets for sale to local residents and tourists. Three individuals had "steady salaried positions with the State," and a few others practiced skills they had learned in Indian boarding schools. Overall, though, the economic picture on the reservation was not sanguine. The average annual income for the 127 Chippewa families living on the reservation was only $198.57.[13]

Health standards and educational opportunities on the reservation also were less than desirable. Many Indians suffered from poor diets and inadequate dental care. Others were plagued by skin diseases, trachoma, and tuberculosis. Alcohol addiction also posed a problem. Moreover, the closure of the Mt. Pleasant Indian School in 1934 "was a blow to the local Indians from which they never quite recovered." Although the Johnson-O'Malley Act of 1934 provided funds to local school districts for the education of Indian students, many Saginaw Chippewa children were uncomfortable in non-Indian schools, and few attended beyond the eighth grade. Most Indians on the reservation were literate, but few had the specialized skills to compete in the mid-twentieth century.[14]

Since the Indian Health Service maintained no facilities near the Isabella Reservation, and the clinic at the Mt. Pleasant Indian School, which had occasionally treated local Indians, had closed in 1934, indigent Saginaw Chippewas received some medical and financial assistance from local agencies. They paid local real estate taxes, except for the few families who still lived on restricted allotments.[15] Some Chippewas complained that the services that local agencies supposedly were to provide them were not forthcoming, and tribal leaders were eager to address their people's problems. After obtaining federal funds through their corporate charter, the Saginaw Chippewa tribal council purchased

410 acres of land, some from tribal members and other parcels from non-Indians, which were then placed under restriction. Using other federal funds in 1939, the tribe built nineteen new homes for lower-income Chippewa families on this acreage and began construction on a new community building.[16]

During World War II, much of the reservation's focus was directed toward the war effort, but the tribal council continued to function "as a credit committee" channeling federal funds (as loans) to tribe members who wished to borrow money to build new homes. Because of increased employment opportunities during the war years, economic conditions improved, and fewer tribespeople received welfare.[17] Due to their limited resources, the tribe relied on state and local authorities for law enforcement on the reservation during these years; however, because the reservation remained subject to federal jurisdiction, the Saginaw Chippewas still retained the right to form their own police force.[18]

In the postwar period, federal officials turned away from the Indian policies championed by John Collier and adopted a policy of "termination" designed to reduce federal services to Native American people and to end the special relationship between tribal governments and the federal government that had been established through the treaty years and the subsequent decades.[19] In 1948, the BIA closed the subagency at Lansing, and R. E. Miller, the acting superintendent of the Tomah Indian Agency in Wisconsin, wrote to the Saginaw Chippewas suggesting that "in order that the Council will not be subjected to further red tape," the tribe should request "the termination of certain powers now vested only in the Secretary of the Interior" which have "resulted in the long delays in the transaction of tribal affairs and in our opinion (have) . . . been very disadvantageous to the tribes concerned." Miller further suggested several procedures in which BIA supervision over the Saginaw Chippewas might be eliminated and informed the Indians that "we should appreciate hearing from you as to the reaction of the Council in connection with the above."[20]

In July 1949, the Saginaw tribal council agreed to Miller's suggestions, but they were justifiably wary of the government's intentions. Although the assistant secretary of the interior assured them that the government only wished to "insure that you will have greater freedom in which to conduct your business" and that "the Interest of this Department in your affairs does not terminate with this action," the council was suspicious that the government might recommend that the tribe be terminated and the Isabella Reservation be abolished.[21] In April 1950, Lucy Pelcher, "Secretary, Saginaw Chippewa Indian Tribe," pointed out that the tribe had a long and proud history and had endured many hardships. They were making progress and were "gradually learning to do business and function economically in the proper business way." But they did not seek termination. According to Pelcher, "It takes time to get used to a new pair of shoes, but be assured, we are traveling in the right direction."[22]

The Saginaw Chippewa opposition to termination was partially fueled by a series of claims they had filed against the United States with the Indian Claims Commission that had not been settled, but the Saginaw Chippewas, like most other tribes, opposed the government's termination policies for other reasons. If terminated, they would lose their status as a recognized Indian tribe. Moreover, the Isabella Reservation would be abolished, and restricted lands on the reservation would be subject to state and local taxation.[23]

Their apprehension was justified. Between 1948 and 1952, the BIA conducted a series of comprehensive investigations of Indian tribes and reservations in the United States to ascertain each community's eligibility and receptiveness to termination. Statistical information was amassed about the Saginaw Chippewas and the Isabella Indian Reservation, and although federal investigators admitted that "the great majority" of Saginaw Chippewas would oppose any termination prior to the settlement of their Indian Claims cases, and that they also opposed any state or local taxation, the investigators still recommended that "this tribe is ready for the complete withdrawal of the Indian Bureau, including land trusteeship." Ironically, the strides made by most Saginaw Chippewas in supporting themselves through off-reservation employment and their improved standard of living seemed to work to their disadvantage. Federal agents reported that their economic status, which "corresponds favorably" to rural working-class whites in Isabella County, had prepared them for termination. Moreover, the BIA investigator pointed out that in July 1949, the Saginaw Chippewa Council had agreed to some of Miller's suggestions and that "many of the supervisory powers of the

Secretary of the Interior" already had been abolished. A precedent had been set. The further termination of the Saginaw Chippewa Tribe and the abolition of their reservation would be relatively easy for federal officials. The Indian Health Service provided the tribe with no services, and, ominously, the investigator admitted that "plans have already been made for sale of allotted lands in the locality."[24] The termination of the Saginaw Chippewas and the dissolution of the Isabella Indian Tribe's and the reservation's ties to the federal government continued.

In the mid-1950s, Indian tribes across the United States, led by the National Congress of American Indians, united in a groundswell of opposition to the policy, and although a few hapless tribes were terminated before the process could be halted, in 1958 Secretary of the Interior Fred Seaton declared that the termination of tribes without their consent was "unthinkable." Legislation formally ending the termination policy did not pass Congress until 1970, but for all practical purposes, the BIA abandoned the policy during the early 1960s.[25]

The Isabella Indian Reservation continued. During the 1960s, the Saginaw tribal council utilized restricted acreage on the reservation as a site for the construction of a federally financed restricted-income housing project financed by the US Department of Housing and Urban Development (HUD). To manage the construction and administration of this facility, the council established the Saginaw Chippewa Housing Authority. The housing project was completed and dedicated in June 1967.[26] Additional housing units, also financed by HUD, were added to the housing project in 1976.[27] The council also discussed the construction of a tribal museum that would be housed on the reservation and used funds from the US Department of Health, Education and Welfare to finance several social programs and establish a reservation youth center.[28] During this era, programs on the Isabella Reservation obviously expanded. After the passage of the Indian Education Act of 1972 and the Indian Self-Determination and Education Assistance Act of 1975, the Saginaw Chippewas used federal funds to establish a Head Start program. Loans were provided to tribe members who wanted to attend college.[29] A "master plan" was formulated for economic development on the reservation and for the establishment of a reservation-based health service.[30] In 1975, additional acreage was purchased with a federal loan and added to the reservation's restricted land base. Three years later, other federal funds were used to finance an addition to the tribal center, which housed tribal offices and conference rooms.

Yet the 1970s also brought some challenges. In 1977 the Saginaw Chippewa tribal council received federal funds to establish a tribal police force. Council members met with local law enforcement agencies in March, informing them of the Chippewas' intentions and explaining that as soon as the tribal police force could be organized, state and local law enforcement agencies would exercise only limited jurisdiction on the reservation. In response, the mayor of Mt. Pleasant complained to Elford Cederberg, the US congressman from Michigan's 10th District.[31] The associate solicitor in the Department of Interior replied to Cederberg (and hence to officials in Mt. Pleasant):

> As a general matter, either the federal government or the tribe has responsibility for offenses involving Indians or Indian property within the interior boundaries of a reservation. The Isabella Reservation consists of the six townships set aside and established as a reservation by the Treaty of October 18, 1864. . . . Absent a specific grant of jurisdiction to the state by Congress, the state has no power to regulate the conduct of Indians in Indian country. Because Michigan has not acquired jurisdiction within the Isabella Reservation, the responsibility for law enforcement there rests with the federal government and the tribe.[32]

The associate solicitor added that "there had been no recent change in law with respect to the Isabella Reservation." The only change was that after obtaining federal funds, the tribe had decided to establish its own police force. The tribe had hired a "highly trained and highly qualified officer" and planned to hire others. The tribal police force would police the reservation.[33]

The inquiry over criminal jurisdiction on the Isabella Reservation was timely, since in June 1977 two homicides were committed on the Isabella Reservation. The victims were Saginaw Chippewas, but James Manier, the defendant in the case, was a non-Indian. Manier was charged and indicted for murder in the US District Court for the Eastern District of Michigan, but his attorney claimed that the indictment should be dismissed since the site of the alleged crime was not under the exclusive jurisdiction of the federal government and therefore not under the federal district court's jurisdiction.[34]

In response, on July 25, 1977, the field solicitor of the BIA in Minneapolis issued a memorandum that elaborated on the assistant solicitor's previous letter to Cederberg. The field solicitor pointed out that "the boundaries of the Isabella Reservation have not been diminished since they were established in 1864." Moreover, "the fact that the lands were allotted to the Indians in severalty does not affect the status of the lands set forth in the treaty; they remain part of the Indian reservation until Congress explicitly diminishes or terminates the reservation." In addition, lands within the original reservation borders sold by alottees to non-Indians also were under the jurisdiction of tribal and federal authorities.[35]

The field solicitor stated that tribal police or the federal government, not state or local authorities, generally exercised criminal jurisdiction over the Isabella Reservation, and pointed out that the attorney general of the state of Michigan, who had recognized tribal or federal jurisdiction over such offenses, agreed with this ruling. Indeed, the state attorney general had expressed "the State of Michigan's willingness to assist those governments in law enforcement" and had summarized his understanding of the relationship between state, federal, and tribal jurisdiction as follows:

1. Tribal law enforcement authorities have exclusive jurisdiction over Indians committing offenses against tribal ordinances on reservation land.
2. State law enforcement authorities have jurisdiction over non-Indian persons charged with offenses against state law on Indian reservations where Indians and Indian property are not involved.
3. Federal law enforcement officers, including members of the tribal law enforcement unit deputized as federal marshals, have jurisdiction over Indians and non-Indians committing federal offenses on reservation land.
4. In emergencies, state law enforcement authorities who witness federal offenses may arrest and charge Indians with federal violations committed on Indian reservations.[36]

In summary, the field solicitor asserted that "the Isabella Reservation was established by Treaty in 1864, and the boundaries set forth in that treaty have not been diminished since then. Jurisdiction over crimes committed by Indians within the original boundaries, therefore, lies not with the state of Michigan but with the tribal and Federal governments."[37]

Following the ruling, tribal and federal law enforcement agents met with state and local authorities and reached a series of general agreements regarding law enforcement on the Isabella Reservation, but questions regarding taxation continued. Local non-Indian township commissioners complained that the Saginaw Chippewas contributed "not one cent to our operating costs," but voted, used local roads, enrolled their children in public schools, and enjoyed local fire protection.[38]

In response, Theodore Krenze, the director of Indian services, explained to local officials that the BIA could not compel the tribe to pay some state and local taxes. The Saginaw Chippewas were immune from taxation on business enterprises earned on the Isabella Reservation, paid no sales tax for purchases on the reservation, and paid no state tax on income earned on the reservation. But they were required to pay income taxes on income earned off the reservation (where most of the Indians were employed), and they paid private property and real estate taxes off the reservation (where most Indians resided). Indeed, "for those Indians working, owning private or real property, operating privately owned vehicles, or making purchases off the reservation the tax contribution and burden is identical to that of other citizens." The Saginaw Chippewas were eligible to vote and send their children to public schools, but he pointed out that the education of Saginaw Chippewa children currently was being funded by over $27,000 "earmarked for the Mount Pleasant School District." In contrast, taxation for highway maintenance, fire protection, and welfare benefits "depends in part on State statutes and local factors."[39]

Obviously, the correspondence during the late 1970s regarding criminal jurisdiction and taxation reaffirmed that the Isabella Indian Reservation's boundaries remained intact. Moreover, opinions by solicitors in the BIA reasserted that the Saginaw Chippewas were under the jurisdiction of state and local law enforcement and taxation when they left the reservation, but they were generally exempt from such jurisdiction when they were on the Isabella Indian Reservation.

Since 1980, many of the issues facing the reservation, and the programs designed to address these issues, have expanded. By 2007 the tribal police force, whose organization thirty years earlier had led to a renewed assertion of the reservation's boundaries and the jurisdiction of federal authority over the region, had grown to a modern tribal police department consisting of twenty-seven police officers, eleven dispatch and corrections personnel, and two administrative staff. They operate from offices in a public safety building on the reservation that also houses a detention facility and a tribal court system. Tribal police and other federal officials have continued to enforce the law on the Isabella Indian Reservation. Between 1992 and 2005, for example, they arrested and charged forty-two individuals for violating the Major Crimes Act or other federal crimes on the reservation.[40]

In 1979, the reservation organized its own volunteer fire department that at first partially supported itself through raffles and lotteries. Initially the fire department was able to provide only limited service, but by 1997 the department had grown to ten full time fire personnel who still were augmented by volunteers on occasion. By 2007, the Isabella Reservation was protected by a fire-fighting team that included a rescue team, a hazardous material team, and a certified fire inspector. The fire station housed seven pieces of equipment, including an eighty-five-foot aerial ladder.[41] As these vehicles cross the reservation, some of the roads they traverse are constructed and maintained through tribal funding.[42]

The Saginaw Chippewas also have continued in their efforts to improve education on the reservation. Using a combination of federal grants and funds generated on the reservation, by 2005 the tribe had established an education department that supervised a series of programs. Some Saginaw Chippewa children were enrolled in public schools in neighboring communities, but others attended a tribally owned and administered daycare facility. The Saginaw Chippewa Academy Binoojiinh Montessori School provided learning experiences for preprimary and elementary students on the reservation. The tribe also financed and administered a tribal scholarship program, an adult education program, and an Ojibwe (Chippewa) bilingual program. In addition, the Saginaw Chippewa Education Department worked closely with the newly formed Saginaw Chippewa Tribal College, which offered college-level courses designed to meet the specific needs of the reservation community.[43]

Tribally financed housing projects that began under federal programs in the 1960s and '70s continued through 1995, as did a series of social programs that had emerged during the same decades.[44] In addition, during the early 1980s the tribal council received federal funds for a substance abuse program, a low-income energy assistance program, and for several Comprehensive Employment Training Act (CETA) programs through which tribal members were trained and employed on the reservation.[45] The scope of these tribally sponsored services has continued to grow. In 2007 a special Office of Behavioral Health Programs focused on substance abuse, while the Anishinaabeg Child and Family Services Program used Title II funds and other resources to "promote the safety and well-being of tribal children, youth, [and] vulnerable adults and elders."[46] In a separate reservation facility, the Sowmick Senior Center provided services to tribal elders and sponsored a series of programs through which their individual and accumulated wisdom could be shared with younger tribe members.[47]

In the early 1980s, the Saginaw Chippewa Council contracted for federal funds previously expended through the Indian Health Service to administer their own healthcare services. Since that time, tribal medical facilities have grown from a small clinic to a community health program that provides a broad spectrum of health services to the tribe. The Nimkee Memorial Wellness Center, which includes a pharmacy, is located in Mt. Pleasant and serves the tribe as a comprehensive medical facility providing a broad range of medical and dental care. In 2005, the center housed three physicians, a nurse-practitioner, and an experienced support staff of nurses and assistants. The tribal Community Health Services works closely with the professional staff of the Nimkee Center to provide tribe members with diabetes screening, educational assistance to pregnant and new mothers, chronic disease counseling, immunization clinics, and other programs. Although part of the funding for the clinic and these programs comes from the federal government, tribally appointed administrators manage the Nimkee Center and outreach programs. According to the clinic's administrators, "our primary goal is to maximize the health and knowledge of Native Americans."[48]

Concerns for the health of reservation residents also emerged in 2000 when the state of Michigan attempted to issue a permit for a wastewater treatment facility within the boundaries of the Isabella Indian Reservation. In this instance, the Environmental Protection Agency (EPA) stated that the state of Michigan was not authorized to issue such a permit on the reservation. According to the EPA, the Isabella Indian Reservation was part of "Indian Country" and not under the state's jurisdiction.[49]

To strengthen the preservation of tribal traditions, in 1998 the Saginaw Chippewas established the Ziibiwing Center of Anishinabe Culture and Lifeways. Located on the reservation, the center contains a museum, tribal archives, meeting rooms, a small restaurant, and a gift store. The center has emerged as the cultural heart of the reservation and is used as a facility where tribal children assemble to learn from tribal elders or where Native American artists and artisans meet with schoolchildren to explain their work and to encourage the children to use art to express themselves. The center boasts a gallery of photos portraying Saginaw Chippewas from the late nineteenth and early twentieth centuries, and the archives contain documents providing valuable insights into the history of the Isabella Reservation. The center is open to the public and has attracted visitors from throughout the United States.[50]

Similar to many other reservations during the past quarter century, the Isabella Indian Reservation has experienced significant economic changes. The origins of these changes emerged in the spring of 1981, when the Saginaw Chippewa tribe began to hold a weekly bingo game at the tribal center on the reservation. Uncertain about their obligations to withhold federal income tax from part-time workers at the bingo games and whether they should provide winners of bingo games with tax forms, the tribal council asked for advice from the field solicitor of the Department of the Interior in Minnesota.[51] In reply, the solicitor's office advised them: "Assuming the bingo is conducted by the Tribe itself, . . . the income to the Tribe is not subject to federal income taxation." Bingo workers employed by the tribe who were paid $84 or more per month would be considered employees and should be provided with W-2 forms. The tribe would be obligated to supply bingo winners with IRS 1099 forms if the winner's aggregate earnings totaled $600 in a calendar year.[52]

Aware that the ruling indicated that they could conduct games of chance on their reservation, and encouraged by the expansion of Native

American gaming throughout the United States, the Saginaw Chippewas seized an economic opportunity. During the past two decades they have exploited it fully. In 1998 the tribe opened the Soaring Eagle Casino and Resort on reservation land near Mt. Pleasant. In addition to bingo, the casino features thousands of slot machines and over seventy game tables for blackjack, craps, roulette, and poker. Saginaw Chippewa gambling enterprises are supervised by the Saginaw Chippewa Gaming Commission, which oversees the daily operation of the casino, inspects and regulates all gaming activities, and ensures that such activities comply with the federal Indian Gaming Regulatory Act.[53]

The hotel adjoining the casino contains hundreds of rooms, and the combined casino and hotel offer several restaurants. The tribe also operates a smaller gaming facility across the street from the casino and several other restaurants and gift shops associated with these sites. Another restaurant and gift shop can be found at the Ziibiwing Center. A large concert hall adjoining the casino hosts performances by well-known entertainers. In 2005, these resort enterprises, including both casinos and the restaurants employed over four thousand people.[54]

The economic impact of the Saginaw Indian Reservation on Isabella County has been profound. Tourists have visited the casino in large numbers to gamble, but they also purchase goods and services from both Saginaw Chippewas and from non-Indian merchants. Obviously, enterprises owned by the Saginaw Chippewas on the Isabella Reservation have profited from this influx of revenue, but so have non-Indians, and the tribe also has shared their good fortune with the larger Isabella County community. Since 1994, they have returned two percent of their profits to local school districts and to neighboring city and township governments. The payments are awarded semiannually. On November 21, 2006, the Saginaw Chippewas distributed nearly $4 million to local governments and school districts. Between 1994 and mid-2000s, they had awarded almost $70 million to similar agencies.[55]

In addition to the large, luxurious hotel that forms part of the Soaring Eagle Casino and Resort, the tribe also owns and operates another lodging facility. The Saginaw Chippewa Indian Tribe Campground, a more modest accommodation, sits on "The Hill" overlooking the casinos and offers a "quiet and peaceful campground with a calming breeze and shaded sites" for both tents and recreational vehicles.[56] It is assumed that patrons of the campground will have arrived at the reservation by motor vehicle, since the sites are arranged to accommodate cars, trucks, or motor homes. It's not surprising that many weekend tourists from Michigan choose to camp at this location and travel by motor vehicle to the reservation. Obviously, most motorists in Michigan are well aware of the Isabella Indian Reservation and its location. It is easy to find—it is well marked on "One Hundred Years of Transportation," the official 2005 Department of Transportation map printed and readily distributed by the state of Michigan.[57]

Following the closure of the Mt. Pleasant Indian School in 1934, the tribal council of the Saginaw Chippewas applied to the BIA for reorganization under the Indian Reorganization Act. Federal officials denied their application as an existing tribal government but declared they were eligible since they were "Indians residing on a reservation." Applying the government's declaration that the Isabella Indian Reservation and its boundaries had remained intact since 1864, the Saginaw Chippewas submitted a constitution and bylaws that were accepted by the BIA, and in 1937 they were recognized as a reorganized tribal government.

During the late 1930s and 1940s, the Saginaw Chippewas used federal funds to purchase additional lands, which were placed in trust on the reservation. The council constructed tribal housing and a community center on part of this land and leased the rest to farmers for agricultural purposes. The council also served as a conduit through which individual tribe members received federal loans. During the early 1950s, the tribal council severed some of its ties with the BIA but preferred to retain federal jurisdiction over the reservation and opposed the government's policy of termination.

In the 1960s, the Saginaw Chippewa Tribe utilized federal funds to develop restricted-income housing, a youth center, and a broad spectrum of social services. Many of these programs, also financed by the federal government, expanded during the last quarter of the twentieth century. In 1977, the tribe used federal funds to develop a tribal police force with jurisdiction over the Isabella Indian Reservation. Discussions with local law enforcement agencies and issues of taxation engendered a renewed declaration by federal officials that the Saginaw Chippewa Tribe and the federal government, not state or local governments, exercised jurisdiction over the Isabella Indian Reservation, and that the original boundaries of the reservation, established in 1864, were still intact. Moreover, federal solicitors pointed out that the allotment of lands within the reservation's borders did not alter the reservation's status.

Since the 1980s, the Saginaw Chippewa tribal council, like other tribal governments in the United States, has pursued gaming as a growing economic opportunity. Under the aegis of the federal Indian Gaming Regulatory Act, in 1998 the tribe opened a casino and resort on the Isabella Indian Reservation. The development of gaming on the reservation has had a beneficial economic impact not only on the Isabella Indian Reservation but also on surrounding communities. As an expression of their sense of community responsibility, since 1994 the Saginaw Chippewas have shared almost $70 million from reservation gaming revenue with local municipal and township governments and with local school districts.

The Isabella Indian Reservation, under tribal and federal jurisdiction, continues to play an important role within the geographic borders of the state of Michigan. It was established as a home for the Saginaw, Swan Creek, and Black River bands of Chippewa Indians. The land base of the reservation emerged from lands set aside for these Indians in a treaty signed on August 2, 1855, but the modern reservation was established by a treaty between these Chippewas and the United States signed on October 18, 1864. Federal officials envisioned the Isabella Indian Reservation as a homeland where the Saginaw, Swan Creek, and Black River Chippewas would be protected from non-Indian intrusion and would learn those tenets of mainstream culture (language, literacy, agricultural techniques, etc.) that would enable them to assimilate into American life. The treaty of October 18, 1864, envisioned that the Isabella Indian Reservation would remain "Indian Country," since it included a provision that after all Chippewas or other Indians who were eligible for allotment on the reservation received their lands, remaining unallotted reservations lands would not be sold and would be allotted to Chippewa children when they came of age. To prevent the loss of Indian lands through fraud or ignorance, Indian agents were authorized to compile a list of all potential allottees who would be classified as "competent" or "not so competent." After ten years, "competent" allottees would receive their lands in fee simple. Those Chippewas designated "not so competent" would be awarded lands, but those lands would be restricted and could not be alienated or sold without the permission of the secretary of the interior. Obviously, the United States intended that the Isabella Indian Reservation would continue as a new homeland for the Saginaw, Swan Creek, and Black River bands of Chippewa Indians.

In the decades between 1864 and 1889, the Isabella Indian Reservation often suffered from inept or fraudulent federal administration. Indian agents such as Mark Stevens (1885–89) valiantly attempted to defend the reservation and the Saginaw Chippewas from fraud and trespass, but other Indian agents proved ineffective or dishonest. Agents compiled lists of allottees and their land selections, then "misplaced" them or became embroiled in disputes with other bureaucrats while the Saginaw Chippewas awaited their certificates of selection or final patents. Records accumulated by the land office or by the BIA in Washington were lost or damaged. George Betts, the Indian agent for the Mackinac Agency between 1871 and 1876, conspired with unscrupulous local businessmen and complicit Indians, and reservation lands were lost or denuded of their timber. The federal government continued its jurisdiction over the Isabella Indian Reservation during these years, but its hegemony was tainted.

The federal government has maintained a relationship with the tribal government of the Saginaw, Swan Creek, and Black River Chippewas from 1865 through the present. Although Article 6 of the treaty of August 2, 1855, supposedly "dissolved" the "tribal organization of said Indians except so far as may be necessary for the purpose of carrying into effect the provisions of this agreement," some historians have argued that this provision was meant to prevent the Saginaw, Swan Creek, and Black River Chippewas from joining with other Chippewas bands in joint negotiations with federal officials. It was not intended to end the Saginaw Chippewas' tribal organization or government.[58] The continued interaction of federal officials with Saginaw "chiefs," "headmen," "tribal councils," and "business committees" in the decades between 1855 and 1937 bears abundant testimony that the tribal political structures functioned during those years. Assistant Commissioner of Indian Affairs William Zimmerman's ruling in 1936 ignored a record of federal negotiation with, and jurisdiction over, a Saginaw Chippewa political structure that is well authenticated by documents from the National Archives. After 1937, when the Saginaw Chippewas restructured their tribal government under the Indian Reorganization Act, their political relationship with the federal government continued.[59]

The federal government has continued to recognize the existence of the Isabella Indian Reservation from its establishment in 1864 until the present. Throughout the period during which the Isabella Indian Reservation was administered under the old Mackinac Agency (1864–89), correspondence and reports by federal agents are replete with commentary mentioning or implying that the reservation was in existence. After 1889, when the BIA abolished the Isabella Reservation Agency, but not the reservation, the commissioner of Indian affairs continued to list the Isabella Indian Reservation as extant in his annual reports. Reports by superintendents of the Mt. Pleasant Indian School and by other officials in the federal government during this period also indicate that these individuals and their agencies saw the reservation as extant.[60] In 1936, Assistant Commissioner William Zimmerman pointed out that the federal government had acknowledged the continued existence of the reservation since 1864.[61] Since 1937 and the reorganization of the Saginaw Chippewa Tribe of Indians under the Wheeler-Howard Act, the federal government has continued to acknowledge the existence of the reservation.

Comments by Indian agents that the Isabella Reservation had been abolished or had ceased to exist generally reflect these agents' reluctance to assume responsibilities associated with the reservation and must be placed in historical context. Most such statements or comments originated from R. A. Cochran, L. E. Baumgarten, and Frank Christy, individuals who served as superintendents of the Mt. Pleasant Indian School. These employees of the BIA saw themselves primarily as school administrators who were forced to assume onerous administrative tasks on the Isabella Indian Reservation in addition to their regular duties as school administrators. In consequence, they attempted to deflect the responsibility for such added responsibilities by claiming that the reservation did not exist, so therefore they should not be responsible for duties associated with it. Ironically, during the same period in which these school superintendents made statements that the reservation was not in existence, these same individuals made repeated references to its continued existence in other correspondence. Comments by Baumgarten that the reservation ceased to exist because it contained allotted lands were refuted by his superiors. In retrospect, the context of these agents' comments that the Isabella Indian Reservation had ceased to exist severely limits their value in any assessment of the continued existence of the reservation.

Moreover, non-Indian citizens in Michigan have continued to envision the Isabella Indian Reservation as extant. Since the reservation's establishment in 1864, a broad spectrum of public correspondence, newspaper articles, and other literature has continued to describe the reservation as in existence. Letters by residents of Isabella County, news items from local newspapers, and descriptions of the Mt. Pleasant Indian School made available by the State Library of Michigan all testify to their authors' belief that the reservation existed. These statements have continued: legal opinions by the Michigan attorney general and, more recently, highway maps printed and distributed by the Michigan State Transportation Commission attest that the state of Michigan also acknowledges that the Isabella Indian Reservation continues to exist.

The Saginaw Chippewa Tribe has continued to assume that the Isabella Indian Reservation remains in existence. Since 1864, correspondence from tribal members to federal Indian agents and other individuals or agencies is replete with references to the reservation as extant. Recent economic development on the reservation bears mute testimony to the assumption by the Saginaw Chippewa people that the reservation will continue.

7

THE SHADOW OF THE LAW

The disposition of the tribe's legal case, *United States and Saginaw Chippewa Indian Tribe of Michigan v. Granholm et al.*, depended on the history laid out in the previous chapters. Briefly, the Saginaw Chippewas argued that the tribe and the federal government had created the Isabella Reservation in the treaties of 1855 and 1864, and the reservation had never been diminished or abolished by any mechanism. However, the state also had its historical experts, who laid out alternative histories that supported the state's arguments that the treaties had not created a classic reservation in which the Saginaw Chippewas held all the land in common; rather, the treaties had created a pool of land from which individual Saginaw Chippewas would select land parcels to hold and farm in the Euro-American manner. Alternatively, the plaintiffs' experts argued that, even if the two treaties had created a reservation, the allotment of land to individual Saginaw Chippewas had diminished the area of that reservation over time.

If the matter had proceeded to trial, the court would have had to decide between these conflicting histories, using the canons of Indian treaty construction laid down by the US Supreme Court. These canons recognize that Indian treaties were rarely negotiated between two equal partners. Alcohol was often provided as part of the negotiations, and often government payments of food and other necessary supplies were often withheld until they agreed to a treaty. Sometimes federal treaty representatives had close ties to the states—usually the tribe's most deadly enemies—in which the Indians resided. Furthermore, the federal government recorded the treaties in English, a language that the Indians rarely understood. On occasion, the US Senate would unilaterally change the treaty terms during the ratification process. Altogether, these circumstances often gave the federal government a decisive advantage in any negotiations.

The canons therefore require all courts to interpret the documents as grants from the Indians to the United States. They must interpret Indian treaties as the Indians understood them at the time, not as Euro-American lawyers interpret them then or now. Furthermore, courts are never to interpret treaties technically or to the prejudice of the Indians. All ambiguities are resolved in favor of the Indians. Additionally, the US Supreme Court has imposed a duty of trust on the federal government to explain the meaning of a treaty to the Indians. These canons of construction deeply inclined any treaty interpretation in favor of the Saginaw Chippewas' position in the Isabella Reservation case.

These canons cast a long shadow over the state's case. The latter depended on Article 6 of the 1855 treaty, which stated in its entirety: "The tribal organization of said Indians, except so far as may be necessary for the purpose of carrying into effect the provisions of this agreement, is hereby dissolved."[1] If the Saginaw Chippewas' tribal organization were dissolved, how could it exercise jurisdiction over the members and a reservation? It could not do so because the tribe no longer existed except for the minimal purpose of facilitating allotment and assimilation. Individual Saginaw Chippewa Indians were to give up their tribal membership and live as U.S. citizens with the help provided by other treaty articles. There was no "reservation" as the term is traditionally understood, or if there was, it was diminished through allotment under the treaty. These arguments were not frivolous, but they depended heavily on the difficult task of proving that the Saginaw Chippewas understood the 1855 and 1864 treaties in that manner.

To understand how this other 1855 treaty affected the outcome of the Saginaw case, it is necessary to track the litigation that occurred in Michigan prior to the negotiation with the Saginaw bands. The state had enjoyed only marginal success in making a similar argument about an

1855 treaty between six Ottawa and Chippewa bands in Michigan. This treaty was negotiated immediately before the Saginaw treaty and by the same federal Indian agent. It contained an article with a first clause identical to the one in the 1855 Saginaw treaty, and the state would argue that it dissolved the tribal organization of the six bands in a series of cases.[2]

The litigation over this latter treaty's meaning focused on the right of the six bands to fish commercially and to use gill nets while doing so. Their assertion of their sovereign rights caused sport fishers to viscerally react because they believed any fishing by the bands would deplete the stock of salmon, and using gill nets would destroy the lake trout fishery.[3] The simmering dispute came to a head in the eastern part of Michigan's upper peninsula when a state conservation officer arrested Albert LeBlanc for commercial fishing without a license for using a gill net in 1971.[4] The latter was a member of the Sault Ste. Marie band of Chippewa Indians, one of the six bands that entered into the 1855 Ottawa and Chippewa treaty.

In the resulting state case, LeBlanc admitted the basic facts but argued that he had a federally protected treaty right to fish under an earlier treaty with the six bands: the 1836 Ottawa and Chippewa treaty.[5] This treaty contemplated the ultimate removal west of the six bands. Until that happened, the Sault band had reserved all the "usual privileges of occupancy," including fishing rights, for itself. Removal never happened, however, and this raised the legal question of whether LeBlanc still had the right to fish commercially using a gill net in the twentieth century.[6]

The state of Michigan challenged LeBlanc's right for numerous reasons; on the one hand, claiming he and the Sault band had never had that right, or, in the alternative, that if the right existed, the band had lost it in the 1855 Ottawa and Chippewa treaty. The trial court found the band had that right under the 1836 treaty but had surrendered it in the 1855 treaty. A Michigan circuit court affirmed the conviction. This second court agreed with the state that the band "had given up" its fishing rights in the 1855 treaty.[7]

LeBlanc appealed his convictions to the Michigan Court of Appeals. A unanimous Court of Appeals reversed the decision, finding that the circuit court had applied a "technical" construction of the 1855 Ottawa and Chippewa treaty to the prejudice of the band. Such a construction was contrary to the canon of Indian treaty construction requiring all courts to interpret all treaties by "how the words of the treaty were understood by this unlettered people [the Indians]." The Michigan Court of Appeals in *LeBlanc* also relied on US Supreme Court precedent that, as the parties to a treaty were not on an "equal footing, . . . the inequality is to be made good by the superior justice which looks only to the *substance of the right,* without regard to technical rules framed under a system of municipal jurisprudence." The decision never discussed the state's argument that the 1855 treaty provided for the Ottawas and Chippewas to become US citizens.[8]

The state appealed to the Michigan Supreme Court, and the highest state court affirmed the Court of Appeal's decision in a four-to-three decision. Applying the same canons of treaty construction as the Court of Appeals, the highest Michigan court found the Sault Ste. Marie band had reserved the right to fish where LeBlanc was fishing in the 1836 treaty and had not surrendered that right in the 1855 treaty. LeBlanc had the right to fish commercially and use gill nets.

Unfortunately, the majority's decision mechanically applied the canons of Indian treaty construction without discussing why the resulting decision, which "suddenly had hunting and fishing prerogatives that were not previously recognized," was fair. In particular, the majority in the Michigan Supreme Court discussed the dissolution clause in the treaty or, more broadly, the state's argument that the 1855 Ottawa and Chippewa treaty was a treaty of assimilation that provided for individuals to give up their tribal membership and become Michigan and US citizens with all their privileges and responsibilities. The majority only held that the 1855 treaty was one of "removal," thereby impliedly rejecting the state's argument.[9]

This failure was glaring because two dissenting judges addressed the state's argument. They wrote: "The intent of both parties was to plan for the future in light of present realities." The dissenters summarized their interpretation as follows:

The Treaty of July 31, 1855, reflects a marked departure from the policy of removal of the 1836 treaty. The Treaty of 1855 provides for the dissolution of the tribal structure of the Chippewa, sums of money and individual allotments of land to individual Indians, and assistance in the settlement and assimilation of the Chippewa into their new lifestyle as settlers. It provides them with schools, blacksmith shops, agricultural implements, carpenter's tools, household furniture, building materials and cattle.

They concluded that the "Chippewa clearly expected that they were to be assimilated into the white society," based on the historical record that showed that several negotiators for the band expected to settle on the soil and become farmers.[10]

This dissenting opinion was problematic encouragement for the state, but it relied on the argument to deny the right of the other five bands to fish on the Great Lakes. This time, the other five bands initiated the ligation by suing in federal court for a declaration of their sovereign right to fish. In a lengthy opinion, a district court judge rejected the state's argument that the 1855 Ottawa and Chippewa treaty provided for the assimilation of band members as state and US citizens. He also rejected the state's argument that the 1855 treaty dissolved the bands' tribal organization by focusing on a second clause in Article 5, which contained the dissolution clause. This second clause described how the federal government would negotiate with each band separately in the future. In light of this clause, the article as a whole served to dissolve an "artificial entity"—the tribe of the Ottawa and Chippewa Indians created by the federal government to negotiate the 1836 treaty—not the tribal organizations of individual bands of Ottawas and Chippewas who came together to negotiate the 1855 treaty.[11]

The state appealed the federal district court's decision. The US Court of Appeals for the Sixth Circuit never considered the state's arguments in depth because, on a preliminary matter, it stated that "reasoning of the Supreme Court of Michigan in *People v. LeBlanc*, 399 Mich. 31, 248 N.W.2d 199 (1976) appears to correctly state the law applicable to gill net treaty fishing by Indians in the Great Lakes." In light of this state-ment, the state abandoned its full appeal and entered into a complicated consent decree regarding the six bands' right to fish on the Great Lakes.[12]

The decisions in the fishing rights cases forewarned the state of the challenges they would face if they made similar arguments in the Isabella Reservation case. Nevertheless, the 1855 Ottawa and Chippewa treaty differed from the 1855 Saginaw Chippewa treaty in a significant way. Article 6 of the 1855 Saginaw treaty contained only one clause, and it simply stated that "the tribal organization of said Indians, except so far as may be necessary for the purpose of carrying into effect the provisions of this agreement, is hereby dissolved." The article did not provide for future meetings with different bands, as did the Ottawa and Chippewa treaty of that same year, and this difference might make it more difficult for the tribe and federal government to argue that Article 6 in the 1855 Saginaw treaty served only to dissolve a fictitious entity.[13] In *Granholm*, the state had its strongest case on the dissolution clause.

The state could also argue that the treaty never created a reservation where the Saginaw Chippewa Tribe held the land in common. Article 1 of the 1855 Saginaw treaty stated that the United States "will withdraw from sale, for the benefit of said Indians," certain public lands. The words "for the benefit of" are general and generic. However, the treaty used the same exact words when it confirmed "the entries of land" by the Missionary Society of the Methodist Episcopal Church. This latter provision, plus the lack of the use of the words "reserve" or "reservation" in connection with the Isabella Reservation, suggests that "for the benefit of" meant in fee simple. Additionally, the 1855 treaty provided that all individuals entitled to patents would have received them after ten years, which showed the parties contemplated a definite end to the tribal relationship.[14] As with all arguments based on treaty language, the state would have to overcome the canon requiring the court to interpret that language in a nontechnical, nonlegal way that would protect the substance of the right held by the Saginaw Chippewas.

The state had other evidence in support of its theory of the case. Professor Anthony G. Gulig found that the Saginaw Chippewas had dissolved their tribal organization and that the treaty's "language was never intended to describe a defined piece of land set aside to be held in common." For example, after 1837 some Saginaw Chippewas had begun buying land individually to remain in the state, and one Euro-American missionary believed that the Saginaw Chippewas needed to own land individually and become citizens in 1855. Regarding the 1864 Saginaw treaty, Gulig found evidence that its primary purpose was to provide land in severalty to minor children; therefore, the parties needed to change allotment provisions to provide for more time. Finally, they would have little use for a reservation held in common if they lacked a tribal organization.[15]

Nevertheless, the state faced a steep climb in proving its case for reasons other than the canons. The language of Article 1 of the 1855 treaty may not have created a traditional reservation held in common, but the 1864 treaty used more direct language, suggesting that there was such a reservation. Instead of merely withdrawing land from sale, Article 2 stated: "The United States hereby agree to set apart [certain lands] for the exclusive use, ownership, and occupancy" of the Saginaw Chippewas. Furthermore, the treaty used the terms "reserve" and "reservation" repeatedly. For example, Article 3 referred to "lands upon the Isabella reservation." Article 3 also spoke of the Saginaw Chippewas "who now reside upon said reservation in Isabella." Finally, the 1864 treaty replaced the ten-year time frame with a more indefinite, seemingly more protective one that required the federal Indian agent to find the individual Saginaw Chippewas competent before they could sell their land allotments.[16]

The question of how the Saginaw Chippewas would have understood "except so far as may be necessary for the purpose of carrying into effect the provisions of this agreement" also remained difficult for the state. Would the Indians have understood that the continued tribal existence after the treaty was limited and would eventually end? If so, what were the preconditions for the tribal existence ending? Was it possible they were keeping their options open as they tried to forge a better future for themselves and their posterity in a changing world? However, the state would have to overcome the canon of Indian treaty construction that a court must interpret any ambiguity in favor of the tribe because the federal government drafted the document.

These difficulties for the state would have tilted any judge toward the tribe's interpretation and required the state to justify its reading of the two treaties with forceful arguments. The best type of evidence would have come from the 1855 and 1864 treaty journals, in which clerks engaged by the government would have recorded the negotiations between the federal government and the tribe. The treaty journal would have recorded the federal representatives' explanations of the government's goals and the treaty provisions. The journal would have also recorded the tribal representatives' responses and statements of the tribe's concerns and goals. Other people sometimes participated in the negotiations for various reasons, and the journal would have recorded who they were and what they said. However, historians have not found either treaty journal. The journal for the 1855 Ottawa and Chippewa treaty is available and could provide some help—as the dissenters in *LeBlanc* showed—but all courts considering the issue had previously rejected the state's arguments based on that treaty's dissolution clause.

The state might have argued that these changes occurred because different agents negotiated the two treaties, but the question is, In what way? Which treaty better reflected the parties' intent—the 1855 or the 1864? The state would have argued that the earlier treaty did, using Gulig's historical evidence and Article 8 of the 1864 treaty. That article stated it was "expressly understood that the eighth article of the [1855 Saginaw treaty] shall in no wise be affected by the terms of this treaty." However, the earlier treaty had only seven articles.[17] Therefore, Gulig opined that Article 8 of the 1864 treaty had to refer to a different article. The best candidate was Article 6 of the 1855 treaty, which, according to the state, dissolved the tribal organization of the Saginaw Chippewas. However, Anderson found that the 1864 treaty removed all ambiguity about whether a reservation existed and ensured that future generations of Saginaw Chippewas would have a place to reside from the same evidence.[18] The court would have to choose from these two starkly contrasting interpretations.

Courts are not well placed to do so. Judges are not typically practicing historians. They lack the training and expertise to interpret historical documents in their full context—even documents written by Euro-Americans in English. Their jobs do not usually require it, and their busy schedules do not allow it. Historians often present the "best face" on the evidence for their clients.[19] This desire to please their clients may obscure areas of agreement and cause issues to slip through the cracks between conflicting reports.

As a result, judges may mechanically apply the canons of Indian treaty construction rather than deeply engaging with the historical record, as the *LeBlanc* majority showed. They rely on neat categories such as whether a treaty is one of removal or one of assimilation rather than investigating how the bands understood their continuing right to meet with the federal government. The *LeBlanc* dissenters did not do better; they reached a factual conclusion based on limited, sometimes equivocal historical evidence.

Therefore, the canons of Indian treaty construction ensure fairness by requiring convincing evidence that the Indians understood they were surrendering one of their aboriginal rights. Indians often considered treaties as part of an ongoing relationship in which the federal government would protect and nourish them, not as controlling snapshots of the relationship. The Saginaw Chippewas likely did so when they approached the federal government to negotiate new treaties to ensure they could remain in their homelands. They may have well thought they had succeeded, but federal Indian agents failed to protect the Saginaw Chippewa lands after the Civil War, allowing Euro-Americans to fraudulently manipulate the process of handing out patents. In the late nineteenth century, Congress also stopped funding the office overseeing the federal government's relationship with the Saginaw Chippewas.

If the court ruled the Isabella Reservation did not exist, the judge would have had to disregard the federal government's support of the tribe having a larger Isabella Reservation—inside and outside of the case. He would have done so contrary to the current federal policy of encouraging and supporting tribal self-determination and would have subverted the Saginaw Chippewas' efforts to maintain their tribal organization and reservation for over a century. The Isabella Reservation would have consisted only of those lands held by the federal government in trust for the Saginaw tribe. The Chippewas would have had to seek relief from Congress instead of the more powerful state.

In summary, the canons of Indian treaty construction protect tribal understanding of their treaties as a matter of fairness. This approach places a heavy burden on states wanting to prove that a reservation does not exist and limits the state's negotiating power. But the state could also argue that Congress had diminished the reservation through a statute or a treaty. The next chapter considers this argument.

8

HISTORICAL CHANGE
AND THE LAW

The parties in *Saginaw Chippewas v. Granholm* also faced the thorny issue of historical change. Assuming the treaties imagined a large Isabella Reservation on which predominantly Saginaw Chippewas lived, and which they controlled to the exclusion of non-Indians, it no longer existed in 2008. In the mid-nineteenth century, non-Indians had flooded the tracts allotted to the Saginaw Chippewas by treaty and had established their own governments to control the land on which they resided. This included much of the land on which the Saginaw Chippewas lived. While the federal government began to take more land into trust for the tribe, thereby depriving the local and state governments of jurisdiction over those lands, it did so on a piecemeal and relatively small basis. Non-Indians would still own the overwhelming percentage of land within the six townships listed in the treaties. They would want to be governed by their state institutions, not tribal ones. The law has approached the general issue created by non-Indians flowing onto a reservation through the legal doctrine of diminishment. However, historical change makes applying this doctrine difficult and uneven, as shown in Michigan cases.

Unlike *Saginaw Chippewas v. Granholm,* where the state alleged a treaty changed the reservation boundaries, diminishment cases usually involve a federal statute that divides a reservation into parcels and then issues a title to Indians on the reservation for particular allotments. The statute makes the rest—called surplus lands—available for purchase by non-Indian

129

homesteaders. The allotment provisions in the two Saginaw treaties are analogous to such a statute in many ways. They divided the Isabella Reservation into parcels and provided for the Saginaw Chippewas to receive title to those parcels. The remaining lands were then opened to purchase by non-Indians, but there was no need to unconditionally commit to compensate the Saginaw Chippewa Indian Tribe for the lands opened for settlement because the treaty theoretically did that. Additionally, only the US Senate approves treaties. The main impact of this latter difference is a reduction in the size of the legislative history; the legislative body sometimes ratified treaties as a group with little discussion.

A lack of evidence and precedent would again challenge the state's argument. The state had already argued that allotment had diminished a reservation in *Keweenaw Bay Indian Community v. State of Michigan*. In that 1991 case, the court held "a clear and unambiguous legislative act [was] required to terminate a reservation . . . created" by an 1854 treaty with the community. It found that a ratified treaty might serve as such a legislative act, but "the presence of allotment provisions in a treaty does not mean the reservation is terminated as a matter of law when allotment takes place."

Furthermore, the court rejected the state's "plain reading of treaty [that a reservation did not contain lands sold before its creation] as too narrow and not intended by either party." Tribal members and friends of the tribe lived on those lands. The members of the Keweenaw Bay Indian Community (KBIC) would not have understood those lands as separate from the reservation they received. Neither party had intended the treaty to be a "form of self-executing land distribution." The treaty also lacked a termination clause stating that the allotted land was no longer part of a reservation.

Nonetheless, the state in the *Granholm* case could distinguish the *Keweenaw Bay Indian Community* case by arguing that the dissolution clauses effectively served as a reservation termination clause. In this argument, the state would rely on the historical report of Professor Theodore J. Karamanski. He concluded—as had Gulig—that the Saginaw Chippewas had never held the Isabella Reservation collectively. They understood that it was not a bounded reservation, and in a petition to the federal government "demanded relinquishment of guardianship over us by the Government." They were Michigan citizens who voted and held office. They held land individually on the Isabella Reservation. Indian agents were incompetent or corrupt, and fraud was rampant on the reservation. Finally, the federal government never enforced the Trade and Intercourse Acts on the Isabella Reservation and eventually, if temporarily, ended its oversight in the late nineteenth century.[1]

The *Granholm* court would have had to choose between the history presented by the state and the often diametrically opposed history of the tribe and federal government, but it is worthwhile to step back for a moment from the case and ask what this history means today. If anyone at the time the treaties were made imagined that the Saginaw Chippewas would assimilate seamlessly into Euro-American society in a few years, it did not happen. It still has not happened. There are a variety of possible, often mutually compatible, reasons. Perhaps the Saginaw Chippewas never intended to do so for good reasons of their own, or sometime between the 1855 and 1864 treaties, they decided to maintain their tribal organization and exercise jurisdiction over whatever land they owned. Maybe the rampant fraud after the Civil War convinced them to maintain their tribal organization. Euro-American society may have rejected their attempts to assimilate. For whatever reason, at least some Saginaw Chippewas maintained their tribal organization and vibrant culture until today.

On the other hand, the federal government and tribe did not maintain their jurisdiction over the entire Isabella Reservation from 1855 until now. Individual Saginaw Chippewas selected land on the reservation and became Michigan citizens by law. Euro-American settlers entered the disputed reservation, and cities grew up on it. Incompetent or corrupt federal Indian agents fostered an environment in which Euro-Americans could defraud the Saginaw Chippewas of their lands—or at least the trees on them. The twentieth century would see airports and interstates. The Saginaw Chippewas would build a casino on the Isabella Reservation that draws in tens of thousands of nonmembers yearly.

No one could have imagined this future in the middle of the nineteenth century, and it is a fair question to ask what role two brief treaties from that period should play in US society today. It is also fair to ask whether the courts should be the body determining that role. However, lower courts rarely engage in such speculations in their opinions. They must do their job. Either the state meets its burden of proof under the canons of Indian treaty construction, or it loses. The tribe holds the rights. Lower courts then enforce their decision. There is little or no room for the court to adjust the treaty considering present realities.[2]

However, the US Supreme Court cannot altogether avoid the issue of historical change as it is presented in the Saginaw Chippewa case. For example, the Supreme Court has struggled with the issue in two cases involving the Oneida Indian Nation. The facts were not in dispute. The Oneida Nation had sold some of its lands to the state of New York in 1795. The sale violated the federal Trade and Intercourse Act's prohibition against any entity buying Indian land without the federal government's approval, but the Oneida Tribe waited until the 1970s to repurchase the land and assert tribal sovereignty over it. Despite the delay, a court majority recognized the Oneida Indians as owning those lands under "aboriginal title," and thus they had sovereignty over them.[3]

A dissent focused on how the Constitution's framers believed "no one ought to be condemned for his forefathers' misdeeds" and how the majority's decision would disrupt land titles. The dissent would have prevented the latter issue by applying a common-law doctrine called "laches," which means "ancient claims are best left in repose." Too much time had elapsed since 1795 for a court to remedy the wrong as a matter of fairness.[4]

The majority in the Supreme Court had not considered the issue of laches in the first case because of procedural reasons.[5] But a different majority partially reversed the first on the issue of laches twenty years later. This time a new majority adopted the dissent's reasoning in the first case. Reviving tribal sovereignty over the illegally acquired land would, "given the extraordinary passage of time, . . . dishonor the historic wisdom in the value of repose." The Oneida Indian Nation had acquiesced to the sale. It would also create an impractical jurisdictional checkerboard that local and state governments could not effectively govern. Furthermore, the federal law provided an appropriate mechanism for the tribe to regain jurisdiction.[6]

Even more recently, historical change may have caused the court to change course again. In a 2020 case, *McGirt v. Oklahoma,* a five-to-four majority rejected an argument that any Indian reservations made after the federal government removed Muscogee Creeks and other Indians from the eastern United States had been diminished. The majority held that the US Congress must unambiguously express its intent to diminish a reservation on the relevant statute's face for diminishment to occur. It also found that Congress had not done so for the reservations in Oklahoma. Breaking promises to the Indians was not enough to establish diminishment. Nor was it enough for various members of Congress or an administration to express an intent to diminish the reservation in the legislative history.[7]

However, only two years later a different Supreme Court majority found that the state could exercise concurrent jurisdiction over nonmembers on reservations. The new majority in *Oklahoma v. Castro-Huerta*, which consisted of the four dissenters in *McGirt* joined by a newly appointed justice, found that time had weakened the legal presumption that only federal courts had jurisdiction over nonmembers on tribal lands. It applied a balancing test to determine whether the state had some jurisdiction over non-Indians instead of the bedrock principle that only the federal government has jurisdiction over nonmembers in Indian country as applied in *McGirt*. Using this balancing test, the new majority found that precedent now supported states having concurrent jurisdiction over non-Indians accused of crimes in some circumstances. It did so even when a nonmember committed a crime against a member of the relevant tribe.[8]

Four dissenting justices—all once in the *McGirt* majority—described the new majority as responding favorably to the Oklahoma executive branch's effort to "portray reservations within its State . . . as 'lawless dystopias'" which allowed the state of "Oklahoma to intrude on a feature of tribal sovereignty recognized since the founding." The new majority was "usurping congressional decisions about the appropriate balance between federal, tribal, and state interests." It was making legislative policy based on inadequate and faulty information. It was ignoring that the relevant tribe and the federal government had responded by increasing their ability to prosecute crimes on the reservations making up 43 percent of the state of Oklahoma. The dissent ended by stating: "One can only hope political branches and future courts will do their duty to honor this Nation's promises" to tribes.[9]

Although the dissenters relied on doctrine to decide the case, they also recognized that they could not resolve the complicated practical issues created by overlapping and sometimes conflicting jurisdictions That was a matter for the federal, state, and tribal governments to work out among themselves once the court determined the basic jurisdictional boundaries using legal principles. As discussed previously, these principles strongly favored tribal claims, thereby encouraging states to settle. In contrast, a balancing test would only encourage the parties to litigate and likely result in more favorable outcomes for the state.[10]

These last two cases were in the future, however, when *Saginaw Chippewas v. Granholm* was decided—principles, not balancing tests—still governed diminishment cases. The state knew it faced an uphill battle. Furthermore, neither party could rely on Congress, nor did they want to rely on a court to resolve complicated policy issues. They wanted to determine on their own how to best live together in a new century. Accordingly, they sat down to try to negotiate a resolution to the case. The conclusion tells the story of what happened next.

CONCLUSION

In 2010, all parties in the *Chippewa Saginaw v. Granhom* case reached a negotiated settlement. Many different aspects of that negotiation need some final clarification. The tribe and the federal government (plaintiffs), and the state of Michigan, the city of Mount Pleasant, and Isabella County (defendants) had many disputes before the tribe filed the lawsuit. The tribe had entered into a state-tribal gaming agreement approved by the federal government, but serous disputes remained, centering on whether the reservation extended beyond federal trust lands. The three defendants maintained that it did not, but the tribe and the federal government believed that the Isabella Reservation encompassed roughly six townships and that the tribe had hunting and fishing rights within those six townships. The tribe also alleged that local law enforcement exercised improper jurisdiction over tribal members. Finally, the tribe asserted that the state improperly sought to have members collect taxes on sales to nonmembers.

While it is true that local governments worked informally with the tribe on numerous issues of concern to both entities, serious problems persisted. The state refused to recognize the historic boundaries of the Isabella Reservation, and the local governments continued to police nontrust land within the reservation. The city, county, and state continued to tax Indian resources when such taxes were considered by some to be illegal. The disagreements and distrust increased until the tribe felt it had no choice but to sue the state in federal court.

The lawsuit produced significant results. Instead of exacerbating the problem as often happens, the lawsuit provided an opportunity for the parties to forge a better future together. Many aspects of the state-county-city-tribe relationship had to be reconsidered and restructured. Foremost among areas of contention was the simple fact that the tribe had a federally recognized "reservation," established by law in 1864 and defined by the treaty ratified by the US Senate that year. A clear thread was demonstrated in the plaintiffs' historical reports (two of which comprise the first six chapters of this book). They defined reservation and its existence: this in itself was a major step forward.

The tribe and the federal government (which came into the case on the side of the tribe) disagreed with the state and local governments over what lands constituted the Isabella Reservation. Once the parties tentatively agreed on the boundaries of the reservation, they could work out how they would respect, protect, and value the people and rights of the Saginaw Chippewas who lived on that reservation. The initial arguments centered on reaching agreement relative to a consent judgment, in which prior state court criminal verdicts would not be overturned. This led further to state and local authorities agreeing to ask permission before entering key areas of the Isabella Reservation on a routine basis. All parties have also clarified their respective criminal jurisdiction and agreed to seek the help of federal authorities in policing the reservation. The federal district court retains jurisdiction to decide any legal conflicts. Thus, the tribal police department is respected and has become integral to law enforcement efforts on the reservation and in the county.

The parties have also addressed other thorny issues. Chief Justice John Marshall famously wrote that the power to tax is the power to destroy, and the Saginaw Chippewas know it down to their very bones. They demanded and received the protection they needed to pursue their economic livelihoods. The parties also identified those specific Indian lands within the county and city of Mount Pleasant that were not taxable by the county and city assessors. This reduced revenue for both county and city governments, and the tribe agreed to mitigate some of the lost revenue for a short period of years. Finally, the parties reached extensive agreements on the difficult issue of collecting state sales and use taxes on Indian land from non-Indian members.

The parties also reached vital agreements that directly addressed the Saginaw Chippewa Tribe's culture and future. The heinous removal of Native American children from their families without tribal permission was ended, but the tribe and state still had important matters to address regarding welfare. Fundamentally, tribal, state, and local governments needed to protect every child regardless of their parents' status as members or nonmembers, and the tribe needed to have the right to teach its children to embrace their Chippewa heritage. This led to an "Indian Tribal Welfare Act Agreement" that recognized an increased tribal role and reduced uncertainty, benefitting all governments and most of all, the children of native heritage.

The tribe also sought to protect environmental resources, particularly when it came to hunting and fishing. The Saginaw people had been hunters and fishers well before Europeans arrived in their lands, and they continue to hunt and fish today. These issues now have a clear legal framework, but the details are often difficult to work out. The parties continue to do so on a day-to-day basis. Additionally, the tribe has also helped restore vital areas of the Saginaw River and Bay area as a natural resource damage trustee. These activities benefit everyone in the county.

The tribe also has plans to further develop its businesses and the tribal government on the Isabella Reservation. Many thousands of people continue to flow onto the reservation to visit Soaring Eagle Casino and other tribal resources and museums. Both parties—Indian and non-Indian—benefit from such activity, and generally, both parties have cooperated collectively to resolve any issues that arise from this activity. But confusion sometimes happens, and the parties generally negotiate zoning laws to further the development of the county.

Just how the native and nonnative citizens of Isabella County view this agreement today is difficult to determine. Efforts to discuss various aspects of the agreement in the spring 2022 led to some clear statements that suggest considerable cooperation, indeed near total acceptance, of the settlement. Aaron Desentz, the city manager of Mount Pleasant, stated openly that the "basic relationship has been good." He, in turn, contacted the city police chief, who asserted that "everything is operating very well." The tribe, for its part, agreed even before the agreement was reached to contribute 2 percent of the earnings from slot machines to community development. Parks, schools, roads, and other infrastructure have all benefited from these funds, and they replace some of the tax revenue that is no longer paid by the tribe. The fund annually contributes millions of dollars to such community enterprises.

Conversations with Isabella County Sheriff Michael Main provoked a similar response. The county sheriff and his deputies have more interaction with the tribe than any other governmental agency. They have worked hard to determine jurisdictional authority and often share it. Tribal deputies go through the exact same training as county deputies; thus, there is no occupational jealousy. And the tribal court system functions at the same level as the nontribal district court. In the agreement, the tribe decided not to contest any convictions determined under the county courts prior to the agreement, fundamentally ending any animosity that might have emerged over former convictions. As Sheriff Main noted in closing, recently tribal funds have been used to purchase police cruisers and to arm every officer with new body cameras. Law enforcement has benefited from the agreement rather than suffered from it.

The tribe's reaction to the agreement was even more favorable. In a press release issued by the public relations director of the Saginaw Chippewa Indian Tribe, dated November 23, 2010, Tribal Chief Vincent Kequom Sr. proclaimed, "This is a very extraordinary day for the Tribe and the Community." He went on to note that the agreement "recognizes our Reservation boundaries and allows for greater understanding of the jurisdictional power of the Tribal Government to direct the growth and well-being or our Native people." Chief Kequom went on to explain that the tribe had "reached its goal" without the expense of a long, legal, court battle. Judge Thomas Ludington expressed mostly the same sentiments, applauding the cooperation that ultimately prevailed among a battery of lawyers representing many diverse interests in northern Michigan.

This panoply of agreements was perhaps more comprehensive than ever seen before in such legal disputes. Indeed, the Chippewa sovereignty case has become somewhat of a role model for future litigation. How did this happen? Some of the answers have been suggested in the preceding chapters, which reveal the history behind the various issues that emerged. But the lawsuit brought every major interested entity together. The federal government, the Saginaw Chippewa Indian Tribe, the state of Michigan, and local governments sat down to find a better way to live together. No one was left outside the tent.

The parties were also fortunate in that they had clear legal principles guiding them. This diminished the uncertainty involved in court and at the bargaining table. The parties rarely took positions because of political or litigation imperatives. By appointing a "special master" to facilitate negotiations and deft handling of motions, the court also reduced uncertainty. The agreements also increased certainty by empowering the court to resolve disputes. Outside the bargaining room, uncertainty about the rules alone can cause neighbors to argue and governments to sue. When combined with injustice, the confusion can produce violence, as it did early in Native American efforts to reassert their treaty rights. Nothing of the kind occurred here in Michigan; when temper disappeared, rational arguments prevailed.

The last sentence hints at something more historically profound. Christopher Columbus landed on an island that he named San Salvador in 1492. He came as a conqueror more than anything else, and those who followed him often did so as well. Wars of conquest preceded Euro-American settlement for the next four hundred years. Federal policy separated Native Americans from the acquisitive newcomers after 1789. Eventually, Euro-Americans prevailed in those wars and imposed their vision on the land. Many people who should have known better spoke casually of the vanishing American Indian.

But the Saginaw Chippewas did not vanish. They never abandoned their tribal government, even when the state government considered it dissolved. The historical chapters that precede this conclusion attest to that. They taught their children Saginaw Chippewa mores, lifeways, and language because those customs were good ones, and in the last quarter century, they have reestablished their treaty rights. The state and federal governments now recognize the tribe's sovereignty. Gaming made much of this possible because it gave the tribe the wherewithal to go to court and protect its rights.

Equally important, gaming has created an ongoing economic, social, and political relationship between the local, state, and tribal governments. This relationship is one that both the tribal and the non-tribal members of the county wish to maintain, for common economic reasons. Nontribal members flow in and out of the Soaring Eagle Casino and the reservation. It has become the county's largest employer, and it also contributes financially to schools and other public resources. The dispute over the Isabella Reservation's boundaries threatened those relationships, but tribal members and state and city officials had enough courage to bring the parties together as citizens, with common goals, living together in peace and justice.

NOTES

INTRODUCTION

1. Jackson to Monroe, March 4, 1817, in Andrew Jackson, *Correspondence of Andrew Jackson,* 7 vols., ed. John S. Bassett (Washington, DC: Carnegie Institute, 1926–35), 2:277–82.

2. Lindsay G. Robertson, *Conquest by Law: How the Discovery of America Dispossessed Indigenous Peoples of Their Land* (New York: Oxford University Press, 2005), 122–39.

3. Mathew L. M. Fletcher, "The Supreme Court's Indian Problem," *Hastings Law Journal* 59 (2008): 579–642.

4. Kathryn E. Fort, "The New Laches: Creating Title Where None Existed," *George Mason Legal Review* 16 (Winter 2009): 357–401.

5. Theodore J. Karamanski, "The Historical and Ethnohistorical Context of Hunting and Fishing Treaty Rights in Western and Northern Michigan," 1.

6. Karamanski, "Historical and Ethnohistorical Context," 185–91.

7. Anthony G. Gulig, "An Historical Analysis of the Saginaw, Black River and Swan Creek Chippewa Treaties of 1855 and 1864," 85.

8. For Gary Anderson's conclusions, see chapters 1–4 of this volume.

9. R. David Edmunds's report, "A History of the Isabella Reservation" appears, with minor edits, as chapters 5–6 of this volume. A fifth report was produced by Professor Frederick Hoxie for the Justice Department, which is not reproduced here.

10. US District Court, Eastern District of Michigan, Northern Division, "Order for Judgement," December 17, 2010.

11. "Order For Judgement," Section 3-A.

CHAPTER 1

1. Ojibwe scholar Anton Treuer from Minnesota prefers the term "Ojibwe" in discussing his people. He believes that most of the Minnesota Ojibwe use "Anishinaabe" in a more general sense, as a term that refers to Indians. Like many Native scholars, he acknowledges that Europeans first crafted the term "Indian" but that it is so commonly used today that it is almost impossible to avoid it. The Saginaw people of central Michigan, Anishinaabe people who first encountered Europeans, use the term "Chippewa," which is what is adopted for this book. See Anton Treuer, *The Assassination of Hole in the Day* (St. Paul: Minnesota Historical Society Press, 2011), xix; and the Saginaw Chippewa Indian Tribe website, http://www.sagchip.org.

2. E. S. Rogers, "Southeastern Ojibwa," in *Handbook of North American Indians,* 20 vols., ed. William C. Sturtevant (Washington, DC: Smithsonian Institution, 1978), 15:760–71.

3. The British anthropologist Robin Fox has studied matrilineal and patrilineal societies, noting the importance of clan identity in preventing incest. While Fox clearly notes the need for such prevention, he cannot explain why such a need developed in tribal society. See Fox, *Kinship and Marriage: An Anthropological Perspective* (New York: Cambridge University Press, 1983), 54–76. The anthropologist Claude Meillassoux has argued that in tribal societies one of the most important decisions made is determining who gets a wife or a husband. See his argument in *Maidens, Meal and Money: Capitalism and the Domestic Community* (New York: Cambridge University Press, 1981), 1–42. Another account of marriage, dependent mostly on observations made by Samuel Champlain, who got his information from traders among the Huron, is found in W. Vernon Kinietz, *The Indians of the Western Great Lakes, 1650–1760* (Ann Arbor: University of Michigan Press, 1965), 93–96.

4. For a good description of the kinship system, see Saginaw Chippewa Tribe of Michigan, *Diba Jimooyung: Telling Our Story, A History of the Saginaw Ojibwe Anishinabek* (Mt. Pleasant, MI: Self-published, 2005), 13–15.

5. By far the best account of Chippewa marriage is found in Ruth Landes, *The Ojibewa Woman* (New York: W. W. Norton, 1971), 51–123.

6. Richard White, *The Middle Ground: Indians, Empires and Republics in the Great Lakes Region, 1650–1815* (New York: Cambridge University Press, 1991), 62–64.

7. See Bruce Trigger, *The Children of Aataentsic: A History of the Huron People to 1660,* 2 vols. (Montreal: McGill-Queens University Press, 1976).

8. This thesis is forwarded in White, *The Middle Ground.*

9. White, *The Middle Ground,* 15–19. A classic example of how Natives treated early French traders is found in the journal of Pierre Charles Le Sueur, who ascended the Mississippi River in 1700 and arrived at the Illinois village just above the river's junction with the Ohio River. The Indians descended on

Le Sueur's boats and forced him to sit on a large buffalo robe, which several men picked up and paraded into the village. Tribal elders then sat next to him and placed food in his mouth, symbolically adopting him into the community. Le Sueur then offered presents of hatchets and other goods that the Indians expected. See "Mémoires de Mr le Sueur," Archives Nationales, Paris, France.

10. White, *The Middle Ground*, 65–66. As White points out, these relationships did cut down on another practice that Jesuit missionaries abhorred—that of polygamy.

11. For a good discussion of the argument, see Maurice Godelier, *The Mental and the Material* (London: Verso, 1984), 18–23.

12. Marshall Sahlins, *Stone Age Economics* (New York: Aldine, 1972), 17. Sahlins studied several different hunting cultures to arrive at a figure of four to five hours a day or twenty-eight to thirty-five hours a week.

13. These views of hunter-gatherers are derived from Sahlins, *Stone Age Economics*. See his chapter "The Original Affluent Society," 1–39.

14. See Francis Jennings, *The Ambiguous Iroquois Empire: The Covenant Chain Confederation of Indian Tribes with English Colonies from Its Beginnings to the Lancaster Treaty of 1744* (New York: W. W. Norton, 1984), 1–112.

15. See Trigger, *Children of Aataentsics.*

16. For general accounts of this period, see R. David Edmunds, *The Potawatomies, Keepers of the Fire* (Norman: University of Oklahoma Press, 1978), 3–23; White, *The Middle Ground*, 75–93.

17. Richard Weybing, "'Gascon Exaggerations': The Rise of Antoine Laumet, dit de Lamothe, Sieur de Cadillac, the Foundation of Colonial Detroit, and the Origins of the Fox Wars," in *French and Indians in the Heart of America, 1630–1815*, eds. Robert Englebert and Guillaume Teasdale (East Lansing: Michigan State University Press, 2013), 77–112; R. David Edmunds and Joseph L. Peyser, *The Fox Wars: The Mesquakie Challenge to New France* (Norman: University of Oklahoma Press, 1993), 47–216.

18. See Gregory Evans Dowd, *A Spirited Resistance: The North American Indian Struggle for Unity, 1745–1815* (Baltimore: Johns Hopkins University Press, 1992), 34–40. See also David Stout, "Ethnohistorical Report on the Saginaw Chippewa," in *American Indian Ethnohistory: North Central and Northeastern Indians, Chippewa Indians V*, ed. David Horr (New York: Garland, 1974), 97–100.

19. White has a good description of this growing lawlessness. See *The Middle Ground*, 300–78.

20. Gary Clayton Anderson, *Ethnic Cleansing and the Indian: The Crime That Should Haunt America* (Norman: University of Oklahoma Press, 2014), 87–90.

21. Anderson, *Ethnic Cleansing and the Indian*, 102–6.

22. Treaty with the Wyandot, etc., 1795, in Charles J. Kappler, *Indian Affairs: Laws and Treaties*, 2 vols. (Washington: GPO, 1904), 2:39–45, online at Tribal Treaties Database (hereafter TTD), https://treaties.okstate.edu/, 7 Stat.,

49, Identifiers RIT_023, NAI_170281462. The Tribal Treaties Database at the Oklahoma State University Libraries hosts the digitized texts of all seven volumes of Kappler's *Indian Affairs*. It is searchable by tribe name and by the "identifiers" listed following the treaty title (e.g., RIT_023, NAI_17028142). See also "Description of the Treaty of Greenville, 1795," Avalon Project, Yale Law School, https://avalon.law.yale.edu/18th_Century/greenvil.asp.

23. Charles E. Cleland, *Faith in Paper: The Ethnohistory and Litigation of Upper Great Lakes Indian Treaties* (Ann Arbor: University of Michigan Press, 2011), 49–51.

24. See the various treaties in Kappler, *Indian Affairs,* 2:60–90; and online at TTD.

25. Treaty with the Ottowa, etc., 1807, Kappler, *Indian Affairs,* 2:93, online at TTD, 7 Stat., 105, RIT_054, NAI_161303994TD.

26. See Robert M. Owens, *Mr. Jefferson's Hammer: William Henry Harrison and the Origins of American Indian Policy* (Norman: University of Oklahoma Press, 2007), 67–127; Anderson, *Ethnic Cleansing and the Indian,* 138–39. While a 1996 biography of Lewis Cass inexplicably fails to mention his role in negotiating the Treaty of 1819—an exceedingly important treaty—it does examine his expedition into the upper Lakes in 1820, a trip that resulted in several other treaties with Indians. William Carl Klunder, *Lewis Cass and the Politics of Moderation* (Kent, OH: Kent State University Press, 1996), 34–38.

27. See the description of Saginaw in Fred Dustin, *The Saginaw Treaty of 1819: Between General Lewis Cass and the Chippewa Indians, Written for the Celebration of the Treaty September 19, 1919* (Saginaw, MI: Committee on History and Records, 1919), 4–5.

28. Treaty with the Chippewa, 1819, Kappler, *Indian Affairs,* 2:185–87, and online at TTD, Stat., 203, RIT_109, NAI_101784571; see also Dustin, *Saginaw Treaty of 1819.* On Cass's complaints regarding the constant drunkenness of Indians, who obtained liquor from the British, see Klunder, *Cass and the Politics of Moderation,* 30–38.

29. The trader who reported the use of whiskey was Louis Campau, whose recorded descriptions of the negotiation are found in Saginaw Chippewa Tribe, *Diba Jimooyung,* 40. See also Christopher Mabie, *Uncle Louis: Biography of Louis Campau, Founder of Saginaw and Grand Rapids* (Walker, MI: Van Naerden, 2007), 25–38. Another account is Bernard Peters, "Hypocrisy on the Great Lakes Frontier: The Use of Whiskey by the Michigan Department of Indian Affairs," *Michigan Historical Review* 18 (1992): 4–5.

30. Peters, "Hypocrisy on the Great Lakes Frontier," 12–17.

31. Lewis Cass to Secretary of War John C. Calhoun, September 30, 1819, National Archives, Record Group 75 (hereafter NARG 75), Documents Relating to the Negotiation of Ratified and Unratified Treaties. An overview of the locations of documents in NARG 75 relating to the Bureau of Indian Affairs

1793–1989, can be found at Guide to Federal Records, https://www.archives .gov/research/guide-fed-records/index-numeric/001-to-100.html#RG075. A breakdown of the content of the BIA archive can be found at https://www .archives.gov/research/guide-fed-records/groups/075.html#75.1.

32. Cass to Calhoun, September 30, 1819.

33. A good description of the issue is found in Cleland, *Faith in Paper,* 52–55.

34. See trader Henry Connor to Schoolcraft, October 24, 1835, NARG 75.15.5, Letters Received (hereafter LR), Mackinac Agency.

35. See 4, *United States Statutes at Large,* 729, the final version being debated in Congress. That debate can be found at House Journal, 23rd Cong., 1st Sess., 645, 833, 852, 869.

36. This ethnic cleansing is the subject of Anderson, *Ethnic Cleansing and the Indian,* 110–72.

37. See Connor to Schoolcraft, October 24, 1835, NARG 75.15.5, LR, Mackinac Agency.

38. Treaty with the Chippewa, 1836 and Treaty with the Chippewa, 1837, in Kappler, *Indian Affairs,* 2:461–62 and 2:501–2; online at TTD, 7 Stat., 503, RIT_207, NAI_148026684, and 7 Stat., 547, respectively.

39. Treaty with the Chippewa, 1837, Kappler, *Indian Affairs,* 2:501–2.

40. Kappler, *Indian Affairs,* 2:450–55.

41. See George Manypenny, *Our Indian Wards* (1880; reprint, New York: Decapo, 1972).

CHAPTER 2

1. Ronald N. Satz, *American Indian Policy in the Jacksonian Era* (Norman: University of Oklahoma Press, 1975), 6; Robert A. Trennert Jr., *Alternative to Extinction: Federal Indian Policy and the Beginnings of the Reservation System, 1846–1851* (Philadelphia: Temple University Press, 1975), vii, 1–3.

2. Francis Paul Prucha, *The Great Father: The United States Government and the American Indians,* 2 vols. (Lincoln: University of Nebraska Press, 1984), 1:191–95, 1:214; Satz, *American Indian Policy,* 9–31.

3. Prucha, *Great Father,* 1:243–69. See also Treaty with the Winnebago, Oct. 13, 1846, online at TTD, 9 Stat. 878, RIT_249, NAI_175516216; and Treaty with the Menominee, Oct. 18, 1848, TTD, 9 Stat., 952, RIT_253, NAI_174683967.

4. Trennert, *Alternative to Extinction,* 18, 29–30.

5. William Medill, *Annual Report of the Commissioner of Indian Affairs,* House Exec. Doc. no. 1, 30th Cong., 2d sess., serial 537, 388 (1848).

6. Trennart, *Alternative to Extinction,* 30–39, 47–51. Orlando Brown served as commissioner of Indian affairs for one year immediately following Medill's departure. Brown advocated for Medill's two-reservation system but was not able

to garner congressional support for this proposal during his short tenure in office. See also Robert M. Kvasnicka and Herman J. Viola, eds., *The Commissioners of Indian Affairs, 1824–1977* (Lincoln: University of Nebraska Press, 1979), 41–47.

7. Luke Lea, *Annual Report of the Commissioner of Indian Affairs*, Sen. Exec. Doc. no. 1, 31st Cong., 2d. sess., serial 587, 35 (1850) (SC012990). See also Trennart, *Alternative to Extinction*, 55–56; Kvasnicka and Viola, *Commissioners of Indian Affairs*, 49–56.

8. James J. Rawls, *Indians of California: The Changing Image* (Norman: University of Oklahoma Press 1986), 141–47. The federal government ultimately chose a different route, relocating Indians onto five military reservations in California starting in 1853. See Albert L. Hurtado, *Indian Survival on the California Frontier* (New Haven, CT: Yale University Press, 1988), 141–42.

9. Trennert, *Alternative to Extinction*, 16–39; Gary Clayton Anderson, *Kinsmen of Another Kind: Dakota White Relations on the Upper Mississippi River, 1650–1862* (Lincoln: University of Nebraska Press, 1984), 229–36.

10. The best discussion of Lea's efforts is in Trennert, *Alternative to Extinction*, chapter entitled "Toward a Reservation System: Whig Indian Policy, 1849–1851," 40–60. The creation of the Texas reservation system is discussed in Gary Clayton Anderson, *The Conquest of Texas: Ethnic Cleansing in the Promised Land, 1820–1875* (Norman: University of Oklahoma Press, 2005), 256–58.

11. Prucha, *Great Father,* 1:316–17; Kvasnicka, *Commissioners of Indian Affairs*, 57–67.

12. George Manypenny, *Annual Report of the Commissioner of Indian Affairs*, Sen. Exec. Doc. no. 1, 34th Cong., 1st sess., serial 810, 338 (1855).

13. Treaty with the Menominee, 1854, Kappler, *Indian Affairs,* 2:465–66, online at TTD, 10 Stats. 1064, RIT_269, NAI_81145645. The Menominee treaty never specially referred to a "reservation" per se, although Manypenny later wrote that "their reservation in Wisconsin has been confirmed to them as a permanent home." Manypenny, *Annual Report of the Commissioner of Indian Affairs*, Sen. Exec. Doc. no. 1, 34th Cong., 1st sess., serial 810, 321 (1854).

14. Treaty with the Kickapoo, 1854, Kappler, *Indian Affairs,* 2:471–73, online at TTD, 10 Stat., 1078, RIT_272, NAI_169512353.

15. Treaty with the Kaskaskia, Peoria, etc., 1854, Kappler, *Indian Affairs,* 2:474–75, online at TTD, 10 Stats., 1082, RIT_273, NAI_169606641.

16. Prucha, *Great Father,* 1:327.

17. Jacob Thompson to the President, November 30, 1860, *Annual Report of the Secretary of the Interior*, Sen. Exec. Doc. no. 1, 2nd sess., spec. sess., 36th Cong., serial 1078, 35–36 (1860). See also Charles Mix, *Annual Report of the Commissioner of Indian Affairs*, Sen. Exec. Doc. no. 1, 35th Cong., 2nd sess., serial 974, 358 (1858).

18. Bradley to General Lewis Cass, December 14, 1852, NARG 75.15.5, M234, LR, Mackinac Agency.

19. For the first two years the land was to be offered at $5.00 per acre. Thereafter, if any land remained unsold, the price was to be reduced to $2.50 per acre for the next three years, and finally to as low as 75 cents. Treaty with the Chippewa, 1838, online at TTD, 7 Stat. 565, RIT_231, NAI_185842570. Because the United States had failed to survey the lands in a timely manner, federal officials now admitted that it would take more than thirty years to dispose of the ceded territory and that the final sale price would fall "very much below the sum which the Indians had expected to receive within just five years." Gilbert and Manypenny to Mix, Aug. 7, 1855, NARG 75.15.5, LR, Mackinac Agency. Henry Schoolcraft, who had negotiated the prior treaties on behalf of the federal government, remarked that "had the lands been promptly surveyed and offered for sale, there would have been no disappointment [in the Indians' expectations]," ibid. (quoting Schoolcraft).

20. Gilbert to Manypenny, March 6, 1854, NARG 75.15.5, M234, LR, Mackinac Agency.

21. Treaty with the Ottawa, etc., 1836, online at TTD, 7 Stat. 491, RIT_201, NAI_198249818.

22. Gilbert to Manypenny, March 6, 1854, NARG 75.15.5, M234, LR, Mackinac Agency.

23. "Executive Orders Relating to Reserves," Kappler, *Indian Affairs,* 3:846.

24. Wilson to Manypenny, December 20, 1854, Kappler, *Indian Affairs,* 2:846–47.

25. Gilbert to Manypenny, April 12, 1855, NARG 75.15.5, M234, LR, Mackinac Agency, M234, Roll 404:625–27.

26. Manypenny to Gilbert, May 10, 1855, NARG 75.5, Records of Commissioner of Indian Affairs (hereafter COIA), Letters Sent (hereafter LS), M21, Roll 51:391.

27. "Executive Orders Relating to Reserves," Kappler, *Indian Affairs,* 3:847.

28. Johnston's address is found in the Johnston Papers, no date, Burton Collection, Detroit Public Library.

29. Johnston Papers, no date, Burton Collection, Detroit Public Library. The money issue emerged during the discussions in June and early July, revealing that some $96,257.72 was owed the Saginaw Chippewas for lands sold under earlier treaties. While this was not the sole reason for including them in the negotiation, it certainly caught the attention of government officials who seemed to be oblivious of the debt. George C. Whiting, acting COGLO, to Charles E. Mix, Acting COIA, July 13, 1855, NARG 75.15.5, LR, Mackinac Agency.

30. "Proceedings of a Council with the Chippeways and Ottawas of Michigan Held at the City of Detroit, by the Hon. George W. Meanypeny [sic] & Henry Gilbert, Commissioners of the United States, July 25, 1855," included in *United States v. State of Michigan,* M26-73CA (SC11277) (hereinafter Ottawa Chippewa Treaty Journal, 1855).

31. Ottawa Chippewa Treaty Journal, 1855. Gen. Lewis Cass, the leading Democratic politician in Michigan, appeared briefly at the negotiations and echoed Manypenny's sentiments: "Now let them make an arrangement; by which they can secure permanent homes, farms, school, churches, & the implements of husbandry."

32. Treaty with the Chippewa of Saginaw, Swan Creek, and Black River, 1855, online at TTD, 11 Stat. 633, RIT_298, NAI_178354861.

33. Treaty with the Chippewa of Saginaw, 1855.

34. Treaty with the Chippewa of Saginaw, 1855.

35. Treaty with the Chippewa of Saginaw, 1855.

36. Treaty with the Ottawa and Chippewa, 1855, online at TTD, 11 Stat. 621, RIT_296, NAI_178331415.

37. During the 1855 negotiations, Waw-be-geeg, a Chippewa leader, confirmed this by stating: "My father I have spoken to our friends the Ottawas saying that we have been brought up together & are merely friends. I can make no laws for them. I can only make laws for myself & my people." Ottawa Chippewa Treaty Journal, 1855, 35.

38. Treaty with the Ottawa and Chippewa, 1836, online at TTD, 7 Stat. 491, RIT_201, NAI_198249818.

39. Ottawa Chippewa Treaty Journal, 1855.

40. Ottawa Chippewa Treaty Journal, 1855.

41. Ottawa Chippewa Treaty Journal, 1855.

42. Gilbert to Manypenny, March 6, 1854, NARG 75.15.5, LR, Mackinac Agency.

43. Ottawa Chippewa Treaty Journal, 1855.

44. Manypenny to Gilbert, June 15, 1855, NARG 75.5, Records of COIA, LS, M21, Roll 52:18–19 (emphasis added).

45. Manypenny, *Annual Report of the Commissioner of Indian Affairs*, Sen. Exec. Doc. no. 5, 34th Cong., 3rd sess., serial 875, 554–832 (1855) (emphasis added).

46. Hendrix to Mix, September 8, 1855, NARG 75.15.5, LR, Mackinac Agency.

47. Gilbert to Manypenny, June 19, 1856, NARG 75.15.5, LR, Mackinac Agency.

48. The plat books for Michigan have survived and are found in Bureau of Land Management Records (hereafter BLMR), Eastern States Office, Springfield, VA. This set of the Isabella plats, dated from the 1830s and with the handwritten notations from 1855–64, is viewable on the Department of the Interior website at http://www.glorrecords.blm.gov/survey.

49. Manypenny to Gilbert, April 25, 1856, NARG 75.5, Records of COIA, LS.

50. For a discussion of the defective surveys, see *Michigan Land & Lumber Company vs. Rust,* 68 F. 155, 156 (6th Cir. 1895).

51. Leach to William P. Dole, April 23, 1862, NARG 75.5, Records of the COIA, Entry 389.

52. Leach to William P. Dole, April 23, 1862; J. M. Edmunds to COIA, March 26, 1862, NARG 75.5, Records of the COIA, Entry 389.

53. D. C. Leach, "Selection of Lands" List, July 19, 1861, NARG 75.15.5, Records of the Michigan Superintendency and Mackinac Agency, Entry 389.

54. Leach, "Selection of Lands" List, July 19, 1861.

55. The list showing the 109 people from the Bay is originally dated October 18, 1864, the day before the signing of the 1864 treaty. But it appears from the handwriting of the new agent, Richard M. Smith, that nothing was done to issue certificates until February 18, 1868. Richard M. Smith "Land Selections, Chippewas of Saginaw, & in lieu of land, Saginaw Bay," February 18, 1868, NARG 75.15.5, Records of the Michigan Superintendency and Mackinac Agency, Entry 398. In July 1869, Commissioner Ely S. Parker sent a long, detailed letter to Agent James Long declaring that 1,344 certificates had been sent to Agent Leach in 1864. This number included Indians from the other Ottawa and Chippewa reservations. The total number of certificates issued to the Saginaw Chippewas in 1864 was just 497. See Parker's Letter, 1869, ibid., Entry 389.

56. Parker's Letter, 1869, Entry 389.

57. J. M. Edmunds to COIA, March 26, 1862, NARG 75.5, Records of COIA, Land Allotments under Treaties of 1855 and 1864, vol. 19-B; Dole to Leach, June 17, 1862, NARG 75.5, Records of COIA, LS; Usher to Edmunds, December 2, 1864, NARG 75.19.60, LR, Michigan Agency.

58. Manypenny to Gilbert, April 29, 1856, NARG 75.5, Records of COIA, LS.

59. All acreage totals for various categories of land within the Isabella Reservation in this section are based on detailed review of the records in the Plat Book for Michigan, BLMR, and the Michigan Agency's tract books. The land records were not well kept, and discrepancies exist between the Michigan Agency's tract books and the Michigan tract books found at the BLMR in Washington, DC. The latter suggest that military warrants accounted for 8,567 acres, individual sales accounted for 6,424 acres, and swamplands accounted for 12,532 acres.

60. Benjamin Horace Hibbard, *A History of the Public Land Policies* (Madison: University of Wisconsin Press, 1965), 299–301.

61. Plat Book for Michigan, BLMR.

62. See *Michigan Land & Lumber Co.,* 68 F., 155–56.

63. See Plat Book for Michigan, BLMR.

64. See "An Act to enable the State of Arkansas and other States to reclaim the 'Swamp Lands' within their limits," September 28, 1850, 31st Cong., sess. 1.

65. See *Michigan Land & Lumber Co. v. Rust,* 168 U.S. 589 (1897).

66. *Michigan Land & Lumber Co. v. Rust,* 168 U.S. 589.

67. Michigan Plat Book, BLMR.

68. Michigan Plat Book, BLMR.

69. Agent Fitch to COIA, Nov. 10, 1858, Mackinac Agency, in *Annual Report of the Commissioner of Indian Affairs*, Sen. Exec. Doc. no. 1, 35th Cong., 1st sess., serial 942, 404–5 (1858); acting Commissioner of GLO A. B. Greenwood, August 30, 1859, NARG 75.15.5, LR, Michigan Agency.

CHAPTER 3

1. Petition of C. F. Williams, E. R. Webb, M. D. Bourassa, and seven others, December 3, 1855, NARG 75, LR, Mackinac Agency, Indian Claims Dkt. No. 13-H.

2. Agent Fitch, Mackinac Agency, in the *Annual Report of the Commissioner of Indian Affairs*, Sen. Exec. Doc. no. 1, 35th Cong., 1st sess., serial 942, 404–5.

3. Gilbert to Manypenny, December 5, 1855, NARG 75.19.55, LR, Mackinac Agency.

4. Petition enclosed in D. C. Leach to COIA, April 9, 1864, NARG 75.19.60, LR, Michigan Agency.

5. The value of the railroads in lumber exploitation is best found in a letter of Henry H. Crapo to William W. Crapo, December 3, 1864, Crapo Papers, Detroit Public Library. Henry told his father that his timber must be marketed that winter, as in the spring of 1865, the mills at Saginaw would provide stiff competition because of the new railroads being built in that region.

6. Forest B. Meek, *Michigan's Timber Battle Ground: A History of Clare County, 1674–1900* (Clare, MI: Clare County Bicentennial Historical Committee, 1976), 46–66. One prominent lumberman from Flint was Henry Crapo, who used his influence to get railroads into Clare and ultimately the Isabella Reservation. See Crapo Papers, Bentley Library, University of Michigan, Ann Arbor.

7. H. C. Potter to Austin Blair, December 14, 1870, Austin Blair Papers, Burton Collection, Detroit Public Library.

8. See Leach to Dole, April 9, June 14, and July 9, 1864, NARG 75.19.60, LR, Michigan Agency; Dole to Leach, May 2 and September 3, 1864, NARG 75.5, Records of COIA, LS.

9. Treaty with the Chippewa of Saginaw, Swan Creek, and Black River, 1864, Kappler, *Indian Affairs*, 2:665–68, online at TTD, RIT_333, NAI_178924954; Alvord report to Dole, October 31, 1864, NARG 75, Negotiation of Ratified and Unratified Treaties.

10. Treaty with the Chippewa of Saginaw, Swan Creek, and Black River, 1864.

11. Treaty with the Chippewa of Saginaw, Swan Creek, and Black River, 1864.

12. See Article 3 in Treaty with the Chippewa of Saginaw, Kappler, *Indian Affairs,* 2:666.

13. See quotations in Prucha, *Great Father,* 412–13.

14. Usher to Abraham Lincoln, January 17, 1865, NARG 48, LS, Records of the Indian Division of the Office of the Secretary of Interior.

15. Lincoln to the Senate, January 17, 1865, 2nd sess. (SC017240).

16. Zachariah Chandler, M. Howard, T. W. Ferry, J. H. Driggs, et al., to Browning, June 5, 1868, NARG 75.19.60, LR, Michigan Agency.

17. Alvord to Commissioner of GLO S. V. Bogy, November 16, 1866, NARG 75.19.60, LR, Michigan Agency.

18. Alvord to Bogy, November 16, 1866.

19. Smith Report, August 28, 1867, House Exec. Doc. no. 1, 40th Cong., 2nd sess., 336.

20. Browning to COIA, April 20, 1868, NARG 75.19.60, LR, Michigan Agency.

21. Chandler, Howard, Ferry, Driggs, et al., to Browning, June 5, 1868, NARG 75.19.60, LR, Michigan Agency.

22. Chandler et al. to Browning, June 5, 1868.

23. N. Mosher, I. A. Francher, Myron McLaren, et el., Petition, n.d., 1869, NARG 75.19.60, LR, Michigan Agency.

24. Parker to Long, July 30, 1869, NARG 75.5, Records of COIA, LS. The Saginaw Chippewas have written a tribal history that outlines the allotment process and the fraud that soon came to dominate it. See *Diba Jimooyung,* 57–58.

25. Whitney to Long, August 13, 1869, NARG 75, LR.19.60, Michigan Agency.

26. Whitney to Long, August 13, 1869.

27. The Rust Purchase is discussed in many sources. See, for example, Long to Parker, November 14, 1869, November 13, 1869, and February 4, 1870, NARG 75.19.60, LR, Michigan Agency. A good newspaper discussion of the purchase, written in support of its validity, is "Another Nest of Lies Exposed," *East Saginaw Weekly Enterprise,* November 3, 1870. The *Enterprise* was a pro-Driggs paper.

28. Ella V. Powers documents these early purchases in "The Saginaw Chippewa Indians" (unpublished manuscript), Clarke Historical Library, Central Michigan. University, 66.

29. Smith to Commissioner of GLO Bogy, January 31, 1867, NARG 75.19.60, LR, Michigan Agency.

30. Long to Parker, July 1 and November 14, 1869, NARG 75.19.60, LR, Michigan Agency.

31. Long to Parker, February 4, 1870, NARG 75.19.60, LR, Michigan Agency. The legal fight is printed in the congressional record at House Miscellaneous Documents, vol. 23, 1–8, https://www.govinfo.gov/app/details/SERIALSET-02429_00_00.

32. House Miscellaneous Documents, 23:1–8; see also the defense of Driggs in "Another Nest of Lies Exposed."

33. Long to Parker, February 4, 1870, NARG 75.19.60, LR, Michigan Agency, M 234, Roll 409:121–153 (SC023204).

34. Long to Parker, February 4, 1870.

35. See "List of New Selections presented by Rev. George Bradley," February 1870, NARG 75.19.60, LR, Michigan Agency.

36. "List of New Selections presented by Rev. George Bradley."

37. Long to Parker, February 4 and March 28, 1870, NARG 75, LR.19.60, Michigan Agency. Long's views on homesteaders are found in a separate letter. He writes: "One of the most pregnant causes of difficulty is the actual settlers claim under the provisions of the homestead act—It is the universal wish of the controlling influences in this state, that these claims may be respected by the government and I have accordingly done so, knowing if I did not, that political influence would accomplish it." Long to Parker, November 8, 1870, NARG 75.19.60, LR, Michigan Agency.

38. G. Bradley to Presisent Grant, October 31, 1870.

39. Commissioner Wilson to Parker, June 11, 1870, and Congressman Ferry to Wilson, August 30, 1870, NARG 75.19.60, LR, Michigan Agency.

40. See "An Appeal for the Indians," by George Bradley, October 31, 1870, and petition of the "Chiefs of the Chippewa Indians of Saginaw, Swan Creek and Black River Bands," December 19, 1870.

41. Driggs to "Dear Gov [Blair]," December 15, 1870, and Indian petition "To His Excellency U. S. Grant, President of the United States," Blair Papers, Burton Collection, Detroit Public Library. Driggs apparently wrote the petition, supposedly signed by twenty Saginaw Chippewa Indians, revealing that Long had bought the mill property, enclosing a copy of the deed, dated December 8, 1870, registered at the county courthouse in Mt. Pleasant. The notary public on the deed was Isaac A. Francher, and the registrar was Cornelius Bennett, both of whom became wealthy through acquiring Indian lands. Indian petition, December 19, 1870, NARG 75.19.60, LR, Michigan Agency.

42. Long to Parker, August 11, 1870, NARG 75.19.60, LR, Michigan Agency.

43. Long to Parker, March 26, 1871, and Indian petition, collected by Hampton Graves, Justice of the Peace for Isabella County, May 8, 1871, and Long's appeal to Senator Ferry, on stationary letterheaded "Longwood Land," dated May 20, 1871, in NARG 75.19.60, LR, Michigan Agency. To "boom" his new town, Long soon developed stationary that even included a Map of "Longwood," which, in turn, revealed the central avenue, "Long Street." See Long to Francis W. Walker, July 12, 1872, in ibid.

44. Smith to Parker, May 27, 1871, NARG 75.19.60, LR, Michigan Agency.

45. Smith to Parker, June 15, 1871, NARG 75.19.60, LR, Michigan Agency.

46. Delano to Smith, September 18, 1871, and Delano to Attorney General A. T. Akerman, September 18, 1871, NARG 75.19.60, LR, Michigan Agency.

47. Brockway to Parker, February 10, 1871, and Knox to Francis W. Walker, December 8, 1871, NARG 75.19.60, LR, Michigan Agency.

48. Long Letter, October 20, 1870, in *Annual Report of the Commissioner of Indian Affairs*, House Exec. Doc. no. 1, 41st Cong., 3rd sess., serial 1449, 779.

49. George W. Lee to COIA, June 30, 1876, NARG 75.19.60, LR, Michigan Agency.

50. Smith to Parker, May 27, 1871, NARG 75.19.60, LR, Michigan Agency.

51. Smith to Parker, June 15, 1871, NARG 75.19.60, LR, Michigan Agency.

52. Delano to the Attorney General A. T. Akerman, September 18, 1871, Delano to Smith, September 18, 1871, and Delano to H. R. Clum, September 19, 1871, NARG 75.19.60, LR, Michigan Agency; A. B. Maynard to Delano, September 14, 1871, Part of H 211, Mackinac I-830; Smith; *Annual Report of the Commissioner of Indian Affairs* (Washington, DC: GPO, 1871), 508–11.

53. The best evidence of how the process worked is detailed in Kemble to Smith, February 22, 1876, H-211, 2496.

54. See report in Kemble to Smith, February 22, 1876, Ct. Cl. H-211, 2496, Suitland FRC. Whiskey freely reached north-central Michigan Indians during the 1860s, but it apparently was even more available during the regime of Agent Long. See A. Porter to COIA, April 17, 1871, NARG 75.19.60, LR, Michigan Agency.

55. The lawyers involved were well known in Mt. Pleasant and included Cornelius Bennett (also registrar of deeds in 1871), Issac A. Francher, Samuel W. Hopkins, Henry H. Graves, William N. Brown, and John C. Leaton. The way in which the land transactions occurred was mostly spelled out in an article entitled "Isabella Indian Lands," published in the *Isabella County Enterprise,* July 30, 1886. Another account that describes the men involved is Powers, "Saginaw-Chippewa Indians," Clarke Historical Library, 66.

56. See Andre Deeds, 1871 and 1872, Bentley Library, University of Michigan, Ann Arbor.

57. Andre Deeds, 1871 and 1872, Bentley Library, UM.

58. Powers, "Saginaw-Chippewa Indians," 67–71.

59. Powers, "Saginaw-Chippewa Indians," 72. It is possible that Brown and Leaton "owned" closer to 40,000 acres. See Agent George W. Lee to COIA, January 20, 1882, NARG 75, LR, Central Files, #1511.

60. D. W. Immanuel to Parker, June 7, 1871, NARG 75.19.60, LR, Michigan Agency.

61. Knox to Commissioner Walker, December 8, 1871, NARG 75.19.60, LR, Michigan Agency.

62. Betts to Walker, January 26, 1872, NARG 75.19.60, LR, Michigan Agency. The figure of 670 new selections at Isabella City comes in Betts to

Walker, September 30, 1872, *Annual Report of the Commissioner of Indian Affairs* (Washington, DC: GPO, 1872), 202–3.

63. Hill to Blair, May 9, 1872, Blair Papers, Burton Collection, Detroit Public Library.

64. Gage to Walker, May 22, 1872, NARG 75.19.60, LR, Michigan Agency.

65. Ryan Johnson and Co. to Commissioner Walker, April 27, 1872, and Betts to Walker, April 26, 1872, NARG 75.19.60, LR, Michigan Agency.

66. Affidavit of Arthur Hill and John C. Leaton, 1872, NARG 75.19.60, LR, Michigan Agency.

67. "Memorial of Charles R. Eddy and 82 others," sent forward by Austin Blair, June 25, 1872, NARG 75.19.60, LR, Michigan Agency.

68. Diggs to Blair, May 9, 1872, Blair Papers, Burton Collection, Detroit Public Library.

69. Betts to Walker, January 20, March 13 and 28, 1872; W. D. Foster (4th District Michigan) to Walker, July 6, 1872; C. H. Gage to Walker, May 11, 1872; and Ryan Johnson (enclosing clipping of the station incident) to Delano, April 27, 1872, all in NARG 75.19.60, LR, Michigan Agency. Betts gives the number of new selections collected as 670 in his annual report, September 30, 1872, in *Annual Report of the Commissioner of Indian Affairs* (1872).

70. Betts to Walker, July 25, 1872, NARG 75 75.19.60, LR, Michigan Agency.

71. Betts to Walker, August 27, 1872, NARG 75 75.19.60, LR, Michigan Agency.

72. See Driggs to Blair, April 3, 1873, Blair Papers, Burton Collection, Detroit Public Library; and Levi P. Luckey to Senator Chandler, February 17, 1874, Zachariah Chandler Papers, Library of Congress.

73. Betts's annual report, September 15, 1873, in *Annual Report of the Commissioner of Indian Affairs* (Washington, DC: GPO, 1873), 174–76. See also GLO Township Plats with notations of Indian Agents Betts and Knox regarding allotment of each parcel on the reservation, NARG 75, Michigan, vol. 61, Box 1 of 3, 11–17; 7 items, National Archives II, College Park, MD.

74. Betts's annual report, September 14, 1874, in *Annual Report of the Commissioner of Indian Affairs* (Washington, DC: GPO, 1874), 184–85.

75. See "Proceedings of Council held at Isabella Mich., 16th inst. relative to selections of lands, etc.," September 16, 1872, NARG 75.19.60, LR, Michigan Agency.

76. Betts's figures should be compared with those of Agent George W. Lee, who estimated that some 70,000 acres had been allotted by 1881 and that Indians still held something like 5,000 acres of allotted land at that time. See Lee to Commissioner, January 20, 1882, NARG 75, LR, Central Files, #1511.

77. Commissioner H. Price to Houseman, March 6, 1884, NARG 75.7, Records of the Land Division, LS, 1884, Land Bureau 123, 25–27. This reports

that 43 patents had been canceled and sent back to Washington, but the real number was over 100.

78. The petition is dated May 28, 1875, NARG 75.19.60, LR, Michigan Agency.

CHAPTER 4

1. The reports of such men form a "Special File," in the BIA records, NARG 75.

2. Betts fought the charges, soliciting letters of support from former agent James Long and from A. R. Arnold, a land speculator who was also the Isabella County surveyor. See the letters in NARG 75.19.60, LR, Michigan Agency. Kemble's report is addressed to Commissioner J. Q. Smith, February 22, 1876, H-211, 2496 (SC001497).

3. Lee to Smith, December 2, 1876, NARG 75.19.60, LR, Michigan Agency.

4. Lee to Smith, March 28, 1877, NARG 75.19.60, LR, Michigan Agency.

5. Lee to Smith, June 30, 1876, NARG 75.19.60, LR, Michigan Agency.

6. Saginaw Chippewa Tribe, *Diba Jimooyung,* 54.

7. Kemble Report, February 22, 1876, Ct. Cl. H-211, 2496, Ziibiwing Center.

8. Acting Commissioner Brown to C. L. Webber, February 16, 1880, NARG 75.5, Records of COIA, LS.

9. Grant's two terms as president were filled with corruption to such an extent that historians argue that his efforts actually weakened the powers of the presidency itself. Robert A. Divine et al., *America: Past and Present,* 7th ed., 2 vols. (New York: Pearson/Longman, 2005), 2:470.

10. S. D. Coon to Price, August 1, 1881, NARG 75, LR, Central Files, 1881, #13,486; Price to Coon, September 1, 1881, NARG 75.7, Records of the Land Division, LS, Letter Book 85, 314–16.

11. See the GLO Records, US Department of the Interior, Bureau of Land Management, https://glorecords.blm.gov/default.aspx.

12. See John R. Robinson to Lee, August 9, 1881, and Lee to COIA, August 11, 1881, NARG 75, LR, Central Files, 1881, #14311.

13. Chief Noge-che-qaw-me to COIA, June 16, 1881; John R. Robinson to George Lee, August 9, 1881, Petition of Saginaw Chiefs, April 20, 1881, Petition of Saginaw Chiefs, January 20, 1882, and Edward P. Allen to COIA, September 5, 1882, all NARG 75, LR, Central Files, 1881, #10,511, #14,311, #7,600, and 1882, #1,511 and #16,360.

14. Lee to COIA, January 20, 1882; and Allen to Price, April 5 and May 14, 1883, NARG 75, LR, Central Files, 1881, #1511, and 1883, #6454 and #8938; and Price to Lee, June 6, 1882, NARG 75.7, Land Division, LS, 1882,

Letter Book 97, 139–46. A second possible reason for Lee's removal was the fact that Brown and Leaton, one of the largest timber dealers in Mt. Pleasant, purchased the downed timber at an auction in Reed City. See Commissioner of GLO Sparks to Atkins, October 8, 1887, NARG 75, LR, Central Files, 1887, #26,772.

15. Allen to Price, October 4, 1883, NARG 75, LR, Central Files, 1883, #18,485.

16. Tinker to COIA, January 30, 1883, NARG 75, LR, Central Files, 1883, #2240.

17. Allen to Price, October 4, 1883, NARG 75, LR, Central Files, 1883, #2240.

18. Price to Allen, May 21, 1884, NARG 75.7, Land Division, LS, Letter Book 125, 476–81.

19. Assistant commissioner GLO to COIA, March 9, 1885; Allen to Commissioner D. C. Atkins, September 25 and October 13, 1885; and Assistant Commissioner GLO to Commissioner Atkins, December 26, 1885, all NARG 75, LR, Central Files, 1885, #5042, #22,687, #24,366 and 1886, #279; COIA to Secretary of Interior, November 17, 1885; and Atkins to Stevens, February 4, 1886, NARG 75.7, Land Division, LS, Letter Book 142, 60–61, and LB 144, 282–83.

20. The certificates for these allotments are in the National Archives. An actual count produces the number 152 in total, for 6,080 acres. The two extra allotments cannot be explained. See Allen report, October 27, 1885, enclosing schedules, NARG 75, LR, Central Files, 1885, #25,463.

21. Commissioner Atkins to Mark W. Stevens, January 14, 1886, NARG 75.7, Land Division, Letter Book 145.

22. Saginaw Chippewa to president, April 6, 1883, NARG 75, LR, Central Files, Box 18 #7600.

23. Secretary of Interior Samuel Kirkwood to COIA, April 18, 1881, NARG 75, LR, Central Files, 1881, #6460.

24. There would later be some question as to what happened to this money. The sale and the destination of the proceeds are recorded in Commissioner of GLO to COIA Atkins, September 5, 1885, NARG 75, LR, Central Files, 1885, #21,086.

25. H. Price to the Secretary of Interior, September 5 and 10, 1881, NARG 75.7, Land Division, LS, Letter Book 85, 390–92 and 439–41; Lee to H. Price, May 14, 1881; and Attorney General to Secretary of Interior, July 28, 1882, NARG 75, LR, Central Files, 1881, #8300 and 1882, #13,978.

26. A. J. Blackbird to COIA, September 23, 1885, NARG 75, LR, Central Files, 1886, #22,475.

27. A. J. Blackbird to COIA, September 23, 1885; and Commissioner of GLO William A. J. Sparks to Atkins, July 2, 1886, NARG 75, LR, Central Files, 1886, #22,475 and #17,295; Commissioner Atkins to Secretary of Inte-

rior, April 16, 1886; and Acting COIA to Stevens, June 7, 1886, NARG 75.7, Land Division, LS, Letter Books 147, no page, and 149, 82.

28. Stevens to COIA, July 14, 1886, NARG 75, LR, Central Files, 1886, #18,819.

29. Stevens to COIA, July 14, 1886.

30. Stevens to COIA, July 14, 1886. See also Attorney General A. H. Garland to Secretary of Interior, June 24, 1886, NARG 75, LR, Central Files, 1886 #16,678.

31. Stevens to Atkins, April 5, 1886, NARG 75, LR, Central Files, 1886, #9597 (SC030909). There was some competition between Stevens and Worden to see who could offer the most evidence.

32. The correspondence regarding these prosecutions is overwhelming. See, for example, Stevens to Atkins, March 17, 1887 (two letters same day), April 27, 1887; and Commissioner William Sparks to Acting COIA A. B. Upshaw, April 20, 1887, NARG 75, Central Files, #7229, #7230, #10,325, #10,982.

33. A. B. Francher and P. F. Dode to COIA, March 14, 1887, NARG 75, Central Files, Box 382, #7007.

34. COIA to the Commissioner of GLO, May 8, 1890, NARG 75, LS, Letter Book 198, p. 254.

35. COIA to Secretary of Interior, November 2, 1888, NARG 75.7, Land Division, LS, Letter Book 178.

36. Virtually all these entries into the plat book were dated September 11, 1888.

37. James Anderson to Secretary of Interior, (received) September 15, 1888, NARG 75, LR, Central Files, #1,888.

38. Petition of Mt. Pleasant Business Exchange, June 2, 1890, NARG 75, LR, Central Files, #17,067.

39. See telegraphs dated September 22 and 25, 1888, NARG 75.7, Land Division, LS, Letter Book 177.

40. Upshaw to Anderson, September 22, 1888, and Upshaw to W. H. Ward, October 9, 1888; COIA to C. W. Perry, October 12, 1888, and Acting COIA to J. H. Porterfield, May 27, 1889, NARG 75.7, Land Division, LS, Letter Book 177, pp. 292, 329, 471, and Letter Book 185, p. 109.

41. See the petition signed by nineteen Saginaw Chippewas, nine of whom signed their names rather than using an "x." (Received) September 13, 1890, NARG 75, LR, Central Files, #26,265.

42. See Acting COIA to Wallace McDonald, April 16, 1888; COIA to Henry Pego, December 21, 1889; COIA to Adelia W. McDonald, January 9 and April 25, 1890, NARG 75.7, Land Division, LS, Letter Book 172, p. 295, Letter Book 192, p. 407, Letter Book 193, p. 98, and Letter Book 197, p. 411; and petition of James Ogemos and others, December 22, 1890, NARG 75, LR, Central Files, #40513.

43. See Maxwell to COIA, June 5, 1890, NARG 75, LR, Central Files, #17,774; and COIA to Maxwell, July 16, 1890, NARG 75.7, Land Division, LS Letter Book 201, p. 341.

44. See COIA to Senator F. B. Stockbridge, July 23, 1890, and COIA to Congressman A. T. Bliss, August 5, 1890, NARG 75.7, Land Division, LS, Letter Book 202, pp. 23, 31; and COIA to E. B. Reynolds, January 23, 1891, NARG 75.7, Land Division, LS, Box 204, pp. 253–60.

45. Reynolds to COIA, February 10 and 18, 1891, and July 1, 1891, NARG 75, LR, Central Files, #5820, #7132, and #23,734.

46. Acting COIA to C. Bennett, June 3, 1891, NARG 75.5, Records of COIA, LS.

47. Stevens to Reynolds, February 17, 1891, and Gruett to Reynolds, November 2, 1891, NARG 75, LR, Central Files, #7, and #50,960. See also Reynolds to COIA, April 28, 1892, ibid., #15,751.

48. Reynolds to COIA, November 7, 1891, NARG 75, LR, Central Files, #40,960; "Isabella Indian Reservation, Selection List," March 26, 1890, ibid., #12,245.

49. Two different lists of this final allotment have survived, one dated December 19, 1891, found in NARG 75, LR, Central Files, and another in the Clarke Historical Library, Central Michigan University.

50. See petition signed by nineteen Saginaw Chippewas, no date (answered September 13, 1890); William Gunn to M. K. Wright, March 22, 1890; petition of James Ogemos and six others, December 22, 1890; and John S. Charrow to Indian Department, March 11, 1891, NARG 75, LR, Central Files, 1890, #13,188, #26,265, and #40513, and 1891, #9656.

51. Sanford to the Secretary of Interior, January 21, 1892; and Mogg to COIA, September 15, 1892, NARG 75, LR, Central Files, #4,845, and Box 910, #34,890; see also Secretary of Interior Morgan to Mrs. F. Helen Tonkin, March 12, 1892, NARG 75, LS, Letter Book 232, pp. 490–91.

52. Acting Secretary of Interior to COIA, October 9, 1893, NARG 75, LR, Central Files, #37,795.

53. See Acting COIA to E. E. Riopel, April 12, 1892, NARG 75, LS, Letter Book 256.

54. See Loretta Fowler, *Arapahoe Politics, 1851–1978* (Lincoln: University of Nebraska Press, 1982), 102–3.

55. For a discussion regarding the age factor and chiefs, see Acting COIA to Indian Superintendent E. E. Riopel, April 21, 1898, NARG 75.7, Land Division, LS, Box 256, 214.

56. James and Sarah Williams to COIA, April 9, 1896, NARG 75, LR, Box 1303, #13,878; and Elk to COIA, June 14, 1900, ibid., #24,536; acting COIA to Daniel Elk, June 4, 1900, NARG 75, LS, Letter Book 442, pp. 99–100.

57. Chief Phillip Gruett (Identified as "Secretary") to COIA, July 16, 1895, NARG 75, LR, Land, Box 1220, #29,905.

58. The "canceled" patent debate is found in Gruett to Department of Interior, July 16, 1895, and to Assistant Commissioner GLO, October 7, 1895, NARG 75, LR, Central Files, #29,905 and #96,318; COIA to commissioner of GLO, September 18, 1895, LS, Letter Book 314, p. 31.

59. COIA to F. H. Dodds, September 5, 1894, NARG 75, LS, Letter Book 287, pp. 381–83.

60. Reynolds to COIA, April 28, 1892, NARG 75, LR, Central Files, #15,751.

61. James A. Cooper to COIA, September 13, 1893, NARG 75, LR, Central Files, #34,934.

62. The issue came up in Wells, Stone & Co. to COIA, December 19, 1893, NARG 75, LR, #47182. See also the answer, COIA to Wells, Stone and Co., December 28, 1893, NARG 75, LS, Letter Book 271, pp. 21–22.

63. Petition of Saginaw Chippewas, signed by twenty-two leaders, June 4, 1869, NARG 75.19.60, LR, Michigan Agency.

64. See Smith report (August 28, 1867 [misdated as 1861]), in *Annual Report of the Commissioner of Indian Affairs*, House Exec. Doc. no. 1, 40th Cong., 2nd sess. (Washington, DC: GPO, 1867), 335–40, 338.

65. Just who acquired the lands was determined in a report filed by Special Agent E. J. Brooks. I. E. Arnold acquired some 250 selections (under the Betts regime), Jerome and Williams had 855 deeds, which included some 30,000 acres (acquired mostly during Long's tenure), and James C. Leaton had title to over 100 selections. Brooks report, January 18, 1878, NARG 75.19.60, LR, Michigan Agency.

66. Hayt report, in *Annual Report of the Commissioner of Indian Affairs* (Washington, DC: GPO, 1878).

67. George Lee to COIA, July 9, 1878, NARG 75.19.60, LR, Michigan Agency.

68. See Leach to the COIA, February 21, 1865; Smith to the COIA, May 1 and June 18, 1867, NARG 75.19.60, LR, Michigan Agency.

69. See petition signed by twenty-two Saginaw Chippewas, June 4, 1869, NARG 75.19.60, LR, Michigan Agency.

70. Petition dated May 28, 1875, NARG 75.19.60, LR, Michigan Agency.

71. Petition signed by thirty-nine Saginaw Chippewas, August 2, 1875, NARG 75.19.60, LR, Michigan Agency.

72. Powers compiled a list of several dozen Saginaw men who served in the Civil War and returned to the reservation.

73. See petitions of April 20, 1881, and June 16, 1881, NARG 75, LR, Central Files, #7,600 and #10,511; and Allen to COIA, September 5, 1882, ibid., #15,360.

74. Lee to the COIA, May 14, 1881, and Council Proceedings, January 20, 1882, NARG 75, LR, Central Files, #1511.

75. Allen to COIA, October 4, 1883, May 12, 1884, and October 13, 1885, NARG 75, LR, Central Files, #18,485, #9326, and #24,366. See also Assistant Commissioner of GLO to COIA, March 9, 1885, ibid., #5042.

76. Secretary of Interior L. L. C. Lamar to COIA, November 13, 1885, NARG 75, LR, Central Files, #27033.

77. See COIA to Secretary of Interior, January 24, 1898, NARG 75.7, Land Division, LS, Box 162.

78. COIA to Secretary of Interior, February 5, 1896, NARG 75.7, Land Division, LS, Box 162, #324.

79. COIA to Secretary of Interior, November 22, 1893, NARG 75, LS, Letter Book 269, pp. 22–30.

80. On the Indian School superintendent, see Acting COIA to Andrew Spencer, May 4, 1896, NARG 75, LS, Box 166, #332.

81. As late as 1903, a Saginaw Indian was denied a patent because one had been issued in 1872 for the same land. See Secretary of Interior to COIA, October 22, 1903, NARG 75.7, Land Division, LS, #68,373.

82. COIA to Secretary of Interior, November 22, 1893, NARG 75, LS, Letter Book 269, pp. 22–30.

83. See George Manypenny, *Our Indian Wards* (1880; reprinted New York: Da Capo, 1972).

CHAPTER 5

1. "Report of the Commissioner of Indian Affairs, 1889," in "Report of the Secretary of the Interior," House Exec. Doc. no. 1, Part 5, 51st Cong., 1st Sess., 502–3. Also see Charles E. Cleland, "Report of the Nineteenth-Century History," 54.

2. E. B. Reynolds to the COIA, March 12, 1891, LR, Office of Indian Affairs (hereafter OIA), 10020–1891; COIA to Adelia McDonald, April 25, 1890, LR, OIA, 11512-1890; Saginaw Chippewas to the COIA, June 12, 1890, LR, OIA, 18339-1890, all at Ziibiwing Center. Also see COIA to E. B. Reynolds, January 23, 1891, Records of the OIA, Land Division, Correspondence, Vol. 5, pp. 253–59, Ziibiwing Center.

3. E. A Hitchcock to COIA, October 24, 1900, NARG 75.5, Records of COIA, LR, 52802-1900. See also Edith Pingatore, "History of the Mt. Pleasant Indian School, 1893–1934." This manuscript can be found in the Clarke Historical Library, Central Michigan University, Mt. Pleasant. Hereafter cited as Pingatore, "History of the Mt. Pleasant Indian School."

4. COIA to E. B. Reynolds, January 23, 1891, Records of OIA, Land Division, Correspondence, vol. 105, pp. 253–59, Ziibiwing Center.

5. E. B. Reynolds to the COIA, March 12,1891, LR, OIA, 10020-1891, Ziibiwing Center.

6. E. B. Reynolds to the COIA, March 24, 1891, LR, OIA, 11503-1891, Ziibiwing Center.

7. James A. Cooper to the COIA, September 13, 1893, NARG 75, Central File, LR, 34934, Box 1022. Also see acting secretary of interior to COIA, October 9, 1893, LR, OIA, 37795-1893, Ziibiwing Center.

8. D. M. Browning to the Secretary of Interior, April 20, 1894, LR, OIA, 10005-1891 (13020-1894); Browning to the Secretary of Interior, April 25, 1894, LR, OIA, 10005-1891 (14915-1894); C. C. Duncan to the Secretary of Interior, May 11, 1894, LR, OIA, 10005-1894 (1878–1894), all at Ziibiwing Center.

9. An excellent sketch of the Mt. Pleasant Indian School can be found in Pingatore, "History of the Mt. Pleasant Indian School." Also see "U.S. Indian School, Mt. Pleasant Michigan," an undated (although obviously written between 1921 and 1934) typescript distributed by school officials to the public. Copies of this manuscript are available in the Michigan State Library in Lansing and at the Clarke Historical Library in Mt. Pleasant.

10. E. B. Reynolds to the COIA, March 24, 1891, LR, OIA, 11503-1891, Ziibiwing Center.

11. R. A. Cochran to the GLO, March 14, 1905, NA-Chicago, RG 75.19.60, Mt. Pleasant Indian School and Agency, Press Copies of LS, Box 1, vol. 1, 132; acting COIA to Carlos A. Reading, February 25, 1908, CCF Mackinac 9620-08, 313, Ziibiwing Center; Joseph Cushway to superintendent of the Mt. Pleasant Indian School, June 22, 1912, NA, LR, OIA, 68080-1912; C. F. Hauke to R. A. Cochran, April 20, 1912, NARG 75.5, Records of COIA, Ziibwing Center.

12. F. H. Abbott to acting COIA, March 23, 1910, NARG 75.5, Records of COIA, LR, 27346-1910; R. A. Cochran to COIA, January 18, 1912, NA-Chicago, RG 75.19.60, CCF-Mt. Pleasant Indian School, Box 12, File 255; Rodney Graham to COIA, March 10, 1898, NARG 75.5, Records of COIA, LR, 11909-1898.

13. F. H. Abbott to acting COIA, March 23, 1910, NARG 75.5, Records of COIA, LR, 27346-1910; R. A. Cochran to COIA, January 18, 1912, NARG 75.5, Records of COIA, LR.

14. "Articles of Agreement . . . between Commissioners . . . and the Chippewa Indians of Saginaw," August 2, 1855, TTD, RIT_298, NAI_178354861.

15. E. B. Reynolds to the COIA, March 24, 1891, LR, OIA, 11503-1891, Ziibiwing Center.

16. C. Benet to the COIA, March 1, 1890, NA, LR, OIA, 8057-1890; David Elk to COIA, May 19, 1890, LR, OIA, 24536-1809; Chippewa chiefs to the secretary of interior, November 10, 1890, LR, OIA, 10005-1891; Charley

Yock to Department of Interior, June 14, 1892, LR, OIA, 22300-1892, all at Ziibiwing Center.

17. E. B. Reynolds to COIA, March 24, 1891, LR, OIA, 11503-1891, Ziibiwing Center.

18. Elijah Cuptawquoodt to COIA, March 23, 1896, NA, LR, OIA, 11246-1896; Rodney Graham to COIA, March 10, 1898, NA, LR, OIA, 11909-1898, both at Ziibiwing Center.

19. Jacob Shawboose to COIA, December 19, 1906, LR, OIA, 111666-1906; acting COIA to Jacob Shawboose, January 12, 1907, NARG 75.5, LS, OIA (6157), both at Ziibiwing Center.

20. Jacob Shawboose to COIA, December 19, 1906, LR, OIA, 111666-1906, Ziibiwing Center.

21. Joseph Bradley to Cato Sells, March 11, 1914, NA, LR, OIA, 26942-1914, Ziibiwing Center.

22. *Isabella County Enterprise*, October 22, 1915; October 29, 1915; November 5, 1915, Ziibiwing Center.

23. C. F. Hauke to R. A. Cochran, April 30, 1917, NARG 75.5, Records of COIA, Correspondence, 1918–1926, Box 2, C62, Heirship Cases, 4-VR-26; William Zimmerman to Elijah Elk, July 9, 1925, NARG 75.5, Records of COIA, Correspondence, CCF Mackinac, 48656-1932-115.

24. In the Court of Claims, *Saginaw, Swan Creek and Black River Band of Chippewa Indians vs the United States*, H-211, Amended Petition, CCF, Mackinac, 33812-1924 (August 2, 1927), Ziibiwing Center; John Collier to Adam N. Smith, May 13, 1933, NARG 75, Records of COIA, Correspondence, L-C, 20377-33, WMW. Also see Alan S. Newell, "An Overview of Federal Relations with the Saginaw, Swan Creek, and Black River Bands of Chippewa of the Isabella Indian Reservation, Michigan, 1910–1934" (Missoula, MT: Historical Research Associates, Inc., 1992), 16–18. This report was prepared for the Environment and Natural Resources Division, Indian Resources Section—Department of Justice.

25. Minutes of a Chippewa Council Meeting held at Mt. Pleasant. Michigan, May 28, 1930, NA, LR, OIA, 29350; John Jackson to the COIA, June 2, 1930, CCF-Mt. Pleasant, 18430-1930: 121, enclosure, Ziibiwing Center; L. E. Baumgarten to COIA, June 16, 1930, NARG 75.5, Records of COIA, Correspondence, A-I, 29637-30, all at Ziibiwing Center.

26. C. F. Hauke to R. A. Cochran, January 16, 1917, NARG 75.5, Records of COIA, Correspondence, CF-6204; L. E. Baumgarten to COIA, March 13, 1929, 68089-1912; R. A. Cochran to COIA, August 27, 1915, NARG 75.5, Records of COIA, LR, 9870-1915; NA-Chicago, RG 75.19.60, Mt. Pleasant Indian School and Agency, Decimal Correspondence Files, 1926-46, Box 3, 005.

27. R. A. Cochran to COIA, February 11, 1921, NARG 75.5, Records of COIA, LR, File C-50, Ed-L & O, 98005-20, CVP.

28. R. A Cochran to COIA, January 26, 1916, NARG 75.5, Records of COIA, LR, 1798-16, 9185.

29. R. A. Cochran to COIA, July 7, 1916, NARG 75.5, Records of COIA, LR, 74175-1916.

30. C. F. Hauke to R. A. Cochran. April 30, 1917, NA-Chicago, RG 75.19.60, Mt. Pleasant Indian School and Agency, Correspondence with OIA, 1918–1926, Box 2, C62, Heirship Cases, 5-1100; R. A. Cochran to COIA, June 23, 1917, ibid.; E. B. Meritt to R. A. Cochran, July 6, 1917, ibid., Probate 61604-1917, LL.

31. M. E. Gorman to R. A. Cochran, November 1, 1923, NA-Chicago, RG 75.19.60, Mt. Pleasant Indian School and Agency, Correspondence with OIA, 1918–26, Box 2, C63; R. A Cochran to M. E. Gorman, November 5, 1923, ibid.; M. E. Gorman to R. A. Cochran, December 20, 1923, ibid.

32. L. E. Baumgarten to COIA, March 13, 1929, NA-Chicago, RG 75.19.60, Mt. Pleasant Indian School and Agency, Decimal Correspondence Files, 1926–1946, Box 3, 005; acting COIA to Payton Carter, August 25, 1932, NA-Chicago, RG 75.19.60, Correspondence of OIA, Mt. Pleasant, Indian School and Agency, File No. 310, Box 15.

33. L. E. Baumgarten to James Po-maw-mee, June 15, 1928, Correspondence of OIA, CCF Mackinac, 28778-1928, 115; L. E. Baumgarten to COIA, December 4, 1928, CCF Mackinac, 54218-1928, 115; L. E. Baumgarten to COIA, December 13, 1928, NA-Chicago, RG 75.19.60, Mt. Pleasant Indian School and Agency, Decimal Correspondence Files, 1926–46, Box 2, 005; L. E. Baumgarten to COIA, June 28, 1929, NARG 75.5, Records of COIA, LR, 83228. Also see Newell, "An Overview of Federal Relations," 18.

34. L. E. Baumgarten to COIA, June 16, 1930, NARG 75.5, Records of COIA, Correspondence, A-I, 29637-30.

35. L. E. Baumgarten to COIA, July 25, 1929, NA-Chicago, RG 75.19.60, Mt. Pleasant Indian School and Agency, Decimal Correspondence Files, 1926–46, Box 3, 005; L. E. Baumgarten to COIA, June 2, 1930, ibid., Box 4, 005.

36. J. Franklin House to COIA, May 15, 1902, NA, LR, OIA, 29495-1902, Ziibiwing Center.

37. E. Reed to COIA, June 10, 1908, NA, LR, OIA, File 150, 30447, Ziibiwing Center.

38. F. H. Abbott to the Assistant COIA, March 23, 1910, NA, LR, OIA, 27346, Ziibiwing Center.

39. Multiple examples are offered in this text and in the notes below.

40. R. A. Cochran to COIA, August 27, 1915, NA, LR, OIA, 870; C. F. Hauke to Elijah Elk, October 12, 1915, NARG 75.5, Records of COIA, LS, CEF, 10-JW-11; Joseph Bradley to COIA, March 13, 1916, LR, 28372-1916.

41. R. A Cochran to COIA, January 26, 1916, NARG 75.5, Records of COIA, 1798–1916, 9185; R. A. Cochran to S. Y. Tutwiler, April 18, 1915, NARG 75.7, Land Division, Land Rules and Regulations File.

42. R. A. Cochran to COIA, February 11, 1921, NARG 75.5, LR, 12814, Ed-L & O, 98005-20, CVP.

43. R. A. Cochran to M. E. Gorman, July 19, 1923, NA-Chicago, RG 75.19.60, Mt. Pleasant Indian School and Agency, Correspondence with OIA, 1916–26, Box 2, C62, Heirship Cases.

44. Assistant COIA to George H. Carpenter, n.d. (1920), NA-Chicago, RG 75.19.60, Mt. Pleasant Indian School and Agency, Correspondence with the OIA, 1916–26, Box 2, C58, 3. Although this letter is undated, it was written in reply to a letter from Carpenter dated January 2, 1920.

45. E. B. Meritt to Joseph Bradley, February 18, 1921, NARG 75.5, Records of COIA, Correspondence, 78083-16; C. F. Hauke to Clarence E. Hildreth, March 18, 1921, NARG 75.15.5, CCF-Mackinac, Land-Allot., 14849-1921, p. 313; C. F. Hauke to Poh-tah-Sunk, May 6, 1926, NARG 75.5, Records of COIA, Correspondence, 4-abm-30.

46. O. Padgett to COIA, November 19, 1924, NARG 75.5, Records of COIA, LR, 85074.

47. L. E. Baumgarten to COIA, March 21, 1929, NA-Chicago, RG 75.19.60, Mt. Pleasant Indian School and Agency, Decimal Correspondence Files, 1926–46, Box 3, 005 (Cir. 2558); Charles Burke to L. E. Baumgarten, May 15, 1929, NARG 75.5, Records of COIA, LR, 12962-1929.

48. Ramona Village Pueblos to Superintendent of Mt. Pleasant Indian School, December 7, 1929, NA-Chicago, RG 75.19.60, Mt. Pleasant Indian School and Agency, Decimal Correspondence Files, 1926–1946, Box 1, 003; L. E. Baumgarten to Ramona Village Pueblos, December 16, 1929, ibid.

49. L. E. Baumgarten to Miss Ethel Frank, February 1, 1930, NA-Chicago, Mt. Pleasant Indian School and Agency, Decimal Correspondence Files, 1926–1946, Box 4, 005.

50. Frank Christy to COIA, October 30, 1933, NA-Chicago, RG 75.19.60, Mt. Pleasant Indian School and Agency, Decimal Correspondence Files, 1926–1946, File 051; Frank Christy to A. C. Cooley, December 6, 1932, ibid., Box 7, 005, both at Ziibiwing Center.

51. R. A. Cochran to the GLO, March 14, 1905, NA-Chicago, RG 75.19.60, Mt. Pleasant Indian School and Agency, Press Copies of Miscellaneous Letters Sent, 1904–10, Box 1, vol. 1:132; R. A. Cochran to John W. Dunn, July 16, 1908, ibid., Box 2, vol. 1.

52. Charles McNichols to COIA, December 13, 1905, NARG 75.5, Records of COIA, LR, 100622-1905, Ziibiwing Center.

53. Acting COIA to Jacob Sawboose, January 12, 1907, NARG 75.5, Records of COIA, LS, 6157.

54. Acting COIA to the Hon. J. W. Fordney, 1909, House of Representatives, NARG 75.5, Records of COIA, LS, 9144-1909.

55. *Annual Report[s] of the Commissioner of Indian Affairs* (Washington, DC: GPO): (1909), 129; (1911), 81; (1912), 100; (1913), 88.

56. F. H. Abbott to the Director of the Geological Survey, November 13, 1912, NA, OIA, Land Sales, 68089-1912; C. F. Hauke to Director of the Geological Survey, July 31, 1912, ibid.; Acting Director of the US Geological Survey to COIA, December 12, 1912, NA, LR, OIA, 1912; R. A. Cochran to COIA, January 18, 1912, NARG 75.5, Records of COIA, LR, 5957-1912; R. A. Cochran to COIA, February 13, 1912, ibid., 15037-1912; C. F. Hauke to R. A. Cochran, February 21, 1912, NARG 75.5, Records of COIA, LS, Education Supplies, 5957-1912.

57. C. F. Hauke to R. A. Cochran, August 24, 1915, NARG 75.5, Records of COIA, LS, 8-CBH-21; C. F. Hauke to the GLO, September 4, 1915, ibid., 9-WG-2.

58. *Annual Report[s] of the Commissioner of Indian Affairs* (Washington, DC: GPO): (1917), 91; (1918), 101, 107; (1920), 83, 89.

59. Edward Clements to COIA, February 16, 1921, NARG, 75.5, Records of COIA, LR, 15015, Ed-L & O, 98005-20.

60. Inspection Report by Washington I. Endicott, November 29, 1920, NARG 75.5, Records of COIA, LR, 98005-1920.

61. E. B. Meritt to Edward Clements, February 4, 1921, NARG 75.5, Records of COIA, LS, Ed-L & O, 98005-20. A copy of this letter also was sent to R. A. Cochran.

62. L. E. Baumgarten to COIA, March 13, 1929, NA-Chicago, RG 75.19.60, Mt. Pleasant Indian School and Agency, Decimal Correspondence Files, 1926–46, Box 3, 005.

63. L. E. Baumgarten to Elliott Collins, March 29, 1929, NA-Chicago, RG 75.19.60, Mt. Pleasant Indian School and Agency, Decimal Correspondence Files, 1926–46, Box 3, 005; Baumgarten to COIA, July 25, 1929, ibid.; Baumgarten to COIA, August 8, 1930, ibid., Box 4, 005.

64. "Annual Statistical Report, 1931," enclosure in L. E. Baumgarten to COIA, September 24, 1931, NARG 75.19.40, Great Lakes Region, Mt. Pleasant Indian School and Agency, Decimal Correspondence, 1926–1946, File 051.0 (selected documents), Ziibiwing Center.

65. Charles Burke to the Secretary of the Interior, April 4, 1929, NARG 75.5, Records of COIA, LS, 1929; C. J. Rhoads to Kenneth B. Montiegel, July 17, 1930, ibid., 7-MS-15; C. J. Rhoads to Elliott Collins, August 19, 1930, ibid., SWL-15; C. J. Rhoads to Elijah Elk, October 15, 1931, ibid., 10-EMB-9; Commissioner of GLO to Secretary of Interior, March 25, 1929, NARG 75.5, Records of COIA, LR, 1929, 3–15-MVD; Assistant Commissioner of GLO to Poh-Fah-Sunk, June 5, 1929, ibid., 29181-1929.

66. C. J. Rhoads to Edward R. Boyles, November 7, 1932, NA, CCF Mackinac, 48656-1932, 115, Ziibiwing Center.

67. Wells Stone to COIA, November 27, 1893, NARG 75.15.5, LR, Central File, Box 1042, 44312; Wells Stone to COIA, December 19, 1893, ibid., 47182; C. Bennet to COIA, March 1, 1893, ibid., Central File, 8057-1993; John Maxwell to the Secretary of Interior, March 26, 1890, NARG 75.5, LR, 9879-1890, Ziibiwing Center.

68. T. McNamarra to COIA, June 2, 1890, NARG 75.5, LR, OIA, 17067-1890.

69. I. A. Fancher, C. Bennet, and J. W. Harnes to the Hon. F. B. Stockbridge, June 6, 1890, NARG 75.5, Central File, LR, Box 642, 21, 923.

70. *Isabella County Enterprise*, September 16, 1892; March 10, 1899; April 2, 1905; October 22, 1915, at Ziibiwing Center.

71. "U.S. Indian School, Mt. Pleasant Michigan" (1925?), Michigan State Library #13 (3 0000 006 127 819), Clarke Library, Central Michigan University, Mt. Pleasant.

72. Edward Gruett to the Commissioner of GLO, May 14, 1890, LR, 16169-1890; Joseph Bradley to the Secretary of Interior and COIA, November 10, 1890, 10005-1891, both at Ziibiwing Center.

73. Petition by the Chippewas, April 8, 1890, NARG, 75.5, Records of COIA, LR, 12679-1891; Charley I. Yock to the Department of the Interior, June 14, 1892, ibid., 22300-1892, both at Ziibiwing Center.

74. Elijah Cup-taw-Quootd to COIA, March 23, 1896, NARG 75.5, LR, 11246-1896; Joseph Bradley to Secretary of Interior, April 3, 1894, NARG 75.5, LR, 1894, both at Ziibiwing Center.

75. Daniel Elk to COIA, May 19, 1900, NARG 75.5, LR, 24536-1900; Jacob Shawboose to COIA, December 19, 1906, NARG 75.5, LR, 111666-1906, Ziibiwing Center.

76. Joseph Bradley to Cato Sells, March 11, 1914, NARG 75.5, LR, 26942-1914.

77. Elijah Elk to COIA, November 8, 1915, NARG 75.5, LR, 120744-1915; Joseph Bradley to COIA, March 13, 1916, ibid., 28372-1916.

78. Pot-Tar-Sung to COIA, December 29, 1921, NARG 75.5, LR, 263-1922.

79. Anna Norman to Department of Interior, April 4, 1932, NARG 75.5, LR, 18540-1932.

80. "Minutes of Chippewa Council Held at Mt. Pleasant Michigan, May 28, 1930," enclosure in L. E. Baumgarten to COIA, June 16, 1930, NARG 75.5, Records of COIA, LR, 32069-1930.

81. E. B. Meritt to Edward Clements, February 4, 1921, NA-Chicago, RG 75.19.60, Mt. Pleasant Indian School and Agency, Correspondence, 1918–26, Box 2, C50, Land Allotments. A copy of this letter was sent to R. A. Cochran.

82. C. J. Boyles to Edward Boyles, November 7, 1932, NARG 75.15.5, CCF Mackinac, 48656-1932, 115.

CHAPTER 6

1. Kenneth R. Philp, "John Collier, 1933–45," in Kvasnicka and Viola, *Commissioners of Indian Affairs*, 273; House Doc., "Transfer of Property of the Mt. Pleasant Indian School to the State of Michigan for Institutional Purposes," Report No. 562, 73rd Cong., 2nd Sess., 1–2; An Act Granting Certain Property to the State of Michigan for Institutional Purposes, Statutes at Large, 48, 353 (1934).

2. Frank Christy to COIA, January 23, 1935, NA-Chicago, RG 75.19.60, Mt. Pleasant Indian School, Decimal Correspondence Files, 1926–46, Box 36, p. 364.

3. R. David Edmunds, Frederick E. Hoxie, and Neal Salisbury, *The People: A History of Native America* (Boston: Houghton, Mifflin, 2007), 379–82.

4. Elmer Simonds to Jere Charlow, January 23, 1935, NA-Chicago, RG 75.19.60, Mt. Pleasant Indian School and Agency, Decimal Correspondence Files, 1926–46, Box 36, 364; Frank Christy to COIA, January 23, 1935, ibid.; "The Constitution of the Saginaw, Swan Creek and Black River Bands of Chippewa Indians of the State of Michigan," enclosed in a letter from Elijah Elk to Frank Christy, January 1935, ibid.

5. Jere Charlow to Elijah Elk, March 6, 1935, NA-Chicago, RG 75.19.60, Mt. Pleasant Indian School and Agency, Decimal Correspondence Files, 1926–46, Box 36, 364; William Zimmerman to the Secretary of the Interior, February 24, 1937, NARG 75.5, LS, Ind-Org., 9609-A-1937.

6. William Zimmerman to the Chairman of the Constitutional Committee of the Saginaw Chippewa Indians, July 31, 1936, NARG 75.5, CCF 9069-A-1936, Tomah 068, Ziibiwing Center.

7. Zimmerman to the Chairman of the Constitutional Committee.

8. Zimmerman to the Chairman of the Constitutional Committee.

9. Jere Charlow to A. B. Daniels, August 21, 1936, NARG 75.15.5, Records of the Michigan Superintendency and the Mackinac Agency, Sault Tribal Operations Office, Saginaw Chippewa Box, File 076—Michigan Saginaw Constitution and Bylaws, Ziibiwing Center; Zimmerman to Chairman, Constitutional Committee, Saginaw Chippewa Indians, ibid.

10. Zimmerman to the Secretary of Interior, April 26, 1937, NA, CCF-Tomah, 1936:068, File 9606-A, Ziibiwing Center; *Constitution and Bylaws of the Saginaw Chippewa Indian Tribe of Michigan* (Washington, DC: GPO, 1937). A copy of the constitution can be found in the NA, CCF-Tomah, 1936:068, File 9609-A, Ziibiwing Center.

11. "Petition for Incorporation," enclosed in Peru Farver to COIA, June 17, 1937, NARG 75.5, LR, 39742-1937; "Certification by Elijah Elk, Elmer Simonds, and Peru Farver," August 28, 1937, NA, CCF-Tomah, 9609-b-1936.06, (August 13, 1937), Ziibiwing Center; *Corporate Charter of the Saginaw*

Chippewa Indian Tribe of the Isabella Reservation of Michigan (Washington, DC: GPO, 1938); Zimmerman to the Secretary of Interior, October 21, 1937, NA, CCF-Tomah, 9606-B-1936.06, Ziibiwing Center.

12. Shirley N. McKinsey and D. D. Mani, "An Economic Survey of the Saginaw Chippewa Indians of Michigan, 1938," 14–15. This report was prepared for the BIA in 1938 by two economists. A copy can be found in the NARG 75.19.116, Tomah Agency file.

13. McKinsey and Mani, "Economic Survey of the Saginaw Chippewa Indians," 35–43.

14. McKinsey and Mani, "Economic Survey of the Saginaw Chippewa Indians,", 44–45. Also see "Johnson-O'Malley Act of 1934," in *The ABC-CILO Companion to the Native American Rights Movement*, by Mark Grossman (Santa Barbara, CA: ABC-CLIO Inc., 1996), 192.

15. McKinsey and Mani, "Economic Survey of the Saginaw Chippewa Indians," 37–38; John Holst, "A Survey of Indian Groups in the State of Michigan, 1939." Holst, Supervisor of Indian Schools, prepared this second (1939) survey, which was "distributed to the Division Heads in the Indian Office and to administrative officers in the Fields affected." A copy can be found in the NA-Chicago, RG 75.19.60, Mt. Pleasant Indian School and Agency records. Also see Vernon J. Brown to Jere Charlow, January 24, 1940, NA-Chicago, RG 75.19.60, Mt. Pleasant Indian School and Agency, Decimal Correspondence Files, 1926–46, Box 34, 302; Frank Christy to Indians of Tomah Jurisdiction, September 1, 1936, ibid.

16. Holst, "Survey of Indian Groups," 9, 17.

17. "Chippewa Indians Aim High in New Program of Living," *Saginaw News,* (1939). A copy of this newspaper clipping can be found in the NARG 75.15.5, Sault, Tribal Operations Office, Saginaw Chippewa Box, Saginaw Chippewa General File, 1939, and in the Ziibiwing Center. "Minutes of Tribal Council Meeting, April 1, 1940," NA, CCF-Tomah, 9609E, 1936.054, Ziibiwing Center; "Minutes of Tribal Council Meeting, March 4, 1941," ibid.

18. R. E. Miller to D. E. Murphy, June 3, 1948, NARG 75.16.7, LR, Minneapolis, CCF File, 8849-1948, Ziibiwing Center; William Warne to Willis Jackson, July 18, 1949, NARG 75.17.1, Records of the Great Lakes Consolidated Agency, LR, 1949; Hans Walker to Elford C. Cederberg, July 14, 1977, NARG 75.16.7, LR, Minneapolis Office, 1977.

19. Edmunds, Hoxie, and Salisbury, *The People,* 406–15.

20. R. E. Miller to Willis Jackson, January 21, 1948, NARG 75.19.116, Records of the Tomah Agency, Correspondence, LS, 949916.

21. William E. Warne to Willis Jackson, July 18, 1949, NARG 75.17.1, Great Lakes Consolidated Agency, LR, 1949.

22. Lucy Pelcher to William Gilbert, April 29, 1950, NA, EBS—Saginaw, 1950, Ziibiwing Center.

23. "Report with Respect to the House Resolution Authorizing the Committee on Interior and Insular Affairs to Conduct an Investigation of the Bureau of Indian Affairs Pursuant to House Resolution 89," House Report no. 2680, 83rd Cong., 2nd Sess., September 20, 1954, pp. 56–57, 342–43. Surplus lands were plowed, planted with crops, the crops harvested, and the money from the sale went into the tribal treasury (172).

24. House Report 2680, September 20, 1954. Also see "Report with Respect to the House Resolution Authorizing the Committee on Interior and Insular Affairs to Conduct an Investigation of the Bureau of Indian Affairs Pursuant to House Resolution 698 (82nd Cong.)," House Report no. 2503, 82nd Cong., 2nd Sess., December 15, 1952; R. E. Miller to D. E. Murphy, June 3, 1948, NARG 75.16.7, Minneapolis Area Office, LR, Central File, 8849-1948, Ziibiwing Center.

25. Edmunds, Hoxie, and Salisbury, *The People*, 406–16.

26. "Tribal Secretary Gives Picture of Present Indian Conditions," newspaper clipping, August 5, 1964, in Clarke Historical Library, Central Michigan University, Mt. Pleasant. Although the name of this newspaper is unknown, it is dated August 5, 1964. Also see Resolution by the Saginaw Chippewa Tribal Corporation, October 17, 1966, NA, BIA-Sault, Tribal Operations Office, Saginaw Chippewa Box, File 310, Real Property Management and Correspondence-Isabella Reservation; "Minutes of the Saginaw Chippewa General Council, April 10, 1967," NA, Sault, Tribal Operations Office, Saginaw Chippewa Ordinance Public Housing File, 064; "Minutes of a Meeting of the Michigan Commission on Indian Affairs, June 30, 1967," Michigan Commission Minutes, vol. 1, June 30, 1967–May 22, 1971, all at Ziibiwing Center.

27. Invitation to dedication of Saginaw Chippewa Housing Authority HUD Project, August 14, 1976, NA, Sault, Tribal Operations Office, Saginaw Chippewa Box, Saginaw Chippewa Tribal Operations File, Ziibiwing Center.

28. "Minutes of the Saginaw Chippewa General Council, May 6, 1963," NA, Sault, Saginaw Chippewa Tribe, Tribal Council Minutes File; "Minutes of a Meeting of the Michigan Commission on Indian Affairs, June 30, 1967," vol. 1, June 30, 1967–May 22, 1971. See also meeting minutes of February 27, 1971, all at Ziibiwing Center.

29. William G. Demmert, "Indian Education Act, 1972," in Mary B. Davis, *Native America in the Twentieth Century* (New York: Garland, 1996), 255–56; Prucha, *Great Father*, 2:1157–62; "Minutes of the Regular Meeting of the Saginaw Chippewa Tribal Council, January 6, 1975," NA, -Sault, Tribal Operations, Saginaw Chippewa Box, File 064; "Minutes—Special Meeting of the Saginaw Chippewa Tribal Council, July 7, 1975"; see also the minutes for the special meetings of the tribal council on January 9 and July 7, 1975, all at Ziibiwing Center.

30. "Minutes of the Regular Meeting of the Saginaw Chippewa Tribal Council, January 6, 1975," NA, Sault, Tribal Operations, Saginaw Chippewa Box, File 064, Ziibiwing Center; Memorandum by Elmer Nitzsche, May 3, 1978, NARG 75, LR, Office of the Field Solicitor, Twin Cities, Minnesota, 1978—27/30.

31. Elford Cederberg to Ralph Reeser, March 15, 1977, NARG 75.5, LR, MC-14-77, 7109.

32. Hans Walker to Elford Cederberg, July 14, 1977, NARG 75.16.7, Office of the Field Solicitor, Minneapolis, LR, 8647-5 (NB), 8675-6a.

33. Walker to Cederberg, July 14, 1977.

34. *United States vs James Arthur Manier*, Criminal No. 77-20066, US District Court, Eastern District of Michigan, Northern Division (1977).

35. Memorandum by the Field Solicitor, Twin Cities, Minnesota, July 25, 1977, NARG 75.16.7, Office of the Field Solicitor, Minneapolis, LR, 8647-5 (NB), 8675-6a.

36. Memorandum by the Field Solicitor, Twin Cities, Minneapolis, July 25, 1977

37. Memorandum by the Field Solicitor, Twin Cities, Minneapolis, July 25, 1977.

38. Michael Fairbanks to Peter Jensen, November 2, 1978, NARG 75.19.60, Michigan Agency, LS, 1978, 025/030; H. D. Bidlack to Elford Cederberg, January 23, 1978, NARG 75.14.18, Division of Tribal Government Services, LR, 1978-732.

39. Theodore Krenzke to Donald Riegle, March 8, 1978, NARG 75.14.18, Division of Tribal Government Services, LS, 1978-BCCO 731. Information on the tribal police department comes from the Saginaw Chippewa Tribe's website: http://www.sagchip.org/police/index.htm. Also see "Cases in Active or Closed Status under Program Categories 065 and 092 Indian Offenses" (2005). This report is available from the US Department of Justice.

40. "Minutes of the Saginaw Chippewa Tribal Council Meeting, June 3, 1980"; "Minutes of the Saginaw Chippewa Tribal Council Meeting, March 7, 1983," both at Ziibiwing Center.

41. "Tribal Fire Department History," http://www.sagchip.org//fire/index.htm

42. "Minutes of the Saginaw Chippewa Tribal Council Meeting, March 7, 1983," Ziibiwing Center.

43. Veronica E. Velarde Tiller, "Isabella," in *Tiller's Guide to Indian Country: Economic Profiles of American Indian Reservations*, ed. Veronica E. Velarde Tiller (Albuquerque: BowArrow, 2005), 591; "Karen Radell to the Tribal Community," July 17, 2007, at Saginaw Chippewa Tribal College, https://www.sagchip.edu/.

44. "Minutes of the Saginaw Chippewa Council Regular Meeting, November 3, 1980," Ziibiwing Center; Tiller, "Isabella," 591.

45. "Minutes of the Saginaw Chippewa Tribal Council Meeting, November 13, 1980"; see also tribal council meeting minutes for June 28, 1982, January 18, 1983, and March 7, 1983, all at Ziibiwing Center.

46. See links for Behavioral Health and Anishnaabeg Child and Family Services at the Saginaw Chippewa Indian Tribe's website, http://www/sagchip.org/.

47. Sowmick Senior Center, Saginaw Chippewa Indian Tribe, http://www .sagchip.org. Also see Tiller, "Isabella." 590–91.

48. "Regular Meeting of the Saginaw Chippewa Tribal Council, November 3, 1980" and January 12, 1981; "Special Board Meeting of the Saginaw Chippewa Tribal Council, October 20, 1981," all at Ziibiwing Center; Community Health Services, http:/www.sag/Nimkee/comhlthsves.htm. Also see Tiller, "Isabella," 591.

49. "Before the Environmental Appeals Board—U.S. Environmental Protection Agency." In re NPDES Permit for Wastewater Treatment Facility of Union Township, Michigan. Docket No. MI-55808-1. NPDES Appeal No. 00-28. Also see *Michigan Dept. of Environmental Quality v. U.S. EPA*, 318 F. 3d 705 (6th Cir. 2003).

50. Ziibiwing Center, Saginaw Chippewa Indian Tribe, http://www .sagchip.org.

51. Peter Otto to Alvin G. Picotte, October 19, 1981, NARG 75, Sault, Tribal Operations Office, Saginaw Chippewa Box, Saginaw Chippewa Federal Tax Obligations Arising Out of Tribal Bingo File—1981, Ziibiwing Center.

52. Jean W. Sutton to Franklin Annette, March 8, 1982, Tribal Operations Office, Saginaw Chippewa Box, Ziibiwing Center.

53. Soaring Eagle Casino and Resort, https://www.soaringeaglecasino.com. Also see Gaming Commission, Saginaw Chippewa Tribe, http://www.sagchip .org/gamecom/; and Tiller, "Isabella," 591.

54. "Soaring Eagle Casino and Resort," http://www.michigan.org/travel /detail.asp?m+2;1&p=G18271. Also see "Soaring Eagle Casino and Resort— World Class Getaway!," http://www.soaringeaglecasino.com/events/hall.htm; and Tiller, "Isabella," 591.

55. "Saginaw Chippewa May 2006 2 Percent Distribution Totals," SCIT, Saginaw Chippewa Tribe, http://www.sagchip.org/revenuesharing/index .aspx; Also see "Final Motion Approved, 11/17/06."

56. "SCIT Spring 2003 2 Percent Awards," Saginaw Chippewa Tribe, http://www.sagchip.org/revenuesharing/index.aspx.

57. Saginaw Chippewa Campground, the Hill Campground, https://www .thehillcampground.com.

58. "One Hundred Years of Michigan Transportation," Michigan Official 2005 Department of Transportation Map. Printed by the state.

59. "Articles of agreement . . . between commissioners . . . and the Chippewa Indians of Saginaw, August 2, 1855," Treaty with the Chippewa of Saginaw, etc., 1855, online at TTD, 11 Stat., 633, RIT_298, NAI_178354861.

60. Cleland, "Report of the Nineteenth Century History," 31–32; E. B. Meritt to Edward Clements, February 4, 1921, NA-Chicago, 75.19.60, Mt. Pleasant Indian School and Agency, Correspondence, 1918–26, Box 2, C 50, Land Allotments.

61. William Zimmerman to Chairman, Constitutional Committee, July 31, 1936, NARG 75, CCF 9609-A-1936-Tomah .068, Ziibiwing Center.

CHAPTER 7

1. Article 6, Treaty with the Chippewa of Saginaw, etc., 1855, online at TTD, 11 Stat., 633, RIT_298, NAI_178354861.

2. Article 5, Treaty with the Ottawa and Chippewa, 1855, online at TTD, 11 Stat., 621, RIT_296, NAI_178331415.

3. Karen Ferguson, "Indian Fishing Rights: Aftermath of the Fox Decision and the Year 2000," *American Indian Law Review* 23 (1999): 97, 97–154. Using gill nets resulted in bycatch of lake trout, which had virtually disappeared from the lower Great Lakes because of invasive species, among other reasons.

4. Matthew Fletcher recounts the struggles of the Grand Traverse band of Ottawa and Chippewa Indians to secure its sovereign rights in *The Eagle Returns* (East Lansing: Michigan State University Press, 2012).

5. Treaty with the Ottawa, etc., 1836, online at TTD, 7 Stat., 491, RIT_201, NAI_198249818.

6. See Arts. 8 and 13, Treaty with the Ottawa and Chippewa, 1836.

7. *People v. LeBlanc*, 55 Mich. App. 684, 686–87 (1974), affirmed, 399 Mich. 31, 56, 248 N.W.2d 199 (1976) (quotation marks removed from some quotations).

8. *People v. LeBlanc.*

9. *People v. LeBlanc*, 399 Mich. 31, 56, 248 N.W.2d 199 (1976); Phillip McM. Pittman and George Covington, *Don't Blame the Treaties* (Farmington Hills, MI: Northmont Press, 1997), 10.

10. *People v. LeBlanc*, 399 Mich. 31, 56, 248 N.W.2d 199, at 69, 71–72 (J. Lindemer, dissenting).

11. *U.S. v. Michigan,* 471 F. Supp. 192, 247 (W.D. Mi. 1979), affirmed with changes, 623 F.2d 448 (6th Cir. 1980), order modified, 653 F.2d 277 (6th Cir. 1981), cert. denied, 454 U.S. 1124 (1981).

12. 623 F.2d at 448 (6th Cir. 1980). The Sault St. Marie band joined the case for limited purposes after it was started.

13. Anderson still made this argument.

14. Articles 1, 3, and 4, Treaty with the Chippewa of Saginaw, etc., 1855, online at TTD, 11 Stat., 633, RIT_298, NAI_178354861.

15. Anthony Gulig, "An Historical Analysis of the Saginaw, Black River and Swan Creek Chippewa Treaties of 1855 and 1864," 28, 43, 65–69, and 85.

Gulig is a professor at the University of Wisconsin–Whitewater. For Anderson's response, chapters 1–3, above.

16. Articles 1, 3, 5, and 6, Treaty with the Chippewa of Saginaw, etc., 1855.

17. Most likely, an error had crept into the printed copy of the 1864 treaty, either in the transcription or printing process. See Francis Paul Prucha, *American Indian Treaties: The History of a Political Anomaly* (University of California Press: Berkeley, 1995), 445.

18. Gulig, "Historical Analysis," 71–72, and chapters 1–3, above.

19. As Anderson states it in the introduction.

CHAPTER 8

1. Theodore Karamanski, "The Isabella Indian Reservation: A History of Allotment and the Saginaw Chippewa, 1870–1934," 3, 4, 21–22, 43–50, 53, 53–55 (internal quotation marks removed from one quotation). Karamanski is a professor of history at Loyola University, Chicago.

2. See Charles F. Wilkinson, *American Indian, Time, and the Law: Native Societies in a Modern Constitutional Democracy* 121–22 (New Haven, CT: Yale University Press, 1987) (where he asks these questions); Wilkinson is quoted approvingly in Prucha, *American Indian Treaties,* 18.

3. *Oneida County v. Oneida Ind. Nation,* 470 U.S. 226 (1985).

4. *Oneida County v. Oneida Ind. Nation,* 262 (J. Stevens, dissenting in part).

5. *Oneida County v. Oneida Ind. Nation,* 244–45, but see note 16 (expressing skepticism about applying the doctrine).

6. *City of Sherril v. Oneida Indian Nation of N. Y.,* 544 U. S. 197 (2005); Kathryn E. Fort, "The New Laches: Creating Title where None Existed," *George Mason Legal Review* 16 (Winter 2009): 357–401.

7. *McGirt v. Oklahoma,* 591 U.S. (2020).

8. *Oklahoma v. Castro-Huerta,* U.S. No. 21-429, slip op. at 9–10, 12–13, 15, and 18.

9. *Oklahoma v. Castro-Huerta,* slip op. at 10–11, 35, 37, 38, 39, and 42 (J. Gorsuch, dissenting). In his dissent, Gorsuch echoes Wilkinson, *American Indian,* 121–22.

10. *Oklahoma v. Castro-Huerta,* slip op. at 10–11, 35, 37, 38, 39, and 42 (J. Gorsuch, dissenting).

BIBLIOGRAPHY

TREATIES

"Description of the Treaty of Greenville." 1795. Avalon Project, Yale Law School. https://avalon.law.yale.edu/18th_Century/greenvil.asp.

Oklahoma State University Libraries. Tribal Treaties Database (TTD). https://treaties.okstate.edu/treaties/.

Treaty with the Chippewa, 1819. 7 Stat., 203, Identifiers RIT_109, NAI_101784571.

Treaty with the Chippewa, 1836. 7 Stat., 503, Identifiers RIT_207, NAI_148026684.

Treaty with the Chippewa of Saginaw, etc., 1855. 11 Stat., 633, Identifiers RIT_298, NAI_178354861.

Treaty with the Chippewa of Saginaw, Swan Creek, and Black River, 1864. 14 Stat., 637, Identifiers RIT_333, NAI_178924954.

Treaty with the Ottawa, etc., 1807. 7 Stat., 105, Identifiers RIT_054, NAI_161303994.

Treaty with the Ottawa and Chippewa, 1855. 11 Stat., 621, Identifiers RIT_296, NAI_178331415.

Treaty with the Wyandot, etc., 1795 [Treaty of Greenville]. Identifiers RIT_023, NAI_170281462.

ARCHIVES

Archives Nationales, Paris
    Le Sueur, Pierre-Charles. "Mémoires de Mr le Sueur."
Bentley Library, University of Michigan, Ann Arbor
    Henry Crapo Papers

Central Michigan University
    Clarke Historical Library, Central Michigan University, Mt. Pleasant
        Pingatore, Edith. "History of the Mt. Pleasant Indian School, 1893–
        1934." Unpublished ms.
        "U.S. Indian School, Mt. Pleasant, Michigan." Unpublished manu-
        scripts [1921–34?].
    Digital Michigan Newspapers. *Isabella County Enterprise*, 1866, 1879, 1887–
        89, 1892, 1899, 1905, 1915. https://digmichnews.cmich.edu/.
Department of Interior
    Plat Book for Michigan. http://www.glorrecords.blm.gov/survey/.
Detroit Public Library
    Burton Collection, Austin Blair Papers
    Henry Crapo Papers
    Saginaw Enterprise, 1870, 1888
Library of Congress
    Zachariah Chandler Papers. Manuscript Division.
        https://hdl.loc.gov/loc.mss/eadmss.ms006046.
National Archives
    RG 48.5.4. Records of the Indian Division, Office of the Secretary of Inte-
        rior, Letters Sent.
    RG 49.12. Records of the Bureau of Land Management. *Plat Book for Mich-
        igan*. Eastern States Office, Springfield, VA.
    RG 75. Records of the Bureau of Indian Affairs
    RG 75.4. Commissioner of Indian Affairs, Letters Sent.
    RG 75.4. Documents Relating to the Negotiation of Ratified and Unrati-
        fied Treaties.
    RG 75.5. Records of the Commissioner of Indian Affairs and His Immedi-
        ate Subordinates.
    RG 75.7. Land Division.
    RG 75.7.2. Surveying and Allotting Records, Land Division.
    RG 75.14.18 Records of the Division of Tribal Government Services
    RG 75.16.7. Office of the Field Solicitor, Minneapolis (in Kansas City).
    RG 75.19.40. Great Lakes Consolidated Agency Records (in Chicago).
    RG 75.19.55. Mackinac Agency, Letters Received.
    RG 75.19.60. Records of the Michigan Indian Agency and Mount Pleasant
        Indian School, including Letters Received (in Chicago).
    Holst, John. "A Survey of Indian Groups in the State of Michigan, 1939."
    RG 75.19.116. Records of the Tomah Indian Agency.
        McKinsey, Shirley N., and D. D. Mani. "An Economic Survey of the
        Saginaw Chippewa Indians, 1938."
Ziibiwing Cultural Center, Mt. Pleasant, MI. http://www.sagchip.org
    /ziibiwing/.

GOVERNMENTAL RECORDS AND REPORTS

"An Act to enable the State of Arkansas and other States to reclaim the 'Swamp Lands' within their limits." September 28, 1850, 31st Cong., sess. 1. U.S. Statutes at Large 519.

"An Act Granting Certain Property to the State of Michigan for Institutional Purposes" 48 Stat. 353 (1934).

Annual Report of the Auditor General of the State of Michigan for the Year Ending September 30, 1874. Lansing: W. S. George and Co., 1875.

Annual Report of the Commissioner of Indian Affairs. https://search.library.wisc.edu /digital/A3YVW4ZRARQT7J8S.

Serial No. 53, 1848
Serial No. 587, 1849–51
Serial No. 875, 1855–57
Serial No. 942, 1858
Serial No. 974, 1858
Serial No. 1220, vol. 5., 1864
Serial No. 1326, 1867
Serial No. 1449, 1869–71
Serial No. 1505, 1871
Serial No. 1560, 1872
Serial No. 1601, 1873
Serial No. 1639, 1874
Serial No. 2637, 1888
Serial No. 2725, 1889
Serial No. 3088, 1892
Serial No. 5747, 1909
Serial No. 6223, 1911
Serial No. 6409, 1912
Serial No. 6634, 1913
Serial No. 7160, 1916
Serial No. 7358, 1917
Serial No. 7498, 1918
Serial No. 7820, 1920

Annual Report of the Secretary of Interior. Senate Exec. Doc. No. 2, 36th Cong., 2nd Sess. (1860). Serial No. 1078.

House Executive Documents. Congressional Records. https://www.congress .gov.

51st Cong., 1st Sess., vol. 2., 1889.

Document No. 1. 40th Cong., 2nd Sess., 1867–68.

House Journal. Trade and Intercourse Act. 23rd Cong., 1st Sess., 645, 729, 833, 852, 869.

Miscellaneous Doc. No. 23. 40th Cong., 1867–68, 1–8.

"Report with Respect to the House Resolution Authorizing the Committee on Interior and Insular Affairs to Conduct an Investigation of the Bureau of Indian Affairs Pursuant to House Resolution 698." House Report No. 2503, 82nd Cong., 2nd Sess., December 15, 1952.

"Report with Respect to the House Resolution Authorizing the Committee on Interior and Insular Affairs to Conduct an Investigation of the Bureau of Indian Affairs Pursuant to House Resolution 89." House Report No. 2680, 83rd Cong., 2nd Sess., September 20, 1954.

"Transfer of Property of the Mount Pleasant Indian School to the State of Michigan for Institutional Purposes." House Report No. 562, 73rd Cong., 2nd Sess., 1934.

BOOKS AND ARTICLES

Anderson, Gary Clayton. *Ethnic Cleansing and the Indian: The Crime That Should Haunt America*. Norman: University of Oklahoma Press, 2014.

———. *The Conquest of Texas: Ethnic Cleansing in the Promised Land, 1820–1875*. Norman: University of Oklahoma Press, 2005.

———. *Kinsmen of Another Kind: Dakota-White Relations on the Upper Mississippi River, 1650–1862*. Lincoln: University Nebraska Press, 1984.

Billington, Ray Allen. *Westward Expansion: A History of the American Frontier*. New York: Macmillan, 1960.

Cleland, Charles E. *Faith in Paper: The Ethnohistory and Litigation of Upper Great Lakes Indian Treaties*. Ann Arbor: University of Michigan Press, 2011.

———. *Place of the Pike*. Ann Arbor: University of Michigan Press, 2001.

Demmert, William G. "Indian Education Act, 1972." In *Native America in the Twentieth Century*, edited by Mary B. Davis. New York: Garland, 1996.

Dustin, Fred. *The Saginaw Treaty of 1819: Between General Lewis Cass and the Chippewa Indians, Written for the Celebration of the Treaty September 19, 1919*. Saginaw, Michigan, 1919.

Dowd, Gregory Evans. *A Spirited Resistance: The North American Indian Struggle for Unity, 1745–1815*. Baltimore: Johns Hopkins University Press, 1992.

Edmunds, R. David. *The Potawatomies, Keepers of the Fire*. Norman: University of Oklahoma Press, 1978.

———, and Joseph L. Peyser. *The Fox Wars: The Mesquakie Challenge to New France*. Norman: University of Oklahoma Press, 1993.

———, Frederick E. Hoxie, and Neal Salisbury. *The People: A History of Native America*. Boston: Houghton, Mifflin, 2007.

Englebert, Robert, and Guillaume Teasdale, eds. *French and Indians in the Heart of America, 1630–1815*. East Lansing: Michigan State University Press, 2013.

Ferguson, Karen. "Indian Fishing Rights: Aftermath of the Fox Decision and the Year 2000." *American Indian Law Review* 23, no. 1 (1999): 97–154.

Fletcher, Matthew L. M. *The Eagle Returns.* East Lansing: Michigan State University Press, 2012.

———. "The Supreme Court's Indian Problem." *Hastings Law Journal* 59, no. 3 (2008): 579–642.

Fort, Kathryn E. "The New Laches: Creating Title Where None Existed." *George Mason Legal Review* 16 (Winter 2009): 357–401.

Fowler, Loretta. *Arapahoe Politics, 1851–1978.* Lincoln: University of Nebraska Press, 1982.

Fox, Robin. *Kinship and Marriage: An Anthropological Perspective.* New York: Penguin, 1983.

Godelier, Maurice. *The Mental and the Material.* London: Verso Books, 1984.

Grossman, Mark, ed. *The ABC-CLIO Companion to the Native American Rights Movement.* Santa Barbara, CA: ABC-CLIO, 1996.

Hibbard, Benjamin Horace. *A History of the Public Land Policies.* Madison: University of Wisconsin Press, 1965.

Hurtado, Albert L. *Indian Survival on the California Frontier.* New Haven, CT: Yale University Press, 1988.

Jackson, Andrew. *Correspondence of Andrew Jackson.* 7 vols. Edited by John Bassett. Washington, DC: Carnegie Institution of Washington, 1926.

Jennings, Francis. *The Ambiguous Iroquois Empire: The Covenant Chain Confederation of Indian Tribes with English Colonies from its Beginnings to the Lancaster Treaty of 1744.* New York: W. W. Norton, 1984.

Kappler, Charles J. *Indian Affairs, 1778–1883.* 2 vols. 1904. Reprint, New York: Interland, 1972.

Kinietz, W. Vernon. *The Indians of the Western Great Lakes, 1650–1760.* Ann Arbor: University of Michigan Press, 1965.

Klunder, William Carl. *Lewis Cass and the Politics of Moderation.* Kent, OH: Kent State University Press, 1996.

Kvasnicka, Robert M., and Viola, Herman J., eds. *The Commissioners of Indian Affairs, 1824–1977.* Lincoln: University of Nebraska Press, 1979.

Landes, Ruth. *The Ojibwa Woman.* New York: Barnes and Noble, 1971.

Mabie, Christopher. *Uncle Louis: Biography of Louis Campau, Founder of Saginaw and Grand Rapids.* Walker, MI: Van Naerden, 2007.

"One Hundred Years of Michigan Transportation." Official 2005 Department of Transportation Map. Lansing: State of Michigan, 2005.

Manypenny, George. *Our Indian Wards.* 1880. Reprinted, New York: Da Capo, 1972.

Meek, Forest B. *Michigan's Timber Battle Ground: A History of Clare County, 1674–1900.* Clare, MI: Clare County Bicentennial Historical Committee, 1976.

Meillassoux, Claude. *Maidens, Meal and Money: Capitalism and the Domestic Community*. New York: Cambridge University Press, 1981.

Owens, Robert M. *Mr. Jefferson's Hammer: William Henry Harrison and the Origins of American Indian Policy*. Norman: University of Oklahoma Press, 2007.

Peters, Bernard. "Hypocrisy on the Great Lakes Frontier: The Use of Whiskey by the Michigan Department of Indian Affairs." *Michigan Historical Review* 18 (1992): 4–5.

Philp, Kenneth R. "John Collier, (1933–45)." In *The Commissioners of Indian Affairs, 1824–1977*. Edited by Robert Kvasnicka and Hermant Viola, 273–82. Lincoln: University of Nebraska Press, 1979.

Pittman, Phillip McM., and George M. Covington. *Don't Blame the Treaties*. Farmington Hills, MI: Northmont Press, 1997.

Prucha, Francis Paul. *American Indian Treaties: The History of a Political Anomaly*. Berkeley: University of California Press, 1995.

———. *The Great Father: The United States Government and the American Indians*. 2 vols. Lincoln: University of Nebraska Press, 1984.

Rawls, James J. *Indians of California: The Changing Image*. Norman: University of Oklahoma Press, 1986.

Ritzenhaler, Robert E. "Southwestern Chippewa." In *Handbook of North American Indians, Vol. 15: Northeast*. Edited by Bruce E. Trigger, 743–46. Washington, DC: Smithsonian Institution Scholarly Press, 1978.

Robertson, Lindsay G. *Conquest by Law: How the Discovery of America Dispossessed Indigenous Peoples of Their Land*. New York: Oxford University Press, 2005.

Rogers, E. S. "Southeastern Chippewa." In *Handbook of North American Indians, Vol. 15: Northeast*. Edited by Bruce Trigger, 760–64. Washington, DC: Smithsonian Institution Scholarly Press, 1978.

Saginaw Chippewa Indian Tribe of Michigan. *Diba Jimooyung: Telling Our Story, A History of the Saginaw Ojibwe Anishinabek*. Mt. Pleasant, MI: Saginaw Chippewa Tribe, 2005.

Sahlins, Marshall. *Stone Age Economics*. New York: Routledge, 1972.

Satz, Ronald N. *American Indian Policy in the Jacksonian Era*. Norman: University of Oklahoma Press, 1975.

Sturtevant, William C., gen. ed. *Handbook of North American Indians*. 20 vols. Washington DC: Smithsonian Institution Scholarly Press, 1978–2022.

Tiller, Veronica E. Velarde. "Isabella." In *Tiller's Guide to Indian Country: Economic Profiles of American Indian Reservations*. Edited by Veronica E. Velarde Tiller, 591. Albuquerque: BowArrow, 2005.

Trennert, Robert A., Jr. *Alternative to Extinction: Federal Indian Policy and the Beginnings of the Reservation System, 1846–1851*. Philadelphia: Temple University Press, 1975.

Treuer, Anton. *The Assassination of Hole in the Day*. St. Paul: Minnesota Historical Society Press, 2011.

Trigger, Bruce. *Children of Aataentsic: A History of the Huron People to 1660.* 2 vols. Montreal: McGill–Queens University Press, 1976.

Wilkinson, Charles F. *American Indian, Time, and the Law: Native Societies in a Modern Constitutional Democracy.* New Haven, CT: Yale University Press, 1987.

White, Richard. *The Middle Ground: Indians, Empires and Republics in the Great Lakes Region, 1650–1815.* New York: Cambridge University Press, 1991.

LAWSUITS AND RELATED DOCUMENTS

Anderson, Gary. "Report on the 'Reservation Status' of the Saginaw Chippewa Tribe of Indians of the State of Michigan." 2007. Revised and reprinted this volume (chapters 1–4).

Cleland, Charles E. "Report of the Nineteenth-Century History of the Saginaw, Black River, and Swan Creek Chippewa." 1992. This report was prepared in conjunction with *United States and Saginaw Chippewa Indian Tribe of Michigan v. Granholm et al.,* Eastern District of Michigan (No. 91-CV-10103-BC). A copy of this report can be obtained from the US Department of Justice.

City of Sherril v. Oneida Indian Nation of N. Y., 544 U.S. 197 (2005).

Edmunds, David. "A History of the Isabella Reservation." 2007. Revised and reprinted in this volume (chapters 5–6).

Gulig, Anthony. "An Historical Analysis of the Saginaw, Black River and Swan Creek Chippewa Treaties of 1855 and 1864." 2007. Submitted to US District Court, Eastern District of Michigan, Northern Division, in *US and Saginaw Chippewa Tribe v. Granholm et al.* https://turtletalk.files.wordpress.com/2008/05/gulig-report.pdf.

Karamanski, Theodore. "The Isabella Indian Reservation: A History of Allotment and the Saginaw Chippewa, 1870–1934." Submitted to US District Court, Eastern District of Michigan, Northern Division, in *US and Saginaw Chippewa Tribe v. Granholm et al.*

Keweenaw Bay Community v. State of Michigan, 784 F. Supp. 418, 427–28 (W.D. Mich., 1991).

McGirt v. Oklahoma, 591 U.S. (2020).

Michigan Department of Environmental Quality v. U.S. EPA, 318 F. 3d 705 (6th Cir. 2003).

Michigan Land & Lumber Company vs. Rust, 68 F. 155, 156 (6th Cir. 1895).

Michigan Land & Lumber Co. v. Rust, 168 US 589 (1897).

Newell, Alan S. "An Overview of Federal Relations with the Saginaw, Swan Creek, and Black River Bands of Chippewa of the Isabella Indian Reservation, Michigan, 1910–1934." 1992. Environmental and Natural Resources Division, Indian Resources Section, US Department of Justice.

Oklahoma v. Castro-Huerta, U.S. No. 21-429, slip op. (2022).
Oneida County v. Oneida Ind. Nation, 470 U.S. 226 (1985).
People v. LeBlanc, 55 Mich. App. 684, 686–87 (1974), affirmed, 399 Mich. 31, 56, 248 N.W.2d 199 (1976).
United States v. Michigan, 471 F. Supp. 192, 247 (W.D. Mi. 1979), affirmed with changes, 623 F.2d 448 (6th Cir. 1980), order modified, 653 F.2d 277 (6th Cir. 1981), cert. denied, 454 U.S. 1124 (1981).
United States and Saginaw Chippewa Indian Tribe of Michigan v. Granholm et al. US District Court, Eastern District of Michigan, Northern Division. Case No. 1:2005cv10296, Document 283. "Order for Judgment," December 17, 2010.

SAGINAW CHIPPEWA TRIBE SOURCES

Annual 2% Distributions. http://www.sagchip.org/revenuesharing/index.aspx.
The Hill (Pow Wow Grounds) Campground. http://www.sagchip.org/campground/index.aspx.
Saginaw Chippewa Indian Tribe. http://www.sagchip.org/.
Saginaw Chippewa Tribal College. http://www.sagchip.edu/.
Soaring Eagle Casino and Resort. https://www.soaringeaglecasino.com/.
Ziibiwing Cultural Center. http://www.sagchip.org/ziibwing/.

INDEX